Turning Toward
Philosophy

Literature and Philosophy

A. J. Cascardi, General Editor

This series publishes books in a wide range of subjects in philosophy and literature, including studies of the social and historical issues that relate these two fields. Drawing on the resources of the Anglo-American and Continental traditions, the series is open to philosophically informed scholarship covering the entire range of contemporary critical thought.

Already published:

Turning Toward
Philosophy

Literary Device
and
Dramatic Structure
in
Plato's Dialogues

Jill Gordon

The Pennsylvania State University Press
University Park, Pennsylvania

Library of Congress Cataloging-in-Publication Data

Gordon, Jill, 1962–
    Turning toward philosophy : literary device and dramatic structure
in Plato's Dialogues / Jill Gordon.
        p.   cm.
    Includes bibliographical references and index.
    ISBN 0-271-01925-5 (cloth : alk. paper).
    ISBN 0-271-01926-3 (pbk. : alk. paper)
    1. Plato—Dialogues.   I. Title.
    B395.G455   1999
    184—dc21   99-34786
                                                          CIP

It is the policy of The Pennsylvania State University Press to use acid-free paper for
the first printing of all clothbound books. Publications on uncoated stock satisfy the
minimum requirements of American National Standard for Information Sciences—
Permanence of Paper for Printed Library Materials, ANSI Z39.48-1992.

For Ada

The play's the thing,
Wherein I'll catch the conscience of the King.
(Hamlet)
William Shakespeare

The wholly unreflective subject is naively convinced
that if only the objective truth stands fast, the
subject will be ready and willing to attach himself to
it. Here we see at once the youthfulness . . . which
has no suspicion of the subtle little Socratic secret:
that the point is precisely the relationship of the
subject. . . . [Truth] is not an immediate and
extremely free-and-easy relationship between an
immediate consciousness and a sum of propositions
. . . the truth is the subject's transformation in
himself.
(Johannes Climacus)
Søren Kierkegaard

We [the readers] are one of the elements of the
dialogue and perhaps the most important one.
Jacob Klein

Contents

Acknowledgments and Note on Translations

The journals *Classical Quarterly*, published by Oxford University Press, and *Philosophy and Rhetoric*, published by The Pennsylvania State University Press, kindly gave permission to reprint parts of previously published work.

The members of the Society for Ancient Greek Philosophy (SAGP) gave constructive feedback on several of the chapters of this book, which I presented at SAGP annual meetings. Gerald Press and Christopher Perricone provided some of those opportunities by organizing panels. Mark McPheran, Mitchell Miller, and Victorino Tejera spoke with me and corresponded about work presented at the SAGP meetings, and Charles Young gave insightful and constructive commentary on a paper that appears here as Chapter 3. Thanks also to the International Association for Philosophy and Literature, the Ontario Society for the Study of Argumentation, Trinity College, and Text & Presentation: Comparative Drama Conference, where I also presented work from this book.

Louis Mackey and Drew Hyland read early versions of the manuscript and were extremely constructive and gracious in their comments. I am most grateful to Louis and Drew, more generally, for their mentoring. Christine Bowditch, more than perhaps anyone else, committed time to reading, rereading, and helping me to improve the manuscript. Without Chris's friendship, encouragement, and interest in my work, the project would have been significantly diminished. The reviewer from Penn State Press, Charles Griswold Jr., and the series editor, Anthony Cascardi, suggested significant improvements to the work, and Sandy Thatcher at Penn State Press helped guide me through the long process to publication.

Katie Quackenbush, my spirited, conscientious, and intelligent research assistant, helped in innumerable ways and prepared the index for the book. Thanks also to Bill Dennen from Colby College's Information Technology Services, Grace Von Toble, who provided manuscript assistance, and Maggie Libby and the entire library staff at the College.

I received financial support from the Marguerite Eyer Wilbur Foundation and Colby College during a sabbatical in 1994–95. This allowed me to write single-mindedly, relieved from teaching duties. The teaching was itself, however, a source of energy and intellectual stimulation. Thanks especially to students in my seminar on Plato, spring 1996, and to students in History of Ancient Greek Philosophy every fall. My department provided a supportive environment, especially through my early years there.

Martin Berger helped me to maintain momentum and good cheer during a particularly difficult phase of the revisions. My parents have consistently supported my academic career and shown great interest in my work and its success. My friends at Colby make sanity in academic life possible through their warmth, friendship, and laughter. My husband, Glenn, is a continuous source of emotional support, good sense, and good humor. Thank you, all.

I have used the translations from the Loeb Classical Library collections for most passages in Plato, Aristotle, and Diogenes Laertius. All exceptions are noted. Where appropriate, I have made changes from the British to the American spelling of some words. Translations of *Meno* and *Protagoras* are my own unless noted otherwise.

Introduction

> Imagine human beings living in an underground,
> cavelike dwelling, with an entrance a long way up,
> which is both open to the light and as wide as the
> cave itself. They've been there since childhood, fixed
> in the same place, with their necks and legs fettered,
> able to see only in front of them, because their
> bonds prevent them from turning their heads
> around. Light is provided by a fire burning far
> above and behind them. Also behind them, but on
> higher ground, there is a path stretching between
> them and the fire. Imagine that along this path a low
> wall has been built, like the screen in front of pup-
> peteers above which they show their puppets. . . .
> Then also imagine that there are people along the
> wall, carrying all kinds of artifacts that project
> above it—statues of people and other animals, made
> out of stone, wood, and every material. . . . Do you
> suppose, first of all that these prisoners see anything
> of themselves and one another besides the shadows
> that the fire casts on the wall in front of them? . . .
> [T]he prisoners would in every way believe that the
> truth is nothing other than the shadows of those
> artifacts. . . . Consider then, what being released
> from their bonds and cured of their ignorance would
> naturally be like. When one of them was freed and
> suddenly compelled to stand up, turn his head,
> walk, and look up toward the light.
>
> *Republic*, trans. Grube (1992), 514a–515c

What exactly frees the prisoners from their chains and compels them to turn
their gaze away from the shadows cast on the cave wall and toward the light
that is the source of those images? Interpreting Plato's allegory, the question
becomes: What could free an individual from a life of uninvestigated experience and routine thoughtlessness to live, instead, the life of philosophy?
Whatever could counteract a lifetime of bondage and be wielded to turn a
soul in a direction toward which it is neither accustomed nor inclined would
have to be alluring and powerful. Clearly, the things that might turn one
toward philosophy, whatever they are, must be at work in Plato's dialogues
since these writings, perhaps more than any others, have been responsible

for setting off myriad individuals, uncountable generations, and even entire communities on the task of doing philosophy. This book aims to discover and examine those elements in the dialogues capable of compelling the turn toward philosophy.

By looking closely at what transpires during the act of reading or hearing a Platonic dialogue, I explain in detail how we are so turned. My argument is that the means through which the turn is effected are what have come to be called by modern scholars the "literary and dramatic" elements of the dialogues.[1] Plato's use of these particular devices is, moreover, not accidental but essential. The view of humanity consistently portrayed in the dialogues is one of inherently limited beings, and the dialogues show clearly that, as a consequence, the means of appealing to humans philosophically must take into account those limitations. Plato uses these devices because they are the most suitable and powerful means available for beings such as ourselves. Contrary to more traditional understandings of "Platonism," therefore, I argue that the dialogues' appeal to humans cannot be through rational means alone—through pure argumentation or logic—but must necessarily operate on extralogical levels in order to have any philosophical effect. I examine what those extralogical means are and the particular philosophical—and, Socratically speaking, psychological—effects they have.

While this work is not explicitly about methodology, it must concern itself with methodology, at least obliquely, insofar as it focuses on the phenomenon of reading a Platonic text. Such a focus naturally leads to questions regarding just what we think it is we are reading, and to what consequent experiences particular reading strategies will lead. Because I wish to focus on literary and dramatic elements as being essential to Plato's philosophical project, I must adopt a reading strategy that recognizes these elements as integral to philosophical writing and integral to the activity of doing philosophy. The manner in which the dialogues have been read and interpreted by many Plato scholars in this century is not particularly well suited to recognizing and exploring the elements that capture our attention and turn our gaze in philosophical directions. I begin, therefore, with an examination of the method of reading the dialogues that has occluded our vision of them, the method that has kept us from discovering, describing, and explaining the function of the elements in Plato's dialogues that turn us toward philosophy.

---

1. I shall have more to say later regarding the suitability of this descriptive label for the elements to which I wish to refer. While I have lumped literary and dramatic together, cf. Berger (1987), who argues that the literary and the dramatic represent distinct levels of discourse.

1. Analysis and Argument-Focused Methods

Some of the most influential contemporary scholarship stems from the application of the tools of logical analysis to Plato's dialogues.[2] It seems fair to say that scholars' application of analytic methods to the dialogues contributed to a renaissance in twentieth-century Platonic studies, but it carried with it unforeseen consequences with regard to what we think the dialogues comprise and, ultimately, what we think it means to do philosophy with them. While logical analysis of the arguments in the dialogues is not always the exclusive focus for interpreters adopting this methodology,[3] it nevertheless exerts powerful influence over the philosophical projects that stem from its use. In particular, adopting this methodology focuses philosophers' attention on the arguments in the dialogues, since the arguments are the repositories of the very logic that is under scrutiny and which are the elements most suitable for logical analysis. This approach presumes that the range of objects in the dialogues over which philosophical activity operates are propositions, arguments, premises, and conclusions; it directs philosophers' attention to issues of consistency, validity, soundness and so forth.[4] It presumes, therefore, almost by necessity, a conception of philosophy and philosophical activity as operating primarily on elements that can be the subject of logical analysis. This approach tends to identify philosophical activity with making and analyzing logico-deductive arguments. While this is certainly a part of philosophical activity, and a part of Platonic dialogues, it cannot be the exclusive or even primary activity of philosophers.

Plato's dialogues, in all their complexity, focus our attention on many factors in addition to the arguments advanced in them. In directing our attention to myriad issues that lie outside the purview of logic and logical concerns, the dialogues recommend a broader conception of philosophy and philosophical activities. While I grant that it is possible for one to be turned toward the philosophical life by an argument in the dialogues, it is unlikely that the arguments alone could have such a compelling influence over individuals. This is especially so if one takes seriously the character flaws exhibited by many of the interlocutors and assumes, as is most certainly the case, that as readers

---

2. For explicit claims to this effect, see, for example, Robinson (1953, vi–vii) and Vlastos (1978, I: 1–2).

3. Vlastos (1978, I: 2–3) is quick to point out that the old strategies of "linguistic and historical" analysis should not be left behind.

4. As examples of the types of conclusions that emerge from analysis of arguments in Plato's dialogues, see Vlastos (1956) and his edited anthologies (1978, I and II).

we exhibit some, if not many, of those same characteristics. This being the case, it is unlikely that one would be compelled to live the philosophical life merely after hearing an argument, or even several, such as those made in the dialogues. What turns us toward the philosophical life includes necessarily the extralogical, and so is not easily named or understood by the analytic method.

Among the argument-focused scholars to whom I refer are many who treat the character, Socrates, as a mouthpiece for Plato. Philosophers who fall into this category range from those who recognize Socrates as a literary character but see him, nonetheless, as representative of Plato's views, to those who actually try to reconstruct and distinguish what the historical Socrates has said from what Plato himself means to say through him.[5] There are difficulties associated with making these kinds of attributions, and many scholars, with whom I am in agreement, have argued against such approaches.[6] The written construction of the dialogues mitigates against any mouthpiece reading of them. Since I would never take Richard III's or Cleopatra's speeches to be indicative of Shakespeare's personal views, nor to be indicative of views held by the historical figures that these literary characters represent, so I adopt the same methodological attitude for Plato and his dialogues. But this need not leave one in a hermeneutic impasse, since the plays *Richard III* and *Antony and Cleopatra* do convey meaning. Our experience and understanding of those plays need not be affected one iota whether or not we ever know how closely they reflect the historical personages they portray nor whether we ever come to know Shakespeare's innermost thoughts on love, betrayal, or political rule. Plato's dialogues also have meaning for us—profound, human meaning—whether or not we ever figure out Plato's or the historical Socrates' views.[7]

Pervasive also in scholarly discussions this century, and often overlapping argument-focused approaches to the dialogues and presumptions about Plato's so-called mouthpiece, are questions about the order in which the dialogues were composed and therefore whether one can detect philosophical

5. For example, Irwin (1977) takes Socrates to be speaking for Plato; Vlastos (1991) makes it the focus of several chapters to distinguish between Socrates who represents the historical person and Socrates who speaks for Plato's later, more mature philosophical views; and Frede (1992), even though he presents an argument for recognizing the importance of the dialogue form and all its complexity, cannot keep from talking about "Plato's argument," "Plato's view," and what "Plato endorses," which he apparently gleans from what Socrates says (201–3).

6. See Berger (1987) and Press (1999).

7. Regarding the analogy between Plato and other dramatists see Strauss (1964, 50–51, 58–59) and Kosman (1992b).

development during Plato's life or whether his views are consistent and unified throughout. Some argue that the dialogues show Plato's progressive
philosophical development, while others say that the dialogues present
Plato's unified and consistent view.[8] My disagreement with both the developmental view and the unitarian view, despite the substantial differences
between them, is aimed at two presumptions they share: they both presume, first of all, that the purpose of the Platonic dialogues is to convey
"Plato's thought" even though Plato, through several devices, has gone to
great lengths to create authorial distance and textual ambiguity. And while
for Plato scholars the task has always been to give a meaningful account of
the dialogues in the face of inconsistency, contradiction, and ambiguity,
these philosophers presume, second, that such features of the dialogues are
to be solved, resolved, or otherwise "fixed" and do not serve some philosophical purpose. Both the developmental and the unitarian projects need
to explain away—although in different fashion and for different reasons—
inconsistency, contradiction, lack of resolution, or ambiguity in order to
save "Plato's thought" from these plagues.

Whereas these qualities might be plagues from one particular perspective
of philosophical writing—one that demands, above all, consistent argumentation, economy of expression, and clarity of meaning—they might be
essential components of another type of philosophical writing. I believe
that they are essential to Plato's philosophical writing. By focusing on the
dialogues' written style, written structure, content, and literary devices, I
draw conclusions about how the written elements of the text engage the
reader or audience in the activity we call philosophy. The elements that are
considered nonphilosophical by contemporary approaches—or, at the very
least, extraphilosophical or extralogical—are the very elements of Plato's
dialogues that can turn a soul toward the philosophical life.

The approaches I have briefly characterized here are so prevalent in contemporary scholarship, and so many of their presumptions go unquestioned,
that the presumptions and the methodology founded upon them have
become nearly invisible. It is therefore worthwhile to expose the underlying
presumptions of such work, and to question the methodological utility of

---

8. Clear examples of work stemming from a developmental view are Irwin (1977) and
Vlastos (1991). Examples of work stemming from the unitarian view are Schleiermacher (1836)
and Shorey (1960). My treatment of the recent history of scholarship is cursory here. Tigerstedt
(1977) and Gonzalez (1995, 1–24) provide excellent accounts and critiques of Plato scholarship. Their accounts are richly detailed and point to subtle differences even among scholars
holding seemingly similar accounts of Plato's corpus.

those presumptions since they limit our conceptions of the dialogue and, ultimately, our conceptions of philosophy. The presumptions that underlie the scholarship about which I speak are:[9]

- The dialogues are intended to convey Plato's thought.
- Socrates speaks for Plato.
- The arguments in the dialogues (usually only Socrates') are the philosophical core of the dialogues and are the (only) appropriate objects of philosophical analysis.
- Logical virtues are philosophical virtues and, likewise, logical vices are philosophical vices.[10]
- Categorizing the dialogues into "early," "middle," and "late" periods in Plato's writing career is not only possible but beneficial to our analysis and improves our understanding of Plato's thought.

All of these presumptions, in one way or another, imply further that a Platonic dialogue is a piece of writing in which the author communicates (relatively) directly and logically "his philosophical view" with the purpose of either informing an audience of what his view is or convincing an audience of that view. But this seems an impoverished conception of the dialogues.

On the contrary, I begin with a conception of the dialogues as pieces of writing whose primary purpose is to turn reader and audience toward the philosophical life by engaging them in philosophical activity in the form of deep self-examination. Beginning with this conception of the dialogues requires a different reading strategy, namely, one that looks for and at the means of philosophical engagement in the dialogues. If the argument-focused approaches keep us from seeing the parts of the dialogues responsible for the turn toward philosophy, an alternative approach that focuses on the written elements of the dialogues—what I am roughly referring to as the "literary and dramatic" elements—is needed if one is to examine how that turn is effected.

---

9. Not every philosopher who could be described as utilizing an analytic or argument-focused approach, or who sees merit in trying to order the dialogues, subscribes to all of these presumptions.

10. Although Plato is sometimes "pardoned" by scholars for his logical gaffes based on the undeveloped nature of the science of logic during his lifetime. See Robinson (1953), Vlastos (1956), Vlastos (1978, Introduction), and Irwin (1979, v). See Tigerstedt's comments on the phenomenon of excusing Plato (1977, 22–24).

2. An Alternative Approach

In contrast to those who subscribe to the approaches I have described above, there are several philosophers who look to literary and dramatic details as a hermeneutic strategy for interpreting individual dialogues. Such studies reject, by and large, many if not all of the presumptions of the argument-focused views.[11] I am wholly sympathetic to these projects, sharing the perspective that their interpretations of the dialogues are richer and more complete than interpretations that practically ignore the dramatic and literary elements. But my aim here is a different one, even from these projects. Whereas theirs are interpretive studies of particular dialogues, resting on the well-founded belief that the literary and dramatic elements are important to forming an interpretation of a dialogue, my work attempts to explain why and how the literary and dramatic elements are important by offering, in part, a phenomenology of reading the dialogues. That is, this book offers a detailed account of the experience of the individual reader or auditor of a Platonic dialogue, and that account focuses on the philosophical effect of specific literary and dramatic devices. The project provides an answer to the question "What are the literary elements *doing* in the dialogues?" The work shows exactly how specific literary and dramatic elements of Plato's dialogues *function philosophically* with respect to the reader or audience.

I reject the presumption of some scholarship that Plato's primary philosophical aim could simply have been to transmit a body of (i.e., his) philosophical knowledge or a system of thought or even several philosophical theories or doctrines. Too many aspects of the dialogues speak against this possibility. If we accept such a view of the dialogues' purpose, we pay Plato no compliments. Imagine the folly of writing what Plato wrote in order to convey a body of philosophical ideas of one's own: Plato presents several views in the voices of several characters who most often disagree with one another; the philosophical conversations in which the disagreement takes place rarely, if ever, reach any single conclusion and leave thorny philosophical problems largely unresolved; Plato creates a central character who is himself not consistent in his views, and who distances himself from many of

---

11. For example, Klein (1989), Strauss (1964), Hyland (1968) and (1995), Gadamer (1980) and (1997), Rosen (1983), Miller (1980), (1986), and (1996), Griswold (1986), and Ferrari (1987). In addition, several anthologies mark an emerging literature that is explicitly critical of what I have called the analytic or argument-focused approach: Griswold (1988), Press (1993) and (1999), and Gonzalez (1995).

the ideas he presents; Plato constructs texts with ambiguous meaning and a vast array of possible interpretations; and finally, Plato fills the dialogues with the seemingly superfluous trappings of myth, metaphor, and colorful image. The combined effect of these strategies would lead one to the uncharitable conclusion that Plato chose the most ridiculous means of conveying *his* ideas and, as one would expect, he has failed to do so.

In one sense, of course, it's all Plato. He contrives the actions, speeches, settings, diction, jokes, images, poetic devices, contradictions, irony, and so on. But in another sense, he erases himself through these very devices. He purposely removes his own voice as a philosophical authority through devices that destabilize univocal readings of the texts. The dialogues thus thwart claims about Plato's philosophical views, thwart claims that the character, Socrates, is a mouthpiece for Plato, and even thwart claims about the historical person, Socrates. More in the manner of great poets, playwrights, and writers of fiction, Plato creates texts that, although meaningful, are not necessarily intended to contain his unmediated philosophical view. The task left to the philosopher is to ask what experience each dialogue affords the reader or audience and what the philosophical significance is of that experience.

Plato is not attempting to get the reader to know and understand what is in his (Plato's) mind when he composes the dialogues.[12] He is attempting to get the reader to know and understand what is in her own mind and, from there, to reassess who she is and how she will choose to live her life. This is not to say that the dialogues are void of any positive philosophical content. It is to say, rather, that the function of the dialogues is altogether opposed to looking for—discovering, clarifying, formalizing—"Plato's thought" as an end in itself.[13] The dialogues' function is to turn us inward, to get us to examine our own beliefs. And even if we turn to what we believe might be "Plato's thought," we are meant to assess it in the same rigorous way that the dialogues recommend that all thoughts, ideas, and beliefs should be tested, so that we can make the decision whether "Plato's thought" is something worth holding as our own, whether it is part of the good human life. To stand before a Platonic text expecting it to be a philosophical authority

12. One of Griswold's insights (1987, 83–84) is that Alcibiades' description of Socrates as the Silenus figure in the *Symposium* is more truly about Plato. For it is Plato who is the real Silenus figure in the dialogues, which he creates but is not a part of, and so remains concealed.

13. For an extensive argument against the dialogues' conveying Plato's thought, see Bowen (1988). Gadamer (1980, 95) says that Socratic discourse "is not merely a clever hiding place for [Plato's] 'doctrines'"; and (1991, xxxiii), "We would be poor readers of Plato if we did not allow his dialogues to lead us to the things, the facts of the matter, themselves, rather than reading them as mere material from which to reconstruct Plato's doctrines of principles."

or to be the repository of "Platonism," and not to see it as an occasion for self-examination, is to engage in behavior as objectionable as any interlocutor's behavior. To do philosophy with Plato is to address ourselves in the deepest, most risky manner, to ask about the beliefs we hold and the lives we live. The turn toward philosophy is, Socratically speaking, a turn inward.

Turning, or more accurately, being turned, occupies an important place in Platonic scholarship. Protreptic—which literally means a turning toward, and figuratively means an exhortation—has been a model in both ancient and modern philosophical circles. In the ancient world, the exhortation to philosophize was made explicit in Aristotle's incomplete work *Protreptikos*, a work intended to provide a compelling argument for engaging in philosophy.[14] Konrad Gaiser is among the first to articulate to a modern audience, in his book, roughly translated, *Exhortation and Admonition in the Platonic Dialogues*, the function of protreptic, the hortatory power of Plato's dialogues.[15] Hans-Georg Gadamer follows in these tracks, speaking of the protreptic type of ethics that urges us toward an ideal,[16] and he refers to the "turning" of the individual toward the life of philosophy in a similar vein.[17] So, the protreptic power of the Platonic dialogues would seem to be a presumption of the approach I advocate here, the approach that is specifically looking for what compels the turn.

In keeping with the inward turn of philosophy, several Plato scholars have recognized that the dialogues have an effect on the reader and audience.[18] I want to take their work further. Beyond recognizing the effect that the dialogues can have on reader and audience, it is philosophically significant to understand how that effect is achieved, that is, through what means and to what end. It is to this understanding that I hope to make a contribution. In turning my attention to the philosophical purpose of constructing a written text in a particular fashion, I must view the dialogues as philosophical pieces of *writing*, as philosophy and as literature, all at the same time.

One literary critic, Terry Eagleton, rejects several definitions of "the literary" before settling on "literature is highly valued writing."[19] Eagleton's

14. See Düring (1961), Chroust (1964), and Hutchinson, (1995, 196–97).
15. *Protreptik und Paränese in den Dialogen Platons*, cited in Gadamer (1980).
16. Gadamer (1991, 4, 10).
17. Gadamer (1997, 33).
18. Schleiermacher (1836), Havelock (1963), Gadamer (1980), Klein (1989), Ryle (1966), and Miller (1980) and (1986). My own work owes a great debt to the insights of Miller, esp. (1980, ix–xix)
19. Eagleton (1983, 10). On philosophy and literature, see Danto (1987) and Kosman (1992b).

simple definition is exceedingly useful for my task: it can be used to distinguish the literary elements in Plato's dialogues from his philosophy and at the same time establish that the two are one. The literary, according to Eagleton, is highly valued *writing*. Plato's work is certainly this. Such a conception of the dialogues specifically draws our attention to their structure, composition, style, voice, device, and so forth, none of which we would ordinarily call "Plato's philosophy." And yet, what we do call "Plato's philosophy" could not be sufficiently understood, and would not have the same effect, without seeing the literary media—the techniques of writing—through which Plato works. Plato conspicuously chose to set the dialogues in specific places, to put arguments in the mouths of distinct characters, to develop those characters, to portray action and relationships among the interlocutors, to make jokes, to tell myths and stories, to leave philosophical problems unresolved, to create paradoxical arguments, to name characters in significant ways, and so on. Each of these writing techniques or devices serves a philosophical purpose and achieves philosophical effects. So, one's conception of the literary need not exclude the philosophical nor vice versa. When the written aspects of the texts come into relationship with Plato's audience, philosophical engagement happens through them and not without them. Plato's writing must be examined and understood therefore as also comprising the philosophy he conveys thereby.

The subtext of this project is, therefore, an implicit argument for the union of philosophy and literature in the works of Plato. But I must, paradoxically, make the very distinction I want eventually to efface. The distinction between philosophy and literature is a modern one,[20] and it is responsible for a great many misconceptions about, and perhaps decades of misreadings of, Plato's dialogues. In discussing the work of A. E. Taylor,[21] Drew Hyland explains a defect in Taylor's reasoning:

---

20. Although the distinction between philosophy and poetry is not modern. I treat the relationship between poetry and philosophy in Chapter 3. The Oxford English Dictionary places the date of the use of "literature," in its earliest meanings in the late Middle English period, 1350–1468. The adjectival term "literary," meaning "pertaining to or having the characteristics of that kind of written composition valued on account of its qualities of form or emotional effect," dates from 1730–69. The meaning of the noun "literature," most relevant to the distinction that philosophers currently make, "That kind of written composition valued on account of its qualities of form or emotional effect," dates significantly later still, 1800–1829. See R. Williams (1977, 45–54), who discusses the history of the term "literature," and cf. B. Williams (1993, 13–14), who claims, to the contrary, that Plato was the first to offer the "categories of 'literature' and 'philosophy.'"

21. Taylor (1959).

The "and" in the epithet, "great artist and great philosopher" is by implication disjunctive rather than conjunctive; the two can and must be separated. The upshot of this view, therefore, is that it gives its adherents license, when speaking of Plato's philosophy, effectively to ignore all those aspects of the dialogues that are judged to be "literary."[22]

The bifurcation of philosophy and literature, in part, grows out of the analytic conception of philosophy. If philosophy is defined as the activity that uses logic and focuses on appropriate objects such as arguments and their constituent parts, then whatever is extralogical is also deemed extraphilosophical. Mitchell Miller articulates the problem in the following way:

> In contemporary writings on Plato it is almost commonplace to remark that he is at once a profound philosopher and a dramatist and teacher. Even by its form, however, this remark may confess more about contemporary scholarship and higher education than it reveals about Plato. In disciplinary terms, philosophy, literature, and pedagogy have been separated as distinct fields. The usual consequence for our study of Plato is that the correlative aspects of his dialogues—roughly, their content, form, and communicative function—are approached in isolation; and this, in turn, results in a significant diminution, if not concealment of each. "Content" comes to mean expressed doctrine, to the exclusion of implicit, subsurface meaning which it is the *function* of expressed doctrine, within the dramatically projected context, to suggest; "form" is reduced to style and the devices of stage-setting and portraiture which enliven, but have no internal bearing on, doctrinal content; and the pedagogical "function" of the dialogues tends to disappear altogether, to be replaced . . . by the expressed pedagogical doctrines of the *Republic*, *Meno*, etc. In short, even when we know and remind ourselves of the integrity of these elements, our modern scholarly predispositions, which begin from their separation, make this integrity extremely difficulty to grasp. And much is lost as a result.[23]

Miller's attention to the pedagogical, in addition to the philosophical and the literary, introduces the dialogues' significant potential to transform individuals

22. Hyland (1995, 92).
23. Miller (1980, ix).

who read or hear them. Arthur Danto underscores the importance of transformation. In discussing just when philosophy is literature, Danto says that literature is "transfigurative" because it is "about each reader who experiences
it. . . . Each work is about the 'I' that reads the text."[24] The contribution that
I hope this book will make is an analysis of the specific means through
which Plato achieves transfiguration and, as a consequence, an implicit
argument against the disciplinary dissection of the dialogues that concerns
both Hyland and Miller. Plato's written works quite successfully guide and
even provoke the reader or audience to philosophical activity, and I wish to
show that the means or media through which he does this are what we have
come to call literary or dramatic devices, and to show further just how that
occurs. What I hope to demonstrate, therefore, is that what to modern eyes
and ears are literary elements of Plato's texts, are the very vehicles necessary
for his philosophy. These qualities of his texts are not embellishments, or
finery, or even mere artistry. Rather, they are necessary for Plato to achieve
his philosophical aim. These elements capture an audience and engage it in
the very activity that is philosophy.

One might ask why I do not simply accept the distinction between literature and philosophy and study the philosophical *content* of the dialogues
and their literary *form*?[25] The implicit understanding behind this question is
that the literary aspects are merely the form of writing whose particular
content is philosophical, and that the two are separate and distinct. As is
implied by Miller in the passage cited above, the distinction between form
and content is, in the context of such a question, parasitic on that between
literature and philosophy and so begs the very question I wish to address
regarding their union.

Even the distinction between form and content, like that between literature and philosophy, becomes blurred on my reading of Plato's dialogues. I
illustrate here with three brief examples that are discussed in fuller detail in
the chapters that follow. First, the use of irony in the Platonic text might
usually be thought of as literary form, but as Plato uses it, irony is also—and
inseparably—philosophy or "content." Irony puts the reader in a position to
understand something about the interlocutor that the interlocutor most
likely does not understand about himself. As a consequence, irony can lead
the reader to insights about the importance of self-knowledge, that is, the
importance of having an accurate self-image and of admitting one's igno-

24. Danto (1987, 18–19).
25. Cf. Schleiermacher (1836) and Gonzalez (1996, 4–5).

rance. The irony itself therefore comprises philosophy and serves not just as its literary form.

Second, the use of images in the dialogues might also be considered literary form, but the fact that Plato uses images rather than arguments to convey particular philosophical insights demonstrates something philosophical about modes of human knowing, about the status of arguments, about possible limits to human knowledge, and about the relationship between images and arguments. We can gain philosophical insight through images, not simply through logico-deductive argument, and the human vision needed to see images is an essential epistemological tool in the philosophical life.

Third, Plato's use of dramatic form in the dialogues, the written form in which characters speak directly and in the context of particular settings and specific (inter)actions, compels the reader of the dialogue, by inducing her to play a role in the drama, to participate in philosophical activity. The reader learns what philosophical activity is from engaging in it. The dramatic form, therefore, *is* philosophical content insofar as it conveys to the reader an experience of philosophy and philosophical activity. Form and content converge in a powerful union in Plato's dialogues, just as do literature and philosophy. While we can understand philosophy and literature as separate and distinct through intellectual exercise, beyond the abstraction, they are unified in their practical effect in Plato's dialogues.

3. The Project

In Chapter 1, I delineate the practice and effects of Socratic dialectic, that is, the means through which Socrates engages his interlocutors. Simply speaking, dialectic is the question and answer depicted in the dialogues between Socrates and the interlocutors. In this simple capacity, dialectic can strip one of the conceit of knowledge, help one to admit one's ignorance, and therefore can put one in a position to inquire after the truth. But in a more complex manner, dialectic can be seen more broadly as the Socratic way of life, which is intellectually open, cognizant of ignorance and human limitations, and always in search of truth. Dialectic is thus more than merely a philosophical method or procedure, and is therefore distinct from *elenchus*, which is conceived of in some argument-focused approaches as logical refutation. Using several dialogues, I focus especially on the extralogical functions of dialectic, explaining how dialectic works through the emotion of

shame—since shame is closely bound to self-image—to force one to reconsider one's self-conception in contrast to one's true identity. I illustrate the
fundamental movement of dialectic, the movement at the root of all turning, through a focused examination of parts of the *Meno*, a dialogue most
exemplary of and explicitly about dialectic activity. I explain, as well, the
fundamental tension in dialectic between strong conviction and professed
ignorance, and thus what it means to come to believe, and to hold beliefs,
Socratically.

I establish at the end of the first chapter that the dialectic relationship
between Socrates and the interlocutors depicted within the dialogues has an
analogue on another level between Plato's text and the reader or audience.
Plato's text engages the reader in a dialectic relationship, analogous to that
between Socrates and the interlocutors, through the use of various literary
devices. This idea, that there is both Socratic dialectic and Platonic dialectic,
becomes the theoretical basis for arguments in subsequent chapters that
examine specific literary devices as the tools of Platonic dialectic.

Beginning where the first chapter leaves off, then, I develop more fully in
Chapter 2 just how dialectic on the Platonic level functions with respect to
the reader, fleshing out the analogy between interlocutors' responses to
Socrates and readers' responses to Plato's texts. I use the contemporary
reader-response theory of Wolfgang Iser to explicate just what transpires in
the act of reading. According to Iser's theory, meaning emerges during the
act of reading and through a relationship formed between text and reader
that is dialectical in nature. I show that Iser's theory describes well the relationship created between a Platonic dialogue and a reader of that dialogue. I
demonstrate further that the dialectic interaction between text and reader
can result in a turning of the soul. I then discuss the dimensions of dialectic,
dialogue, and the act of reading, that reveal the power to transform the self.
The turn toward philosophy rests on the possibility of this transformation.

In Chapter 3, I address directly the dramatic structure of the dialogues. I
demonstrate that by ancient Greek standards, Plato is to be considered a poet
and his work poetic. I show that Plato uses the dramatic and poetic elements
of the dialogues to turn the reader or audience toward the life of philosophy.
I explain how specific dramatic and poetic elements of the dialogues—such as
character naming, authorial distance, the reader's adopting a dramatic role,
and lived philosophical experience—function so as to achieve this aim. Then,
using Aristotle's functional definition of tragic poetry as a model, I attempt to
provide a parallel, functional definition for Socratic dialogue in an effort to
expose what is often concealed in philosophical treatments of the dialogues—

that they do have a function. They aim to do something or accomplish something through particular means using a specific medium, with respect to some audience. I conclude this chapter by using the notions of *drama* and *poesis* in their literal Greek senses of "a doing" and "a making," and I argue that Plato's dialogues "do" and "make" with respect to the reader: we do philosophy with them, and they attempt to make us into philosophers.

In Chapter 4, I take up the literary device of character development through a close examination of the *Meno*. This dialogue, through subtle dramatic details, compels the reader to examine the literary technique of character portrayal, and I argue that the dialogue portrays a change in Meno's character. I rely on the semantic ambiguity (that exists in English and Greek) of the term "character," which can refer to both a moral personality and a literary or dramatic persona, in order to make the case that this particular device in Plato's writing has significant philosophical import. By examining how and at what point this change in Meno's character occurs, I demonstrate that this dialogue reveals answers to its central questions, "Is virtue teachable?" and "What is virtue?" Those answers help us not only to see the connection between the life of virtue and the life of dialectic but also provide insight into Plato's philosophical project and his use of the literary device of character development in that project. I conclude that there is a double phenomenon of character development. Plato works on character development in the reader and audience, and he accomplishes this through a medium that works on character development as a literary device. While Plato is developing his literary characters in writing, he attempts to develop the moral characters of his readers.

In Chapter 5, I treat the literary device of irony, which has been the focus of great interest among Plato scholars recently. I argue against Gregory Vlastos's notion of "complex irony," showing it to be incomplete because it fails to embed and understand irony in the dramatic and literary context in which it occurs. I give several clear examples of irony that are not captured by Vlastos's conception of complex irony. I suggest an alternative conception of irony, irony as dramatic incongruity, which not only improves upon Vlastos's notion of complex irony but helps to explain just how irony functions with respect to the reader or audience of the dialogues and how it engages one in philosophical activity. Plato's employment of irony distinguishes those who understand the irony *as irony* from those who remain oblivious to it; those who "get it" perceive a quality in the interlocutors to which they initially feel superior (e.g., an interlocutor's ignorance), but their feelings of superiority are soon checked if they truly "get it," since the irony forces them to (re)consider whether they themselves exhibit that same quality. If one is to appreciate the irony, then—whether as interlocutor or reader—one must confront honestly one's shortcomings. Following the pattern of dialectic, irony thus works on shame in many cases, and it forces a reconsideration of one's identity. Irony is therefore another literary device Plato uses to turn one toward the life of philosophy through dialectic movement.

In the final chapter, Chapter 6, I treat Plato's use of images in myth, metaphor, analogy, and the like. Plato's use of these devices appears to belie aspects of what we have come to consider "Platonic" metaphysics: the senses are inferior to the intellect, the visible is inferior to the invisible, and only through pure reason, apart from the senses, can we come to know the highest truths. This chapter addresses explicitly human limitation, a theme introduced in Chapter 1 on dialectic, and it links that limitation with the very writing devices that Plato employs. I investigate the motivation for and the effect of Plato's use of images, as well as the role that vision might play in philosophy, and the manner in which images turn the reader or audience toward the activity of philosophizing. I discuss in some detail several dialogues that show consistently that images are the appropriate medium for an embodied soul to have philosophical insight, which implies that vision must play a role in philosophical activity. This underscores the idea developed earlier that philosophical activity goes well beyond logico-deductive reasoning. Moreover, Plato's images captivate and engage us in a manner that mirrors dialectic movement. No longer can we understand philosophy—at least philosophy practiced by humans—to be pure reason or pure argumentation, estranged from the particularities of our embodiment. Plato's dialogues indicate clearly that, as the limited beings we necessarily are, we must rely on image and vision for philosophical insight since pure rationality is not a possibility and argumentation will eventually fail us. Philosophy must necessarily include images and image-making. This conclusion opens the door for a reconsideration of all media available for the practice of philosophy.

Thus I conclude in section 4 of Chapter 6—"Epi-Logos"—that the dialogues recommend means for philosophical insight that lie beyond the traditional view of "Platonism." To understand Plato's project, one must go beyond the logic-centered scholarship, and only in doing so can one observe the extralogical devices that Plato uses in order to achieve his philosophical aim, which lies not in presenting winning or convincing arguments, nor in presenting or defending his own philosophical position.

Plato understood the great power of words and images. They can go directly to the soul and make deep and lasting impressions. Plato uses all of the tools of the poets and image-makers, and he appeals to his readers in several capacities beyond the purely rational or logico-deductive. He does so from a deep understanding of human psychology—our limitations, our concerns, our motives. Plato's profound insight into the tools of the poets and image-makers, and the interlocutors' warnings of the potential danger of those tools, mark Plato's respect for the power they wield. While recognizing the potential danger of the tools of the poets and image-makers, he sees more clearly their potential compelling power. They are so compelling as to turn us toward the philosophical life. The dialogues ask us to broaden our repertoire of philosophical media to include all these devices whose great power Plato often alludes to, and whose power he harnesses—aware of the risk involved—in order to turn us toward philosophy. The literary and dramatic devices of Plato's dialogues are the instruments he uses to free individuals from the bondage of ignorance and to turn their gaze toward philosophy.

1

Dialectic

The god, then . . . handed down to us this mode of
investigating, learning, and teaching one another. . . .

Philebus, 16e

Whether he repels us, engages us, maddens us, charms us, or stirs some
strange mixture of these reactions in us, Socrates is undeniably one of the
most intriguing and captivating characters in Western literature. We wrestle
with him; he turns us upon ourselves; he pins down our arguments; we struggle to escape his hold and, just when we believe we can break free, he makes
a move that places us back under his grip; we bend, twist, and writhe uncom-
fortably in his hold; we are seemingly overpowered by the self-confessed
weakling who turns out to be the strongest and most wily wrestler who
knows the holds most effective against our every move. And when we are not
in his presence, we still feel we are under his powerful grip. The contest is,
ultimately, a struggle with ourselves.

How does Socrates establish this relationship with us? It would seem an
important exploration to uncover reasons why his life and his person have

such a profound effect on all those with whom he comes in contact. As readers of Plato's dialogues—like Socrates' fellow Athenians—we rarely react dispassionately to Socrates' persona. Socrates creates a compelling, and sometimes ambiguous, relationship with his audiences, and he establishes that relationship through an activity that lies at the heart of the philosophical life: dialectic.

Dialectic rests fundamentally on question and answer, the give and take of philosophical conversation and investigation. Argument-focused conceptions of dialectic emphasize its argumentative aspects—particularly its refutative qualities—which are certainly significant, but dialectic really includes many tropes, behaviors, and ways of being that are embodied by Socrates. Dialectic is the Socratic existential stance. Since the Socratic life is held up as a worthy human life, and since the Socratic life is an embodiment of dialectic, it is imperative to inquire further into the details of just what dialectic is, how one engages in it, and why one ought to engage in it.

I hope to accomplish four goals, each of which corresponds to one section of this opening chapter. First, I want to advance our understanding of dialectic beyond the logical or argumentative conception of it that is most common in argument-focused Platonic studies. Dialectic is not simply a logical method for pointing out inconsistencies in interlocutors' belief sets. There is an essential aspect of dialectic that aims at the emotional response of the interlocutors; in particular, dialectic effects shame. Second, I introduce what constitute the necessary ingredients in dialectical engagement, which are most clearly enunciated in the dialogue *Meno*, but that are exhibited and valorized throughout the Platonic corpus as human ideals for living and learning. Since *Meno* links knowledge and virtue, my discussion of dialectic in this section touches on the moral and epistemic consequences of dialectic (which, Socratically speaking, are not truly distinct from one another). Third, I discuss how one becomes convinced of beliefs dialectically, what it means to hold one's beliefs dialectically, and, faced with the possibility of skepticism, I demonstrate the need for commitment to belief in human life and the nature of dialectic conviction. Fourth, I establish a parallel between what I call Socratic dialectic and Platonic dialectic. Socrates' effects on his interlocutors provide insights into Plato's philosophical project, his means of carrying out that project, and its possible effects. The mode in which Socratic dialectic is intended to function with respect to the interlocutors is mimicked or echoed in the relationship between Plato's text and his reader. At the conclusion of this chapter, therefore, I move outside the confines of the dialogue itself—outside the dialectic that occurs between Socrates and his interlocutors—to an investigation of the Platonic level of dialectic, the dialectic that occurs between the Platonic text and the reader.

1. Beyond Logic: Dialectic Tools and Practices

Many scholars use the term "elenchus" exclusively to denote a method of cross-examination or refutation they perceive Socrates to be using. Some have even examined Socrates' conversations in a formal way, looking to schematize them or to find consistencies in their logical structure.[1] The kinds of conclusions these studies are left to draw are primarily conclusions about the consistency of the belief sets of his interlocutors and the soundness or validity of Socrates' arguments. Certainly there are patterns and structural similarities one can find among Socrates' arguments, but these kinds of investigations neglect or, at best, diminish the full impact of dialectic; they do not capture its real import. While dialectic might include elenchus, conceived as a means of refutation, it goes significantly beyond it. Dialectic's fundamental impact on an individual's life comes exactly from the force it exerts at points beyond the elenchus or refutation.[2]

What is often deemed "literary" in Plato's texts is what appears to be extralogical. It is a narrow conception of philosophy and philosophical activity—as only what is identifiably "logical"—that encourages philosophers to discount, devalue, or even scrap entirely elements of the dialogues which they deem extraneous. If Socratic dialectic goes beyond "pure" logos,

---

1. See for example, Robinson (1953); Irwin (1979); Vlastos (1956), (1982), and (1983). See especially Vlastos's discussion (1956, xxvi–xlv) and compare his use of "logic" with my own in the following discussion. On not looking to logic as a hermeneutic strategy, see Gadamer (1980, 5).

2. Jaeger (1971) refers to two devices of "Socrates' talk," exhortation and examination (elenchus), which "are just different stages of one spiritual process" (36). He says further that "examination is the necessary complement to the exhortation: it loosens the ground in preparation for the seed, by showing the examinee that his knowledge is only imaginary" (62). Cf. Teloh (1986, 1–5), who claims that dialectic comprises two parts: refutation and soul-leading. While my view is consistent with Teloh's and Jaeger's, I delineate aspects of Socratic dialectic not included in the two parts of dialectic that they describe. Gadamer (1980, 93) grounds dialectic in dialogue and contrasts it with Hegelian dialectic, which is based on thinking in contradictions and is monological rather than dialogical. See also Gadamer (1986, 33–44). For an earlier critique of the approach that focuses on argumentation to the detriment of Plato's dialogues, see Hyland (1968). For discussions between scholars who favor an analytical approach to the dialogues and those who do not, see Griswold (1988). See also Press (1993).

then there is a case to be made for not extracting the "literary" from the philosophical. So, if Socrates' dialectic proves to contain, necessarily, extra-logical elements, and Plato mimics Socratic dialectic in his relationship to the reader, then what is philosophical in the dialogues can in any case be extralogical.

Richard McKim argues that it is not by logical but psycho-logical means that Socrates aims to persuade his interlocutors, and shame is his psycholog-ical tool. McKim demonstrates that Socrates shames his interlocutors into their positions in the *Gorgias*.[3] Callicles states that everyone really believes that doing injustice is naturally better and only social convention shames us into saying otherwise. McKim argues that, to the contrary, both Callicles and Polus believe deep down that it is harmful to the wrong-doer to pursue injustice, and Socrates shames them into admitting their true beliefs. McKim rightly characterizes Socrates as a psychological strategist[4] and shows that it is "shame and not mere logic" that is the weapon he wields to deliver the final blow to Callicles, the blow that makes him concede that he really does believe that to live the life of virtue is better than to live the life of vice.[5]

McKim breaks important ground, and I believe that his core idea can and should be taken even further. There are interactions in many of the dialogues similar to those McKim describes in the *Gorgias*, and shame, in addition to being used to get the interlocutors to confess to specific beliefs, is a common inducement on which Socrates relies to encourage his interlocutors to engage in dialectic practices and to turn toward the philosophical life.

Shame has two aspects, according to Gary Thrane: "On the one hand it is an intimate feeling deeply connected with personal ideals and self-conception. . . . Yet, on the other hand shame is peculiarly social. It seems closely related to 'facing the others.'" Thrane explains that

> shame is always relative to some ideal or standard of conduct. Shame results from failure to achieve or possess the (admired) ideal. The image of the shameful is failure, shortcoming, diminishment. . . . Moreover, one will not feel shame in the face of failure to live up to any ideal. For ideals must be "embraced" as personal before one can feel ashamed of falling short.[6]

---

3. McKim (1988). As a nice complement to McKim's article, see King (1987).
4. McKim, 45.
5. Ibid., 42.
6. Thrane (1979, 142–43); Thrane's emphasis.

In this respect, shame is closely connected to personal identity, and when one is shamed, it is a blow to one's self image by one's own judgment. But at the same time, a necessary ingredient of shame is a vision of oneself in a social context, a vision of oneself against the backdrop of the judgment of others. Bernard Williams advances the view that a kind of moral imperative among the Greeks stems from this social aspect of shame, that is, from a particularized conception of self and from being seen by a particularized other.[7] I argue, in a manner consistent with Thrane's and Williams's ideas, that shame is one of the primary psychological tools Socrates uses to induce one to give an account of oneself and to confront questions about one's true identity, essential components of dialectic.

The character of Alcibiades in the *Symposium* expresses his sense of shame movingly and in remarkable harmony with Thrane's assessment of the phenomenon.

> But nothing like this ever happened to me: [other great orators] never upset me so deeply that my very own soul started protesting that my life—*my life!*—was no better than the most miserable slave's. . . . [Socrates] makes it seem that my life isn't worth living! . . . he makes me admit that my political career is a waste of time, while all that matters is just what I most neglect: my personal shortcomings, which cry out for the closest attention. So I refuse to listen to him; I stop my ears and tear myself away from him, for, like the Sirens, he could make me stay by his side till I die.
>
> Socrates is the only man in the world who has made me feel shame—ah, you didn't think I had it in me, did you? Yes, he makes me feel ashamed: I know perfectly well that I can't prove he's wrong when he tells me what I should do; yet the moment I leave his side, I go back to my old ways: I cave in to my desire to please the crowd. My whole life has become one constant effort to escape from him and keep away, but when I see him, I feel deeply ashamed, because I'm doing nothing about my way of life, *though I have already agreed with him that I should.* Sometimes, believe me, I think I would be happier if he were dead. And yet I know that if he dies I'll be even

---

7. B. Williams (1993). Williams argues against the modernist conception that a Kantian type of moral imperative, that is, one that is deemed "autonomous" rather than "heterono-mous," is somehow a sign of moral progress or superiority. Williams aims to undermine the progressivist view of morality in general and show instead the fundamental moral and cultural similarities between ourselves and the Greeks.

more miserable. I can't live with him, and I can't live without him. What can I do about him? (215e–216c)[8]

This passage illustrates that Socrates uses shame to affect his interlocutors and that, consistent with Thrane's views, shame is a Socratic practice specifically aimed at personal identity. Socrates and the philosophical life provide for Alcibiades the admired ideal to which he subscribes, or at least to which he believes he should subscribe, and which he cannot achieve. In the presence of Socrates he is highly aware of his shortcomings, painfully aware that he falls terribly short of this ideal. Moreover, Alcibiades tells us that he is not the only one who feels this way in Socrates' presence (215d, 215e, 216c).

Socrates also demonstrates the importance of shame in his interactions with Meno. At the peak of his frustration, Meno lets it be known that he is confounded by the perplexity Socrates has thrown him into since he has on several occasions given many fine speeches about virtue to large audiences (*Meno*, 80b). Then, at the point in the slave demonstration where the slave has just admitted his ignorance, Socrates uses Meno's own words to great effect: "Now, he [the slave] would be pleased to find out, since he does not know, but before he might have easily thought to give fine speeches, before many people and often, about doubling an area, saying that one must double the length of the side" (84b–c). Meno's own words must now resonate in another manner than when first spoken.[9] What Meno made as a proud and confrontational boast now puts him to shame. Meno is just as ignorant about virtue as his slave is about geometry, perhaps even more so. Meno would be just as ridiculous expounding on virtue to the masses as the slave would be were he to lecture to large crowds that when we double the length of the side of a square we thereby double its area. Furthermore, to be compared—and unfavorably at that!—with one's slave would certainly be cause for shame for someone of Meno's social position.[10]

---

8. Translated by Nehamas and Woodruff (1989). First italics are translators' emphasis; second are my emphasis. Nehamas and Woodruff translate αἰσχύνω in its various forms as "I feel shame." One could also translate αἰδώς as "shame." The point here is a phenomenological one, not a philological one: what Thrane describes as shame is what Alcibiades and other interlocutors experience in Socrates' presence.

9. Compare Meno at 80b, καίτοι μυριάκις γε περὶ ἀρετῆς παμπόλλους λόγους εἴρηκα καὶ πρὸς πολλούς, καὶ πάνυ εὖ, ὥς γε ἐμαυτῷ ἐδόκουν, with Socrates at 84b, . . . τότε δὲ ῥᾳδίως ἂν καὶ πρὸς πολλοὺς καὶ πολλάκις ᾤετ'ἂν εὖ λέγειν . . .

10. Alcibiades' speech cited above confirms this: ". . . my life—*my* life!—was no better than the most miserable slave's. . . ."

Thrasymachus, who brazenly defends the advantages of the life of vice, is seemingly Socrates' most shameless interlocutor.[11] He even mocks Socrates meanly when he enters the conversation in the *Republic*:

> "Tell me, Socrates, have you got a nurse?" "What do you mean?" said I. "Why didn't you answer me instead of asking such a question?" "Because," he said "she lets her little 'snotty' run about driveling and doesn't wipe your face clean, though you need it badly, if she can't get you to know the difference between the shepherd and the sheep." (343a)

Thrasymachus goes on to defend the view that political rulers rule solely for their own advantage, not for the sheepish masses who are subject to them. Justice, he says, is the advantage of the stronger (343c). We are shocked therefore by the stunning portrayal of Thrasymachus's shame a bit later in the *Republic*. After a lengthy exchange between the two of them, Socrates leads Thrasymachus to conclude that "the just man has turned out on our hands to be good and wise and the unjust man bad and ignorant" (350c). Socrates turns back to his narration of the events that took place that day, and he describes the scene in the following manner: "Thrasymachus made all these admissions not as I now lightly narrate them, but with much balking and reluctance and prodigious sweating, it being summer, and it was then I beheld what I had never seen before—Thrasymachus blushing" (350d). While Thrasymachus is hardly won over by Socrates' arguments, he is annulled from here on out in the dialogue. After he blushes, he no longer defends the life of injustice in the shameless manner with which he began. Rather, he simply agrees to whatever Socrates proposes, indicating that he is doing so simply to please Socrates and not to offend him by differing (352b). Although his apparent compliance is a determined effort to thwart participation in authentic examination, the abrupt change in his behavior, signaled by the blush, draws notice.

That Socrates shames these interlocutors is true whether or not his doing so succeeds in changing their views or getting them to participate in dialectic. Alcibiades feel shame, but he fails to change his behavior accordingly. The same is true, I would argue, of Thrasymachus. It is not immediately obvious whether or not Meno actually feels the shame of being compared

---

11. With Callicles in *Gorgias* giving stiff competition. McKim's work (1988) demonstrates the manner in which Socrates uses shame with Callicles.

unfavorably to his slave.[12] While Alcibiades, Meno, and Thrasymachus represent interlocutors who resist dialectic despite having been shamed, and are therefore not Socratic success stories, there are other types of examples.

The opening scene of the *Protagoras* portrays a young man, Hippocrates, who, contrary to most other interlocutors, does exhibit a proper sense of shame and is therefore well disposed to the positive effects of dialectic.[13] What we learn first about Hippocrates is that he is so zealous in his desire to meet with Protagoras and to ask him to "make him wise" (310d) that he shows up at Socrates' house well before dawn hoping Socrates will introduce him to the great sophist. With the approaching dawn, Hippocrates, too, becomes enlightened as to how important a possession his soul is and what the significance and possible consequences are of entrusting it to someone such as a sophist (or to something such as sophistry) of which he is ignorant. Hippocrates' enlightenment is the direct result of his engagement in Socratic dialectic and the use of shame.

Socrates puts Hippocrates to the test (311b), questioning him regarding what he wants from Protagoras and what Protagoras will provide him. Ordinarily one seeks instruction from a professional in order to become a professional in that same capacity; one takes a course of instruction from a doctor, for example, in order to become a doctor (311b–e). Socrates wonders whether Hippocrates seeks instruction from Protagoras in order to become a sophist. At the unhappy conclusion that he might become a sophist through his association with Protagoras, Hippocrates blushes in shame (312a). He confesses that, even though Protagoras offers his instruction *qua* sophist, a sophist is not what Hippocrates wishes to become. This vivid portrayal of Hippocrates' shame portends his capacity to be turned by and toward dialectic. He clearly exhibits behavior that Socrates often encourages his interlocutors to display.

As Socrates continues the test, Hippocrates proves to be unable to explain the subject matter about which a sophist would make him a clever speaker, and he explicitly admits his ignorance (313c). When he ventures an opinion

---

12. I argue in Chapter 4, however, that Meno's shame does induce him to take part in dialectic in the latter half of the dialogue and to take some small interest in philosophical matters.

13. Theaetetus also fits this mold of a willing philosophical partner who is properly shamed; see *Theaetetus*, 183e, 189e, and 196d. See also *Charmides*, 158c. Charmides blushes, and Socrates takes it to be a sign of his modesty. Klein (1989, 24n) understands this scene to indicate not just Charmides' modesty, but to mark in him the particular virtue, *sophrosuné*, under discussion in this dialogue. For a different reading of the character Hippocrates, in *Protagoras*, see Roochnik (1996, 212ff.).

he is tenuous and not mistakenly over-confident or self assured ("I think I know," 312c). Moreover, he is willing to engage in dialectic early on, asking real, philosophical questions of Socrates such as, "What is a mind fed?" (313c). These behaviors distinguish Hippocrates from many other interlocutors.

As they set off finally for Callias's house, where the great sophist, Protagoras, is staying, Socrates and Hippocrates are engaged in some conversation, the topic of which is not mentioned. Socrates makes note of the fact, though, that they finish their conversation, reaching a mutually agreeable conclusion, before knocking on the door (314c). This is a remarkable detail in the drama.[14] Hippocrates' great eagerness to meet Protagoras just a short while ago seems to have been severely dampened. Recall that he arrived at Socrates' house well before dawn and wanted then to set out immediately to meet the sophist. But now, just moments—and inches—away, he patiently finishes a conversation with Socrates. This shows his serious involvement in their conversation despite his earlier preoccupation with meeting Protagoras. Since the topic of their conversation seems relatively unimportant to Socrates (he does not bother to relate it to the "Friend"), this dramatic detail says something about Hippocrates' character and about dialectic in general. It shows the power of shame to turn the young man to dialectic engagement and, in turn, it shows the power of dialectic more generally since it has compelled a zealous young man to bring a conversation to a mutually agreeable conclusion. That there was any agreement at all tells us that Hippocrates is someone with whom Socrates can reason and someone who is capable of the give and take required of one engaging in dialectic. One need only contrast Hippocrates here with many other interlocutors to see the great significance of this small act of waiting outside the doors to Callias's home—with Protagoras just inside—to finish a conversation and to come to an agreement with Socrates.

Finally, this brief mini-drama with the young Hippocrates, a prelude to the scene in Callias's house which occupies the rest of the dialogue, distinctly opposes the remainder of the drama. Inside Callias's house we see grand speech making, eristic discourse, pedantry, and obsequious sycophancy, none of which conduces to dialectic inquiry. The major dramatic tension between

14. And yet, one does not find many commentaries that take notice of it. For example, while Gagarin (1969) claims that "it is necessary to make a detailed analysis of the dialogue" (134), he simply says of this passage, "The preliminary conversation ends as Socrates and Hippocrates set off" (139). He then moves to the scene following the one that I presently discuss. Likewise, Grote (1888, 264) ignores this episode.

Protagoras and Socrates is the former's unwillingness or inability to engage in dialectic, and twice the inquiry nearly ends because of it (335b–338e and 348b–c). Moreover, the dialogue ends conspicuously with no mutually agreeable conclusion between Socrates and Protagoras, but instead with Socrates stating their opposing viewpoints (361a–362a). The unphilosophical and disagreeable ending of the *Protagoras* contrasts with the philosophical and agreeable beginning centered around Hippocrates' shame.[15]

Shame, then, plays an important role in the psychological dimension of dialectic. It works on a personal, existential level to compel interlocutors to reflect more deeply about who they are, what they believe, and how they choose to live their lives. It induces interlocutors specifically to engage in the give and take of question and answer and, more generally, to live the philosophical life. There are other dimensions of dialectic that operate on this existential level as well, and they indicate that while Socrates may be urging his interlocutors to reject inconsistent belief sets on one level,[16] he is exhorting them more importantly to live better lives. Better lives are lived, Socratically speaking, based on better beliefs, ones thoroughly tested by dialectic. But we ought not focus on the logic of beliefs at the expense of the lives lived according to them. All of Socrates' examinations are about how, ultimately, we will choose to live our lives, and how our beliefs will inform that life.

Of all the dialogues, the *Apology* makes it most explicitly and poignantly clear that dialectic is not about argumentation or logic, simply speaking, but about testing and improving the soul. Dialectic or questioning is a way to protect the soul not from beliefs repugnant to logic, but beliefs repugnant to good human living. Dialectic forces persons not to give good arguments but to give good account of themselves and the lives they have chosen to live.

After telling the jury that he is unwilling to give up the practice of philosophy Socrates admonishes the Athenians for not caring for their souls:

> [A]re you who are a citizen of Athens, the greatest of cities and the most famous for wisdom and power, not ashamed (οὐκ αἰσχύνει) to care for the acquisition of wealth and for reputation and honor, when you neither care nor take thought for wisdom and truth and the perfection of the soul? And if any of you argues this point, and

---

15. Hippocrates is not the only one shamed in this dialogue, however. After giving "no indication as to which course he would take" in his conversation with Socrates, Protagoras is chided by Alcibiades. Socrates thinks that Protagoras is shamed by this chiding and, once shamed, Protagoras "prevail[s] upon himself to take up the debate" (*Protagoras*, 348b–c).

16. See note 1 above.

says he does care, I shall not let him go at once, nor shall I go away, but I shall question and examine and cross-examine him (ἐλέγξω), and if I find that he does not possess virtue, but says he does, I shall rebuke him for scorning the things that are of most importance and caring more for what is of less worth. (*Apology*, 29d–30a)

After his death sentence has been announced, Socrates speaks prophetically to the jurors: "[Y]ou hoped that you would be relieved from rendering an account (ἔλεγχον) of your lives" (39c). Clearly the examining and testing is aimed at correcting the Athenians' lives, compelling them to care for the most important things. Socratic dialectic thus clearly is about one's goodness and it forces one to give an account of one's life not one's logical acumen.

A description of Socrates from the *Laches* underscores this same quality of dialectic as a means of giving an account of a human life, not of refuting arguments. Nicias tells Lysimachus,

[W]hoever comes into close contact with Socrates and has any talk with him face to face, is bound to be drawn round and round by him in the course of the argument—though it may have started first on a quite different theme—and cannot stop until he is led into giving an account of himself (αὐτοῦ λόγον), of the manner in which he now spends his days (ὅντινα τρόπον νῦν τε ζῆ), and of the kind of life (βίον) he has lived hitherto. . . (*Laches*, 187e–188a).[17]

We are not reproached by Socrates for holding inconsistent beliefs, but for living bad lives. Likewise, we do not hear of Socrates testing beliefs or arguments or definitions. Socrates, and therefore dialectic, test us and our lives.

Just as the logic of the arguments is less important than Socrates' aims in engaging someone in question and answer, likewise the definitions sought after in the dialogues (e.g., piety, temperance, justice, courage, and so on) are of less importance than what lies behind the search for them. On one level, the dialogues can be seen as a search for definition, but on a deeper and ultimately more important level, they are a search for identity. Socrates may be asking Meno, Hippocrates, and Protagoras "What is virtue?," on one level, but he is forcing them to ask themselves "Who am I?," on another level. In the process of addressing questions about virtue, justice, knowledge,

17. Although it is used in a different context, the use of this quotation was suggested to me by Seeskin (1984).

piety, or temperance, these and other Socratic interlocutors must also face questions about the types of persons they are, the types of persons they perceive themselves to be, and the types of persons they ought to become. This is why shame, which challenges personal identity, is so powerful and necessary a tool of dialectic. Dialectic involves Socrates' interlocutors on a personal level by forcing them to recognize something about themselves; it then demands that they confront their beliefs and whether they are living the good human life in an honest, personally risky, and sometimes shameful way. In short, dialectic demands that interlocutors address the question, "Who am I?" at the deepest level.

As further evidence that Socrates' questions are about who one is, I should like to call attention to the *Phaedo* where Socrates comes near to stating explicitly that dialectic is not about assessing arguments but about judging oneself. In the context of warning Cebes and Simmias not to be misologues, haters of argumentation, Socrates says that it is pitiable

> if a man, because he has met with some of those arguments which seem to be sometimes true and sometimes false, should then not blame himself or his own lack of skill, but should end, in his vexation, by throwing the blame gladly upon the arguments. (*Phaedo*, 90d)

And further,

> [L]et us not admit into our souls the notion that there is no soundness in arguments at all. Let us far rather assume that we ourselves are not yet in sound condition and that we must strive manfully and eagerly to become so, you and the others for the sake of all your future life, and I because of my impending death. (90d–e)

In these passages, Socrates clearly shifts the young men's focus away from philosophical arguments that might "fail" them and turns them toward an examination of their faulty souls. Passages such as these point us beyond the aporetic "arguments" in the dialogues to an examination of ourselves and our souls. The dialogues are personal because they revolve around the investigation and testing of oneself, not arguments or definitions.

Richard Robinson, who wants to stress, among other things, the *personal* nature of the elenchus, claims that the most striking aspect of Socrates' behavior is that "[h]e is always putting to somebody some general question, usually in the field of ethics."[18] But Robinson's observation is ironic. How personal can the elenchus be when it engages someone in conversation about "some general question, usually in the field of ethics"? Socrates' questions are not "general" questions at all, but rather personal questions, and usually quite specific to the personalities and situations surrounding a particular conversation. Socrates is always speaking to his interlocutors about themselves, about who they are, often in contrast to who they think they are. Moreover, to speak about "the field of ethics" in this manner and context seems to be a misunderstanding of the existential nature of the dialogues. Socrates' questions are not as academic as Robinson seems to indicate and do not address any modern "field" or "discipline." They address entire lives and ways of living.

Socrates' arguments are often formulated with the particular interlocutor's identity in mind, and tailored to be effective on him. In this respect, much of his dialectic is *ad hominem.*[19] Necessarily then, Socrates' arguments are of a rhetorical nature. He attempts to persuade his interlocutors of beliefs to which he himself is committed,[20] and he is committed to such beliefs because they have so far withstood the test of dialectic and continue to do so. Withstanding such a test lies at the heart of the logic and rigor of dialectic.

Logic and rigor carry specific meaning when applied to dialectic that they would not carry in a traditional analysis of mere arguments. If one continues to ask questions—of one's reasoning processes and of the conclusions that result from them—only those beliefs worth holding remain. In this way, dialectic acts as a continuous check on itself and the beliefs that can be distilled through its use, and it implies something about the inherent fallibility of humans.[21] Dialectic's internal logic is thus self-regulating and self-correcting.

18. Robinson (1971, 78).

19. In this regard, I am mostly in agreement with Teloh (1986, 1), who claims to argue several theses in his book: "(1) Socrates invariably fits his logoi (words, statements, or arguments) to the conditions of the psyche (souls) of the persons with whom he talks, (2) Socratic dialectic frequently is *ad hominem* in the way in which it tests the beliefs of an interlocutor, (3) One must look at the specific character of each interlocutor both to appreciate what each says and to understand how Socrates attempts to educated them, and (4) Socratic dialectic (question and answer) has two major aspects: *elenchus* (refutation) and *psychagogia* (psyche-leading); how Socrates uses these aspects depends upon the specific character—psychic condition—of a particular interlocutor." See note 2 above on my exception to the fourth thesis.

20. For example, that it is better to live the just life than the unjust life, that the unexamined life is not worth living for a human being, that doing wrong harms the soul of the wrongdoer, that good souls suffer no evil fate after death.

21. For a detailed and far reaching treatment of human limitations in Platonic thought, see Hyland (1995).

By subjecting her beliefs to dialectic, the individual performs a kind of test whereby those beliefs that stand up to dialectic ought to be kept—albeit always and continually subject to further examination—and those beliefs that cannot stand up to such questioning ought to be discarded. Herein lies the meaning of logic when applied to the whole practice of Socratic dialectic.

Hippocrates poses a question to Socrates in the *Protagoras*, "What is a mind fed?" whose answer helps to elucidate the self-corrective logic of dialectic, and therefore points to dialectic's ability to improve the soul. In cautioning Hippocrates about the care of his soul, Socrates makes the following elliptical analogy: When one is in the market place buying foods in order to feed the body, the vendors are praising all of their wares, whether they are good for the body or bad. And unless one is an expert on health or nutrition, one does not know what to buy so as to benefit the body. One could, however, take away in a separate container the goods one wishes to buy and allow an expert to examine them first, before ingesting them. It is likewise with the sophists who hawk their wares. They praise all of their courses of instruction equally, and unless one is an expert in care of the soul, one cannot know which are good and which are bad for the soul (*Protagoras*, 313c–314b).

Socrates implies but does not explicitly complete the analogy. Hippocrates and we are left to wonder what the analogy is to taking away in containers the things we might learn so that we may test them to determine whether they are good for the soul or not. I suggest that dialectic is that analogue. It forestalls the ingestion of ideas directly and allows us to test them. In this way dialectic performs a duty to the soul like some expert who tests food to see whether it is healthy and may be ingested, or whether it ought to be discarded because of its poisonous or unhealthy influence on the body. This elliptical analogy hints at the self-corrective qualities of dialectic. Dialectic, which is the subtext of the *Protagoras*, can test beliefs for the soul before they are ingested, aiding us in rejecting those beliefs that do not pass the test of dialectic and keeping those beliefs that do, but always subjecting them to further testing.

There is, likewise, a rigor to dialectic, but it is not a logical rigor strictly speaking. Rather, it is a rigor that stems from its continual and unrelenting use throughout a lifetime. The rigor of dialectic arises from the consistent and abiding way in which it is lived, and Socrates' life remains a paradigm of such rigor. Dialectic is a philosophical way of life in addition to being a philosophical procedure. For example, the questioning procedure taken to its limits and lived thoroughly develops into a questioning posture and results in life-as-quest. Moreover, Socratic ignorance, rather than being simply a one-time admission, becomes an existential stance, an attitude which is the source from which life-as-quest springs and reflection develops. The dialectical life is also, therefore, the self-regulating life. One's beliefs and values are continually inspected in an effort to improve them. Life-as-quest is a life lived in search of an answer to the question, "Who am I?" And the evaluation of who one is is measured against who one can and ought to be as a human being.

Socrates' life is the epitome of what I describe here, a paradigm of life-as-quest. So, in exhorting his interlocutors to dialectic, Socrates is exhorting them to live better lives. When engaging an interlocutor, Socrates works through dialectic to tear away old beliefs and behaviors and to replace them with better ones; at the same time he tries to give the interlocutor the means by which he himself can maintain the life of inquiry and learning, namely, dialectic. Dialectic is not merely a tool of logical analysis, nor simply a method of breaking down an interlocutor in argument. Dialectic, as practiced by Socrates, is the fundamental moral enterprise that comprises the Socratic way of life.[22] In practicing it, Socrates benefits his soul and, ideally, the souls of his interlocutors are opened up to the same possibility. Dialectic's aim is the improvement of those who engage in it, and it has the capacity to transform those who put it to use.

To learn through dialectic is to live the examined life as Socrates intended it. Dialectic gives us both a way to live and a way to learn—a way to be and a way to know. It is therefore a learning process that exposes the inseparability of the personal and the intellectual—the ethical and the epistemological. Thus understood, dialectic underscores that virtue is knowledge. In dialectic what (and how) one believes and who one is are conjoined. It is in living the dialectical life that virtue and knowledge become one.

2. Dialectic in the *Meno*

That virtue and knowledge are one is intimated in the *Meno*.[23] This dialogue shows the link between dialectic as a philosophical procedure used to examine ideas and dialectic as moral engagement used to examine and improve the

22. Cf. *Apology*, 20e–23b.
23. For a more detailed treatment of this dialogue, which is not my aim here, see Chapter 4. For my purposes here, I shall address in brief only those aspects of this dialogue that aid me in fleshing out the concept of dialectic.

souls of those who engage in it. The *Meno* asks explicitly what virtue is and how one becomes virtuous, but lurking in this dialogue is the quandary that virtue might be some kind of knowledge and yet not be teachable. Both the quandary and its solution center on the practice of dialectic. The portrait of dialectic that emerges from this dialogue shows just how one might become virtuous through engagement in dialectic and, consequently, how virtue can be knowledge and yet not be teachable. The *Meno* demonstrates how we ought to engage in dialectic and justifies why we ought to engage in it. In the *Meno* we see most clearly what is implicit in all other Platonic dialogues, namely, that dialectic is the key to turning toward the philosophical life. Since it provides an excellent example of Socratic dialectic and an explicit discussion about dialectic interaction, I therefore turn to that dialogue now as a means of illustrating in a more detailed and concrete manner the workings of dialectic.

In the first third of the dialogue, Meno repeatedly fails to give an adequate definition of virtue. When Meno reaches a high point of frustration due to Socrates' questions and his inability to respond adequately, he attempts to throw a wrench in the works. He presents Socrates with a thorny dilemma,[24] posed in such a way that either choice is one Socrates would not want to make: no man can search either for what he knows or for what he does not know; he cannot search for what he knows, for he knows it and there is no need to search for it; neither can he search for what he does not know, for he does not know what to search for and will not know it when he comes upon it (80d5).[25] Meno's dilemma says that inquiry and, consequently, learning are impossible. It therefore threatens to forestall the present inquiry in process between him and Socrates (What is virtue? Is it teachable?), and ultimately it threatens all inquiry. The story of recollection is Socrates' direct response to Meno's challenge, and it is reasonable, therefore, to expect that the story will at the very least show *that* learning is possible—and this it does. In addition, the story of recollection provides an explanation and a paradigm for *how* learning is possible. Recollection explains the learning process in a manner that saves inquiry and learning from Meno's skeptical challenge and that points toward the virtuous life in a single motion. It is Socrates' account of recollection that also ultimately solves the riddle of how virtue can be knowledge and yet not teachable.

24. Meno's dilemma is sometimes referred to as "Meno's Paradox." Meno's motivation for introducing the dilemma, and the consequences of Socrates' response to it, are taken up in detail in Chapter 4.

25. It is, in fact, Socrates who states the dilemma in its strongest form at 80e.

Socrates gets around Meno's dilemma—either we know something already and don't have to search for it or we do not know it and will not recognize it when we discover it—by arguing that it presents a false dichotomy. The story of recollection puts human knowledge in neither of these two states categorically (known or not known). Socrates tells us that the soul, being immortal, has seen all things both here and in the underworld; there is nothing that it has not learned (81c–d). So all learning on the part of the soul, once it is embodied, is a kind of recollection or memory. Since we have always already known the truth, and yet have been caused to forget it at birth, learning then becomes an act of re-covery rather than dis-covery. There is a way to search for something when one does not know it; one will re-cognize it when one comes upon it. Learning is therefore possible, contrary to the implication of Meno's challenge.

But *how* are we to learn? Socrates' exchange with the slave—as well as the dialogue as a whole—demonstrates how learning is possible through the question and answer of dialectic. The dialogue presents four elements that are necessary, although probably none sufficient, to learn dialectically:

(1) To begin with, ignorance is the starting point for learning. Learning can take place only when the walls of self-righteous arrogance are torn down and one admits one's ignorance. Without such an admission, the interlocutor remains stuck with his previous presumptions and erroneous views with no incentive to move beyond them. After a series of questions, the slave is reduced to a position of ignorance from which he states explicitly, "I don't know" (84a). Socrates then turns to Meno and gains his assent that the slave has now been made better off because when he did not know and was unaware of his ignorance he would not search, but now that he is aware of his ignorance his search can begin (84a–d). The puzzlement or aporia that one experiences after being questioned is a necessary and positive component in the learning process. An awareness of one's lack of knowledge is what spurs one on to inquire. The search continues with the slave, solely through Socrates' questions, and the slave is successfully brought to a point of recollecting the diagonal's relationship to the area and length of the sides of the square.

(2) Dialectic learning comes through self-examination and the learner is therefore the mediate source of knowledge. Built into the story of recollection is the notion that the soul recollects from itself what it has already known. Socrates exhorts Meno, telling him that he who is brave in the search for knowledge pursues it for himself (αὐτὸν, 81d) and, even more explicitly, he says that the individual must learn *from* himself (ἐξ αὐτοῦ) not

having been taught but only questioned (85d). I describe the learning subject as the "mediate" source of knowledge, as opposed to the "ultimate" source of knowledge, since the latter must be the form (εἶδος, 72c) to which the individual looks, but each individual has access to knowledge through self-examination. There is no subjective relativism implied. Dialectic is subjective only insofar as the learning subject recollects from herself, not a source external to her, but the objects recollected are presumably external, universal, and absolute.

(3) Socratically speaking, one must submit to question and answer if one is going to learn. Questioning strips one of any conceit of knowledge and thus one arrives at the starting point of learning. Meno is eager early in the dialogue to hear and give long speeches, but this sophistic method, which he presumably acquired from Gorgias, stands in stark contrast to Socrates' dialectic question and answer in which Meno is not particularly adept or willing to participate (75c, 76b, 76c). Socrates explicitly distinguishes dialectic question and answer—inquiry and response—from teaching. Socrates stresses repeatedly and conspicuously that he will only question the slave, not *teach* him anything about geometry (82e, 84c–d, 85d). Teaching, as Socrates understands it here, would seem to be telling.[26] The activity of questioning stirs the memory, and so one recollects or learns. We can assume that at an early stage another person may be involved in the learning process as someone who asks questions, but over time, the individual might assimilate this method into her own life and develop further to the point of being able to ask herself and others questions.

And (4), one cannot learn dialectically from an authority. Authority is eschewed by the elements of recollection that place the individual's own soul as the object of investigation and as the mediate source of knowledge. We should look to our own souls and to the realities themselves in order to learn. Questioning and answering, as opposed to teaching (as telling) function similarly and shun authority. While not actually present at the scene, Gorgias's presence as an authority figure for Meno looms large in the early portions of this dialogue. The dialogue goes to great lengths to establish that Meno's view is assumed to be the same as Gorgias's on the subject at hand (71d, 73c, 79e), but Socrates tries to move Meno away from reliance on Gorgias's authority (71c–d). Meno is exhorted to learn absent of authority and the slave serves as a model of learning independently of any authority.

---

26. This language is used by Teloh (1986, 2ff.). Clearly, Socrates accepts the distinction between teaching (telling) and questioning.

Recollection thus solves the difficulty brought up in Meno's challenging dilemma. It shows that learning and inquiry are possible, and it presents a model for how to search for what one does not know. In addition to the powerful presentation of recollection, two questions are put forth explicitly in the *Meno*: What is virtue? and Can it be taught? The dialogue in its entirety intimates that virtue is knowledge, but knowledge which is not taught, and which comes about in a special way, that is, dialectically. Virtue would seem, therefore, to come through dialectical enterprise, and dialectical knowledge is a kind of knowledge which cannot be taught. It comes through self-examination, by question and answer; it must occur in the absence of authority, and from a position of recognized ignorance. But dialectic entails much more than cognitive activity. It can work through the emotions for its desired effect, as we saw with shame. It is a mode of examining the whole person, forcing her to take stock of her entire life through an examination of beliefs, psychological states, relations, and actions.

3. Dialectic and Belief: The Socratic Disposition

Understanding dialectic helps to understand the manner in which Socrates holds his beliefs and the nature of his commitment to them. Dialectic is an appropriate means of investigation, and an appropriate way of life, in part because of the fragile nature of human knowledge. But dialectic is also powerful enough to provide Socrates with unmatched vigor in defending his beliefs. A strong tension thus pervades the dialogues between their portrayal of the tenuous human grasp on wisdom and the tenacious conviction with which Socrates holds certain beliefs. The nature and function of dialectic stand at the very pressure point of this tension.

The manner in which Socrates' views are presented in the dialogues is, I think, indicative of the manner in which he holds them. Neither are they presented positively nor are they held dogmatically. The dialogues are dramatic pieces containing myth, irony, and humor, and beliefs embedded in such a context are never posited directly. Rather, they emerge in a qualified manner from the text. Socrates has often heard theories from others, he interprets in novel ways the words of the traditional poets, he tells myths, he makes analogies, he sometimes contradicts himself, and his philosophical discussions end aporetically. What needs discussion then is what it means to hold a belief Socratically.

To believe something Socratically is, first of all, to subject that belief to the test of dialectic. Presumably, Socrates' beliefs have thus far withstood the rigors of questioning. But dialectic, remember, is no finite process or algorithm for testing and holding beliefs. So, by being subject to dialectic, these beliefs are constantly open to revision. There can be no closure to a so-called system of Socratic beliefs. There must always be, therefore, an air of fallibility surrounding Socrates' beliefs and all human beliefs. Moreover, in light of the possibilities of fallibility and the consequent need for constant revision of beliefs, we are compelled to take seriously Socrates' claim of ignorance. The paradox of Socratic ignorance is that in it resides his wisdom, a human wisdom (*Apology*, 23a–b). Dialectic, as embodied in Socrates, joins human ignorance and human wisdom in one being. Dialectic is at the same time the means to discovering one's ignorance as well as the means to moving beyond it.[27]

In spite of human fallibility, however, we cannot assume Socrates' commitment to his beliefs to be a weak one. Simply because dialectic takes shape in question and quest, it need not lead to skeptical ends. Socrates' recognition of human fallibility leads neither to epistemological nor ethical skepticism.[28] Rather, we observe in the dialogues Socrates' deep commitment to beliefs, and to a way of life, which fly in the face of either kind of skepticism. In an effort to stave off epistemological skepticism, Socrates reminds Cebes and Simmias and all others assembled in his jail cell that they ought not to fall into despair when rational discourse seems to be failing them.

> Then you know, those men especially who have spent their time in disputation come to believe that they are the wisest of men and that they alone have discovered that there is nothing sound or sure in anything, whether argument or anything else, but all things go up and down, like the tide in the Euripus, and nothing is stable for any length of time. (*Phaedo*, 90b–c)

This passage immediately precedes the passage cited earlier (90d) in which Socrates urges the young men not to become misologues. Epistemological skepticism, far from being the result of dialectic inquiry, is the enemy of dialectic and the philosophical life. Simmias has perhaps already grasped this lesson, for he is the character who, just prior to the discussion of misology,

---

27. Cf. Hyland (1995).
28. I use "skepticism" here in its ancient sense of an unwillingness to assent to beliefs.

provides a wonderful metaphor for human wisdom and dialectic. He reasons that, although precise knowledge about certain things is impossible or extremely difficult in this life, we nevertheless should show strong spirit and conduct a thorough investigation. Once we adopt "whatever human doctrine is best and hardest to disprove" then "embarking upon [this doctrine]," we should "sail upon it through life in the midst of dangers, unless [we] can sail upon some stronger vessel, some divine revelation, and make [our] voyage more safely and securely" (85c–d). Beliefs are vessels on which we navigate the dangerous waters of human existence, and dialectic provides a means for testing the sturdiness of those vessels. Our beliefs must be open to revision so that when, after dialectic discourse, a firmer vessel presents itself, we let go of our current vessel, and sail on board the sturdier craft.

Socrates is committed to certain beliefs not only because they have withstood the test of dialectic, but because, if we hold them, they help us to lead better human lives. The manner in which Socrates holds his beliefs therefore repels ethical skepticism, as well as epistemological; for many of these beliefs their ultimate justification is ethical. Meno is inclined to believe the cynical view of the debaters that one cannot learn, so Socrates recounts for him the story that our immortal souls already have the knowledge we need and we must only recollect it. The story of recollection is most commonly understood to be an epistemic one. Consequently, we might expect an epistemic or metaphysical justification to underlie the story. But, Socrates vouches for the story by twice invoking an ethical argument. Just after introducing his theory of recollection Socrates says,

> So we must not hearken to that captious argument: it would make us idle, and is pleasing only to the indolent ear, whereas the other [i.e., recollection] makes us energetic and inquiring. Putting my trust (πιστεύων) in its truth, I am ready to inquire with you into the nature of virtue. (*Meno*, 81d–e; Loeb trans., 1990)

Then, after the demonstration with his slave, Meno concedes that the story of recollection does seem to make some sense to him after all. Socrates responds:

> And so it does to me, Meno. Most of the points I have made in support of my argument are not such as I can confidently assert (διισχυρισαίμην); but that the belief in the duty of inquiring after what we do not know will make us better and braver and less helpless than the notion that there is not even a possibility of discovering

> what we do not know, nor any duty of inquiring after it—this is a
> point for which I am determined to do battle, so far as I am able,
> both in word and deed. (86b–c; ibid.)

While not devoid of metaphysical or epistemological implications, the story
of recollection clearly and ultimately rests, by Socrates' account, firmly on
ethical grounds. The justification for the story is that we will be better people if we believe it. Socratic commitment to such beliefs, as well as his justification for them, provide strong evidence that dialectic does not lead to
ethical skepticism. Quite the contrary, ethical considerations justify dialectic
endeavor.

Socrates' relentless commitment to certain beliefs is clear in the *Apology*
where his willingness to accept the death penalty for the sake of his convictions is most acutely portrayed. Socrates claims to be utterly committed to
serving the god, that is, practicing dialectic among the Athenian citizens. "I
gladly embrace you, Athenian gentlemen, and I love you. But, I shall obey
the god rather than you. And while I am still breathing and able, I shall not
stop philosophizing, exhorting and explaining" (29d2–6). Ethical, or perhaps in this case, religious, compulsion drives Socrates to lead the life of
dialectic. This paradoxical mixture of openness to revision in one's beliefs
and total commitment to them at the same time captures an essential element of what it means to hold a belief Socratically. The commitment to
beliefs comes from a strong trust in dialectic's self-corrective capacities, and
the openness to revision stems from the presumption of fallibility that
underscores our need for dialectic in the first place. What Socrates' paradoxical commitment ultimately betrays is a total faith in dialectic as a method
and as a way of life.

And "faith," I believe, is an accurate description.[29] One can easily make
the case that Socrates' way of life is indeed religiously motivated insofar as it
is lived in service to the god, as the *Apology* makes clear repeatedly. In
response to the god's message that no one is wiser than he, Socrates begins his
examination of himself and others. He infers that the god's riddle must have
been intended to set him out on this very mission (20c–23b). And this is perhaps the best context in which to understand the brief passage from the
Philebus that heads this chapter. The god has provided Socrates, and through
him, the rest of Athens and humankind, "this mode of investigating, learning,

---

29. See Grote's discussion (1888, 248–49), which refers to the "worship of dialectic" and
thus rightly implies that the philosophical life, when pursued indefatigably, is of a religious
nature. Cf. McPherran (1996).

and teaching one another." Moreover, Socrates' life takes on faith its mode of operation: The one thing that is *not* subject to question is dialectic itself. In fact, to question the dialectic process is to engage in it. The best endeavor to which one can devote oneself is care of the soul, and dialectic is the means by which one may accomplish this. In its broadest interpretation, this way of life can clearly be said to be based on a kind of faith.

It is never lost on Socrates, however, that devotion to such a life holds great risk. To recognize human ignorance and fallibility while living a life of conviction is to expose oneself to the possibility of having held the wrong convictions, of having lived the wrong life. But never to have taken the risk is a worse human life. The single best known line from the Platonic dialogues tells us that the unexamined life is not worth living for a human being (*Apology*, 38a). It is not insignificant that the full statement Socrates actually makes in that context is that few people will believe him when he says that the unexamined life is not worth living for a human being. The significance of the full statement lies in Socrates' understanding of the unusual nature of his life and the profound difficulty of sustaining the life he is recommending. Moments before ending his life, Socrates again speaks with the strange mixture of uncertainty and conviction about the risk of belief:

No sensible man would insist (διισχυρίσασθαι) that these things are as I have described them, but I think it is fitting for a man to risk (κινδυνεῦσαι) the belief—for the risk is a noble one—that this, or something like this, is true about our souls and their dwelling places since the soul is evidently (φαίνεται) immortal. (*Phaedo*, 114d)[30]

Socrates understands the meaning of risk—at this point in his life, especially. As he prepares to drain the cup of hemlock, while not willing to insist on everything he has claimed, Socrates risks his eternal life on his convictions that his soul is immortal and that his death cannot be unpleasant since he has lived a good human life.

Socrates judges the worth of that human life through and with dialectic. Socrates goes beyond admitting his ignorance; he adopts ignorance as part of his basic existential stance in dialectic. He devotes his life to question and answer, searching his soul in order to recover the forgotten ideas still accessible within him, while urging others to search likewise. His convictions have thus far withstood the test of dialectic. Socrates' beliefs are, as a consequence,

30. Translated by Grube (1981).

reasonable, not shameful, and lead to the improvement of his soul. Socrates' life is a preparation for holding convictions in the face of fallibility and this is the aim of the philosophical or dialectic life.

4. Platonic Dialectic: A Look Ahead

Perhaps the greatest tribute we have to the value of dialectic are Plato's dialogues themselves. That Plato chose to write in the dialogue format—that format that most closely resembles Socrates' interpersonal dialectic—lends support to the view that dialectic is at the core of philosophical activity. Within the dialogues we get to see philosophical problems in the process of being worked out. We see into the workings of dialectic through Socrates and his interlocutors, and we see Socrates' life as the paradigm of life-as-quest.

Most significant to my argument here is that dialectic occurs doubly in the dialogues: Plato composes dialectic within the dialogues between Socrates and the interlocutors, but Plato creates a kind of dialectic as well between reader and text. The effects of dialectic on the participants in Socrates' conversations are mirrored in Plato's created effect on the readers of his dialogues. What Socrates tries to convey about human life to his interlocutors, Plato tries to convey through dialectic to his readers and audience. In the next chapter, I shall discuss the dialectic that takes place between the reader and text. Just as Socratic dialectic exhorts interlocutors to live better lives by turning toward philosophy, Platonic dialectic attempts to engage the reader with similar ends in mind.

Initiating the discussion of Plato's dialectic relationship with the reader of his text leaves us at the jumping off point for the chapters that follow. In those chapters, I focus directly on the literary and dramatic qualities of the dialogues, and I demonstrate how they function philosophically with respect to the reader. The remainder of the work rests on the thesis that the literary and dramatic qualities of Plato's texts are the means through which he establishes the dialectic relationship with the reader, and therefore the means through which he realizes his philosophical project to turn individuals toward the philosophical life.

2

Reader

A (Platonic) dialogue has not taken place if we, the
listeners or readers, did not actively participate in it;
lacking such participation, all that is before us is
indeed nothing but a book.

Jacob Klein (1989)

What transpires when Socrates engages an interlocutor? What do we experience when we read one of Plato's dialogues? The answers to these questions are parallel; by understanding the desired effect of Socrates' dialectic on his interlocutors, we can also understand that of Plato's dialogues on his readers. Furthermore, reader-response theory, one contemporary approach to literary criticism, is a powerful tool for gaining insight into Socratic dialectic and Plato's dialogues. While response theory is most commonly applied to the modern novel, it proves highly useful in shedding light on the dialogues and how they function with respect to the reader.[1] I introduce briefly here

A version of this chapter appeared as "Dialectic, Dialogue, and Transformation of the Self," *Philosophy and Rhetoric* 29, no. 3 (August 1996).

1. Hershbell (1995, 31) argues that the dialogues, appearing as they do during an historical transition from orality to literacy, are "an ostensibly oral phenomenon." Although in this chapter

the work of one response theorist, Wolfgang Iser, and I go on to show how his theory can enrich our understanding of Socratic dialectic and of the Platonic dialogues. Iser's work provides a model for a phenomenology of reading, showing that the act of reading, like dialectic interaction, holds the power to transform the reader.

1. Response Theory

Reader response theory begins from the premise that the reader's role in bringing meaning to a literary work has traditionally been ignored. Traditionally, the text has been seen as containing some meaning or message (hidden or otherwise) that is objectively there for the reader to extract. While there are important differences among them, reader response theorists want to remove the myth of objective meaning from the reading process.[2] Rather, they agree, meaning emerges from some relationship between text and reader, and from neither independently.

Response theory resists any kind of discussion broken down into categories of the reader, the text, and meaning since these three elements are woven together in the process called reading. For simplicity's sake, however, I shall try to speak roughly in these terms with the caveat that a discussion of any one of these elements necessitates talk of the other two. The reader, in Wolfgang Iser's view, takes on a wandering viewpoint which is both perspectival and temporal;[3] the reader wanders among many perspectives within the text and moves among various parts of the text temporally during the reading process. The text contains many perspectives—for example, the narrator's, the protagonist's, other characters', or perhaps an invisible person to whom the work is addressed.

I treat the dialogues more as literal phenomena than oral phenomena, I will treat them in the following chapter as oral and aural phenomena, that is, as dramas, and I will treat them as visual phenomena in Chapter 6. My argument regarding the function of the dialogues with respect to the reader or the audience holds in all cases. Hershbell discusses the differences among dialogues, dramas, symposia, and the elenchus. He also reviews several earlier contributions on this issue, among them Havelock (1963) and Ryle (1966).

2. By "objective meaning" I intend to refer to meaning that exists wholly external to and independent of the reading subject. To reject objective meaning is not to reject the possibility of meaning altogether, as this chapter will later argue.

3. Iser (1978, 108ff.), hereafter cited in text as *Act of Reading*.

[T]he wandering viewpoint is . . . situated in a particular perspective during every moment of reading, but—herein lies the special nature of the wandering viewpoint—it is not confined to that perspective. On the contrary, it constantly switches between the textual perspectives. . . . But if the wandering viewpoint defines itself by way of the changing perspectives, it follows that throughout the reading past perspective segments must be retained in each present moment. . . . As the wandering viewpoint is not situated exclusively in any one of the perspectives, the reader's position can only be established through a combination of these perspectives. (*Act of Reading*, 114, 115)

The reader does not merely internalize the various positions in the text, but rather is "induced to make them act upon and so transform each other as a result of which the aesthetic object begins to emerge."[4] This makes the literary text somewhat distinct from other aesthetic objects, which Iser labels "given" objects. Whereas one always stands outside the given object and experiences it qua object, a literary text requires the participation of the subject inside of the object in order to constitute the aesthetic experience (*Prospecting*, 109). The reader wanders about through the text viewing it from all of these perspectives and attempting to synthetize[5] meaning in some way. The reader's viewpoint is in this way a product of other perspectives in the text, but (since the reader moves among the various perspectives from the wandering viewpoint) is not identical to any one of them.

The temporal movement of the reader's viewpoint is not direct, linear, or smooth; rather it is leaping and irregular. During the act of reading, the reader's viewpoint is unstable, changing and being continually formed: "[R]eading does not merely flow forward, but . . . recalled segments also have a retroactive effect, with the present transforming the past" (*Act of Reading*, 115). While moving thus within the text, the reader works at what Iser calls consistency building and searches for the text's "connectability." The wandering viewpoint "permits a process through which the aesthetic object is constantly being structured and restructured. As there is no definite frame of reference to regulate this process, successful communication must ultimately depend on the reader's creative activity" (112). The reader is quite literally making sense out of the text.

---

4. Iser (1989, 40), hereafter cited in text as *Prospecting*.
5. Iser introduces this term (*Act of Reading*, 111).

But what is the nature of this text that the reader is making sense out of? What role does the text itself play in the reading process? According to Iser, the text contains indeterminacies that stimulate the synthetizing activity. The indeterminacy of the text is the fundamental precondition for reader partici- pation (*Prospecting*, 10); it "sends the reader off on a search for meaning" (27). Iser talks about two particular kinds of indeterminacies: blanks and negations (*Act of Reading*, 182ff.). A blank can be an abrupt transition in the narrative or perspective, a hiatus or disruption of the flow of the novel, or simply a confusing or obscure portion within the text. Iser claims that blanks refer to suspended connectability in the text (*Prospecting*, 37). They stimulate the reader toward consistency building, so within the framework of Iser's response theory, each blank is also a potential connection.

Like the blanks or interruptions in the text, negations also serve as poten- tial construction points for the reader. Each text must incorporate an external reality, a context in which it is embedded, which Iser calls the "repertoire" of the text. It consists of the historical, social, or cultural norms from which the text arises and which provide a frame of reference. Negations may revoke, modify, or neutralize the knowledge presented or invoked by the repertoire (*Act of Reading*, 227). Negations in the text therefore serve to dislocate the reader from social and cultural norms. The reader finds that "hitherto famil- iar positions—contemporary norms and the given world—are continually negating each other" (215). Negations "invoke familiar and determinate ele- ments or knowledge only to cancel them out. What is canceled, however, remains in view, and thus brings about modifications in the reader's attitude toward what is familiar or determinate—that is, he is guided to adopt a position in relation to the text" (*Prospecting*, 34). The reader brings to her reading of the text certain experiences, dispositions, and views about herself and the world (her own viewpoint); her viewpoint acts upon, and is acted upon by, the reading process. The reader struggles with the negations and strives for reconciliation between the traditional social and cultural ground- ing and possible alternatives to it. Negations thus compel the reader to stand in a new relation to those norms and thus in relation to the text. Meaning arises from the reader's response to the indeterminacies in the text, from her attempt at consistency building in the face of blanks and negations, and from doing this work from the wandering viewpoint. The reader strives to create a connected and coherent experience in her reading of the text, and meaning emerges from that experience.

One might object that Iser's response theory opens the door to a kind of relativism—that any text can be interpreted in any way by anyone—but Iser implicitly defends his theory against such objections. Just as there are inde-terminacies in the text, there are determinate elements as well. While blanks and negations are in one sense indeterminate elements of the text in that they create the opportunity for meaning to be constructed during the act of reading, they are for the same reasons determinate elements as well. They structure the very response they elicit. The elements of indeterminacy enable the text to communicate with the reader in the sense that they induce the reader to participate in both the production and the comprehension of the literary work. The determinate elements exercise a kind of regulation over the reading process. Acts of comprehension are guided by the structures of the text, but these structures, or determinate elements, can never exercise complete control. They regulate but do not enforce the reader's experience of the text. It is the mixture of determinacy and indeterminacy that condi-tions the interaction between text and reader, and this dialectical process, according to Iser, therefore cannot be arbitrary.[6]

While Iser's theory need not imply relativism, it does open the way for a kind of subjectivism. His theory implies subjectivism insofar as the textual meaning is dependent in part on the subject, an engaged and active reader, but this in itself need not imply any kind of radical relativism in interpretive theory, an "anything goes" kind of hermeneutic.[7] The traditional theory gives hegemony to the text which has some message or meaning that the reader must discover. Any radically relativistic theory gives this same hege-mony to the reader. Iser places himself between these two positions arguing for a dialectic relationship between text and reader.[8] Iser then opens the pos-sibility for multiple readings and an indeterminate number of these might be "good" readings, but any adequate interpretation must bridge the gaps and answer the contradictions in the text.

Some literary critics have difficulties with the dialectic nature of Iser's the-ory. Elizabeth Freund has argued that

> [t]he dyadic shape of [Iser's] theory is both its strength and its weak-ness. On the one hand we have a determinate textual structure which

---

6. The ideas in this paragraph come from Iser (*Act of Reading*, 24), but Iser elaborates these same points in (*Prospecting*, 33–34).

7. Fish, another response theorist, wholly embraces hermeneutic relativism (1972).

8. Although the sense of "dialectic" as I use it in this context is not precisely the same as the term as it is explicated in Chapter 1, my hope is that the fundamental connection between the two uses will become clear as the present chapter develops the ideas about the reader's inter-actions with the text. Suffice it to say at this point that both uses of "dialectic" connote a move-ment expressed in give and take, back and forth, question and answer.

guides and instructs the reader's response. On the other hand, the life of the text depends entirely on the interpretation. This doubleness is vital for establishing the interactive text-reader relationship, whilst managing to avoid the question of interpretive authority.[9]

But Iser's dialectic view of text and reader, interacting in the above manner, does address the issue of interpretive authority; it simply does not result in any single, monolithic authority. Interpretive authority is granted on the grounds of bridging the textual gaps and making sense of the text's inconsistencies. A solution to this general problem of interpretive authority also lies within the structure of Plato's dialogues and mirrors Iser's view as described here. I shall argue below that the dialogues have a self-correcting capacity through dialectic that guides us to an answer to the question of interpretive authority.

The process of filling in blanks and confronting negations—the act of reading—can, potentially, transform the reader. The reader may be in a different state during and after the reading process, changed by the very experience called reading. The reader is drawn into the text, but she is also drawn away from her habitual dispositions. She makes new discoveries in the act of reading and finds that they are incongruous with her habitual disposition, as well as with her social and cultural presuppositions. She is then suspended between them, impelled to make a choice between standpoints. This incongruity can be removed only by an emergence of a third dimension which is perceived as the meaning of the text. When the habitual disposition experiences a correction, the reader achieves a new balance (*Act of Reading*, 218–19). There is potential then for real growth on the part of the reader. It seems clear from Iser's stand on the transformative power of the act of reading that he attributes a moral dimension to that act. The character and judgment of the reader act, and are ultimately acted upon, in the reading process.

Iser describes one case of this potential transformation in the reader of Henry Fielding's *Joseph Andrews*:

> If the reader feels superior to the worldly-wise characters because he can see through them, from the Adams perspective he is then forced to see through himself, because in a similar situation he knows he would have reacted like them and not like the parson. But if he

9. Freund (1987, 147). Fish takes Iser's dualism to be only a weakness in his theory and not a strength. See the exchange between Fish (1981) and Iser (1981) on this issue.

wishes to see through Adams and not himself, in order to maintain his superiority, then, as we have seen, he must share the viewpoint of those whom he is continually unmasking. (*Act of Reading*, 218)[10]

Either way the reader chooses to interpret the text, she must come to learn something about herself. This in turn might initiate a transformation of self or, if not a full-blown transformation, a kind of self-knowledge that could be considered a first step toward transformation.

2. Dialogue and Dialectic: A Phenomenology of Reading

Iser's theory can help to explain the relationship between a Platonic dialogue and the reader. From there one can see the parallels between Platonic dialogues (with respect to the reader) and Socratic dialectic (with respect to the interlocutor). I begin again with Iser's "wandering viewpoint."

   The dramatic form of each dialogue, a determinate element, structures the reading so that the reader sees the perspectives of the interlocutors through what they say and what they do. The reader experiences Socrates' viewpoint in the same manner and, in her active role as participant in the dialogue, she articulates her own viewpoint. She then works with all of these perspectives in an effort to understand the text. The reader of the *Meno*, for example, can see the topic of discussion and the interaction among the interlocutors from a number of perspectives. Most obviously, she can take on the perspective of Meno or Socrates. Since these perspectives differ from one another considerably, the reader must work at consistency building with the dialogue. From Meno's perspective, and perhaps the initial perspective of the reader, virtue seems a simple enough concept to get hold of. But then the reader must grant Socrates' objections to Meno's attempted definitions. The reader could even empathize with Meno's frustration at Socrates' role in the conversation, a phenomenon witnessed by anyone who uses Plato's dialogues in the classroom. In a less developed manner, the dialogue portrays Meno's slave and Anytus, but these two characters also present distinct perspectives which provide the reader with yet a broader conception of the issues at stake and the context in which they are discussed. Seeing issues from these many

   10. This passage makes clear also how Iser imagines the perspectival elements of the wandering viewpoint to function.

perspectives, the reader must attempt to make sense of virtue, its meaning or definition, what knowledge is, who can have it, in what manner one comes to have it, what its relationship is to virtue and so forth. Consistency building from various perspectives thus shapes the reader's experience of a Platonic dialogue.

Moreover, the temporal element of the wandering viewpoint is evident as the reader must move forward and backward within the text in order to construct meaning, as Iser's response theory suggests. I return, by way of illustration, to the scene discussed in the Chapter 1 in which Socrates uses Meno's very own words to admonish him for speaking about virtue when he is as ignorant about it as the slave is about geometry:

> We have made some progress as it seems, toward finding out the situation here. Now, he (the slave) would be pleased to find out, since he does not know, but before he might have easily thought to give fine speeches, before many people and often, about doubling an area, saying that one must double the length of the side. (*Meno*, 84b–c)

In order to appreciate the impact of what Socrates says here, the reader recalls something earlier in the text that Meno said at the height of his arrogance. "And indeed, I have given many speeches about virtue on thousands of occasions, and before many people—and quite good ones as they seemed to me" (80b). As we saw in the last chapter, the similarity is unmistakable and even conspicuous between Meno's boast and Socrates' description of the slave. Whereas there I discussed the impact on Meno of hearing his own words used this way, and I used the passage to illustrate the manner in which Socrates relies on the shame of the interlocutor to induce him to engage in dialectic, here I wish to focus on the reader standing outside of the dialogue's dramatic scene, that is, what impact recognizing the parallel between Meno and the slave has on the *reader* of the dialogue. The words Meno originally introduced as a boast are turned into an insult later—a connection in the text that could be made only by the reader's movement temporally forward and backward within it. The temporal movement within the text is a necessary step for the reader to take in order for fuller meaning to emerge from the reading of this passage.

The *Meno* provides a second example illustrative of the wandering viewpoint. After Socrates has finished speaking briefly with Anytus, Socrates and Meno agree that good and virtuous men often have despicable sons, despite their efforts to provide them with proper educations. Furthermore, Socrates and Meno agree that public affairs are not governed by knowledge; Athenian statesmen, as well as the Athenian electorate, are ignorant. With these agreements in mind, let us look backward at Socrates' introduction of Anytus into the dialogue:

> Let us share our search with [Anytus]; naturally we should share it. For Anytus here is, first of all, the son of a wealthy and wise father, Anthemion, who acquired his wealth, not automatically nor as a gift from someone . . . but through his own wisdom and care. And furthermore, in other matters, he seemed not to be an arrogant citizen nor egotistical nor annoying, but rather a well ordered and well behaved man. Then he raised and educated quite well Anytus here, as it seems to most Athenians: they choose him to fill the highest offices. (*Meno*, 89e–90b)

Now if the reader remembers Socrates' earlier introduction of Anytus, or can return to it in the reading process, the later discussion with Meno takes on significant meaning that it would not otherwise take on, and that meaning relies on the reader's ability to remember and to move back and forth among dramatic scenes. These scenes demonstrate not only the temporal aspect of the wandering viewpoint, but the perspectival as well. From Anytus's perspective, the introduction is complimentary, but from Socrates' perspective the introduction of Anytus in this manner is not complimentary (and is tinged with irony).[11] The reader constructs meaning after seeing the introduction from the different perspectives and after hearing the later discussions of whether good men can pass their virtue on to their own sons and the status of those who succeed in Athenian public affairs. With the later passages fresh in the mind of the reader, praising Anytus's father and saying that Anytus is popular as a statesman are meaningful in ways they would not otherwise be. This type of meaning is clearly constructed from the wandering viewpoint as Iser describes it.

In addition to synthetizing meaning from the wandering viewpoint, the reader of a Platonic dialogue interacts in specific ways with the dialogue form itself, and this interaction recreates the method and the effects of Socratic dialectic. The interaction between dialogue and reader is parallel to that between Socrates and interlocutor insofar as it contains the elements

---

11. Irony in the dialogues depends on the reader's ability to adopt specific perspectives. I return to this issue below, in Chapter 5.

necessary for dialectic illustrated in the *Meno* and outlined in Chapter 1. The reader interacts with a dialogue under ideal conditions when she does so (1) in the context of recognized ignorance, (2) in "subjective" fashion insofar as the learning (reading) subject plays the central role in learning, (3) through question and answer, and (4) without relying on an authority who teaches by telling. We are confronted with characters, motives, actions, settings, circumstances, and conversations; nowhere does Plato present his own philosophical views directly.[12] As readers, we are thrust back upon our own reflections and thoughts in our efforts to understand the dialogues. The dialogue form, therefore, cannot teach by telling us anything; rather, we discover and learn by reflection and self-examination. Whereas other philosophers might put themselves in positions of authority, Plato does not. The reader then cannot properly rely on the Platonic text as unmediated authority due to its many perspectives and its dramatic sophistication. Even to consider Socrates as a mouthpiece for Plato is oversimplified and an injustice to the complexity of Plato's project.[13] In addition, the dialogues encourage the reader quite literally to play a role in the drama, to interact with it and to philosophize along the way. Insofar as we play a role in the drama, we must ask questions of ourselves, not only the same questions put to the interlocutors by Socrates, but other questions that take us beyond those: Do I know what (virtue, piety, courage) is? Am I arrogant in the way (Meno, Euthyphro, Laches) is? What could Socrates mean by these strange claims? Why is there this inconsistency in Socrates' words? Why is this question never answered in the dialogue? The dialogues in this way engage the reader in question and answer. Finally, the dialogues ideally induce a recognition of one's ignorance. If we are answering our own questions honestly when we interact with the text, then we realize that we probably do not know what virtue is, that we are best off keeping ourselves open to inquiry, and that we ought not to deny our affinity with the interlocutors.

Returning to Iser's characterization of the moral dilemma of the reader of *Joseph Andrews*, we can see in similar fashion how the reader wants to feel her superiority over the interlocutor, while she knows that the Socratic

12. The dialogue form makes it plain enough that Plato's views are not being presented as such; it is what distinguishes the dialogue form most fundamentally from direct discourse. Although, to some interpreters of Plato, this is a controversial claim. For an extended argument that Plato's views are not directly presented in the dialogues, see Bowen (1988). For a representative view that Plato's ideas are discernible in the dialogues—and that those of the "historical" Socrates can be distinguished from Plato's views—see Vlastos (1991), esp. chaps. 1–3. See also Nails (1999).

13. Cf. Vlastos (1991).

lesson is fitting for her too.[14] Most readers want to avoid the uncomfortable alliance with the interlocutors who are portrayed, for the most part, unfavorably. But if the reader is to distance herself from the interlocutors, she must picture herself as one without the conceit of knowledge and admit her own ignorance. At the same time, even if she is willing to confront her own ignorance, the reader must realize her shortcomings relative to Socrates' own example. In the dialogues, the interlocutors are ignorant and unaware of their ignorance—one of the worst states for human beings to be in. The reader might take comfort in the fact that she has realized her ignorance and is now ready for the search for truth. Tragically, however, in the presence of Socrates one is constantly reminded of one's moral shortcomings and the kind of life one ought to lead. Even the good and aware reader of the dialogues is suspended somewhere between Socrates and the interlocutors.

Beyond the dramatic form of the dialogues there are other, more specific elements of the dialogues that condition reader response. While the remaining chapters are devoted to explaining the philosophical role of literary devices—determinate textual elements—in Plato's project, I discuss a couple examples briefly in the context of reader response theory in order to make concrete the effect that such devices can have on the reader. Aporia and contradiction are two such devices that help us to understand Iser's concepts of determinate and indeterminate elements. These literary elements are determinate in Iser's sense insofar as Plato's construction of them in the text is fixed; these determinate elements guide and limit response.[15] Through the use of these determinate elements, however, Plato creates indeterminacies in the text. These aspects of the text throw the reader into confusion and frustration, and they create opportunities for meaning to be constructed. Briefly, they function in the following manner.

Many of the dialogues appear to be broaching a specified topic or question, but the problem initially introduced is most often left unresolved. While the reader is expecting to find an answer to the problem introduced, that expectation is frustrated. This is why the dialogues are deemed aporetic. For

14. Plato provides the conditions or opportunity for the reader's (false?) sense of superiority through certain literary devices such as irony, which I discuss below. Such a device lets the reader in on something to which the interlocutor remains oblivious.

15. Fish would argue that even these two so-called determinant elements to which I refer are actually constructed by readers, that is, even they are not objectively there in the dialogues. While one may choose to dispute this aspect of Fish's theory, it is not necessary to do so in making the case I do here. Whether they are determinate elements as in Iser's theory, or constructed elements as in Fish's theory, does not bear on the point I wish to make here, which is *how they function* with respect to the reader.

example, the *Meno* addresses the questions "What is virtue?" and "Is virtue teachable?," but without any explicit answer or resolution. Likewise, with the question "What is knowledge?" in *Theaetetus*, "What is piety?" in *Euthyphro*, "What is courage?" in *Laches*, "What is temperance?" in *Charmides*, and so forth. The reader is left with no apparent way out of the difficulty that they present, no explicit answer from within the dialogues themselves. The reader must strive not only to answer such questions but to understand why they are left unanswered. The aporia experienced by the reader is much like what the interlocutors seem to experience when Socrates subjects them to dialectic. Just as the interlocutors do with Socrates, the reader might become frustrated with the text and with trying to understanding it; the reader might even choose not to finish reading it. Such behavior on the part of the reader mimics that of interlocutors such as Callicles, Meno, Protagoras, or Thrasymachus who act out against Socrates, trying to subvert dialectic in various ways, or Euthyphro, who abruptly departs the scene. But if the reader can be open to the text dialectically, she might accept the aporia and she might even attempt to leave a state of ignorance in a quest to understand the dialogue.

Aporia as experienced by the reader, therefore, can be likened to Iser's blanks. It is a potential construction point in the text. And just as aporia leaves a gap (ignorance) that is necessary as a first step in the interlocutor's learning process, so aporia leaves the reader with a gap in the text to be filled with meaning. By trying to answer the questions posed by the text, and by trying to understand why the dialogues have left them unanswered, the reader gains insight into the Platonic conception of philosophical activity. Sometimes Plato even gives guidance to the reader in this direction. In the *Theaetetus*, for example, Socrates addresses explicitly the aporetic ending of his conversation with Theaetetus:

> *Socrates*: Then does our art of midwifery declare to us that all the off-spring that have been born are mere wind-eggs and not worth rearing?
> *Theaetetus*: It does, decidedly.
> *Socrates*: If after this you ever undertake to conceive other thoughts, Theaetetus, and do conceive, you will be pregnant with better thoughts than these by reason of the present search, and if you remain barren, you will be less harsh and gentler to your associates, for you will have the wisdom not to think you know that which you do not know. So much and no more my art can accomplish. (*Theaetetus*, 210b–c)

At the same time that Socrates' words encourage Theaetetus to continue philosophical pursuits despite a seemingly unproductive outcome, his words provide similar solace and resolve to the reader. The reader ought not be disappointed in the aporetic dialogue, since she will be better in her future pursuits because of the experience. Socrates even holds out the possibility that, from the blanks in the text, the reader might gain a kind of wisdom.

The reader can also be moved toward this type of wisdom through another kind of blank: apparent contradictions. These at first confound the reader and then later reactivate the process of consistency building. Take, for example, the seeming contradiction in the *Meno* that virtue is teachable, but is not knowledge. The contradiction emerges from the assumption that if anything were teachable, knowledge certainly would be.[16] Careful reading of the *Meno* can reconcile the apparent contradiction through understanding how it is exactly that virtue is knowledge and yet not teachable. If virtue is the knowledge obtained through dialectic, then virtue can be knowledge and yet not teachable.

Speaking through Socrates' voice, the personified Laws of the *Crito* give at least one argument that seems to contradict Socratic views expressed earlier in that dialogue (and elsewhere). The personified Laws argue that Socrates, if he were to escape, would bring about great risk to his friends who would "be exposed to the risk of banishment and the loss of their home in the city or of their property" (*Crito*, 53a–b). But earlier, when Crito brings up similar concerns about property and loss of material advantage, Socrates chides him. These are lowly concerns that only occupy the thoughts of senseless people, the Many (48c).[17] The reader who recognizes this apparent contradiction is forced to ask why it is there, and what possible meaning the dialogue might have in light of it. Do the Laws speak for Socrates? If not, then for whom? Why does Socrates use this indirect method in order to persuade Crito?[18] There are other contradictions in other Platonic dialogues, and a brief look at the abundance of secondary literature provides overwhelming evidence that they function so as to stimulate reader response in all the ways that Iser

---

16. Socrates remarks near the end of *Protagoras* how odd it is that he should have begun the conversation with Protagoras arguing vehemently that virtue is not teachable, and end it by arguing that virtue is knowledge (361a–c). Socrates thus makes explicit in *Protagoras* the same contradiction that is only implied in the *Meno*.

17. For an excellent work on the *Crito* that addresses, among other things, this very contradiction, see Miller (1996).

18. Miller addresses these specific questions, in ibid.

describes. Through aporia and contradiction, therefore, Plato's dialogues provide indeterminacies in the form of blanks for the reader. In searching for the connectability of the text and in working at consistency building, the reader takes part in creating meaning for the dialogues.

Interlocutors and readers are also affected through negation. Much as Iser describes, Socrates often aims at getting the interlocutors to see traditional ideas in new ways, to break away from their usual opinions which are grounded in traditional norms. Socrates often begins with some belief, accepted by "the Many," and then proceeds to turn it on its head. To give one example, the traditional Greek maxim that one ought to do harm to one's enemies and good to one's friends is rejected in favor of the Socratic views that one ought never to harm anyone and that it is better to suffer harm than to inflict harm. Versions of this view appear, for example, in *Crito*, *Gorgias*, and *Republic*. Many Socratic interlocutors resist the Socratic alternatives to the traditional ideas because the Socratic ways of thinking are contrary to what Iser calls the "repertoire" or cultural background against which we might place them.

In parallel fashion, Plato attempts to get the reader to see things differently. The ideas presented in the dialogues certainly oppose the repertoires of Plato's contemporaries and, in a remarkably similar way, even ours in the Western world of the late twentieth century. In addition to helping us to reconsider harm and wrong doing, the dialogues take issue with traditional understandings of such terms as "benefit," "virtue," "knowledge," "justice," "honor," "courage," and so on. In reading the *Phaedo*, for example, we are challenged to understand death as something not to be feared, but to be faced with dignity and, if we are philosophers, maybe even happy resignation. The *Republic* forces us to confront political cynicism and to consider what true political motivation consists of. The *Apology* undermines our relentless pursuit of material comforts, social advancement, and public esteem, urging us to regard our souls with more care and concern. As the reader participates in the dialogue, she comes to question her own beliefs, to compare them to those of the interlocutors and to those of Socrates. The interlocutors and Plato's readers—even twentieth-century readers—are thrown back or alienated from traditional beliefs or social norms that until now they had not questioned.

Plato's dialogues thus induce us to engage in dialectic while we are reading them. In addition, they convey to us the tools necessary for living the life of dialectic beyond the act of reading. If we take seriously the moral component of Socratic dialectic as a way of life, then Plato's dialogues act in a parallel fashion to exhort the reader to live the Socratic or philosophic way of life. The act of reading one of Plato's dialogues, therefore, can serve as the beginning of a transformation.

3. Transformation of the Self

Interpretation and transformation are thus coextensive. But, since the transformation of the reader is linked to the function of various literary devices, any problems in interpretation would necessarily have consequences for the mode of, and possibility of, transformation. That is, literary concerns necessarily become philosophical concerns. I return, therefore, to some putatively distinct literary concerns in order to clarify further the manner in which the reader is turned toward philosophy by the dialogues.

Plato, the moral absolutist and the epistemological idealist, might seem a strange bedfellow for Iser, a late twentieth-century literary critic. One might object that Plato's belief in universals cannot lie beside Iser's attention to the subjective nature of the interpretive act.[19] Can reader response theory still be a useful framework for examining the function of the dialogues if we wish to retain a particular view of the human reader, universalism, and Plato's project? The answer, I believe, is yes, and furthermore the answer points us in a direction helpful for understanding the transformative power of the act of reading.

There is in Plato a marriage of ideas that seems paradoxical to modern sensibilities. Whereas modern thinkers are accustomed to dichotomies such as objectivism versus subjectivism and personal versus universal and, furthermore, are accustomed to think of these pairs not only as oppositional but also as comprising members that are exclusive of one another, such is not the case in Plato's work. The dialogues conjoin the objective and the subjective as well as the personal and the universal. Apprehension is both objective and subjective, personal and universal. While the forms themselves exist independently of human thought,[20] and are, therefore, in the modern

19. I am indebted to Drew Hyland for directing me to address issues of universality. These are my own attempts at resolving some of the difficulties, although I remain convinced that questions surrounding universality, authorial intent, and interpretive authority are worth pursuing further than I am able to do here.

20. I do not wish to enter the debate regarding the putative difference between what Socrates expresses in the so-called early dialogues and the full blown, presumably Platonic,

sense "objective," the mode of apprehension is distinctly subjective and personal. What do the dialogues tell us except that only through personal, self-reflective dialectic can the individual subject gain access to the universal? Plato is therefore a subjectivist (although not therefore a relativist) as well as an objectivist—a personalist and a universalist. The upshot of this argument is that in reading Plato we do not have to give up our objectivism if we want to retain the subjectivism involved in the act of reading. We can cling to the personal and idiosyncratic aspects of the reader without having to relinquish claim to a text that is universally, humanely meaningful. In fact, Socratic dialectic presents a model of inquiry that relies on the personal and idiosyncratic. Socrates does not interact with everyone in the same manner. He molds dialectic to fit the personality of the interlocutor in order to be most effective. Understanding Plato in this way allows us now to revisit the issue of the reader's interpretive authority, which, in turn, has fundamental implications for self-transformation.

The problem of interpretive authority arises as a consequence of the subjective nature of interpretation. One is led to wonder whether interpreters and readers can ultimately distinguish between good and bad interpretations of dialogues and, if so, how. One might argue that there are two possibilities with respect to the interpretations that readers form of a dialogue. Either there is one correct interpretation of it (which the reader may or may not come up with) or there is no correct interpretation and any one is as good as any other. Both of these options seem undesirable—the one being too restrictive and deeply seated in the traditional myth of the objective "message" of the text, and the other being too inclusive and thus rendering interpretation and meaning rather empty concepts. But it is possible to understand reader response theory in a coherent manner while, Socratically speaking, trying to reconcile these two possibilities. We could say that the above possibilities—that there is one correct interpretation and that there are many correct interpretations—are both true and consistent claims. The "one" correct interpretation of the dialogues is any one that results in the reader's seeing the life of dialectic as desirable and that turns her toward the philosophical life. But, beyond that, there are many and various ways to interpret Plato's dialogues, and we can argue the merits of each interpretation in different ways. Regardless of which interpretation of the many possible we come to hold,

---

"theory of Forms." What I describe here is consistent with either forms or Forms. It should be clear that I do not accept any complete or systematic theory that is attributable to Plato, nor do I think it is possible nor philosophically constructive to distinguish between "Plato's" beliefs and "Socrates'" beliefs.

however, the dialogues themselves compel us to hold them dialectically. Dialectic, with its self-corrective quality, grants the reader interpretive authority, but of a self-limiting kind. The reader must stick to interpretations with the commitment they are due insofar as they stand up to further dialectical investigation. But the reader must also be prepared to revise her thinking about the dialogues when faced with a reasonable challenge.[21] Paradoxically, then, the "one" correct interpretation of the dialogues, since it commits one to dialectic, is the interpretation that compels us to be open to "all other" reasonable interpretations of the dialogues, and reasonable interpretations would be those that stand up under the scrutiny of dialectic.

The parallels among the act of reading, dialectic, and dialogue are striking. Terry Eagleton describes Iser's theory in the following way:

> Rather than merely reinforce our given perceptions, [what Iser considers] the valuable work of literature violates or transgresses these normative ways of seeing, and so teaches us new codes for understanding. . . . [A] reader with strong ideological commitments is likely to be an inadequate one, since he or she is less likely to be open to the transformative power of literary works. . . . If we modify the text by our reading strategies, it simultaneously modifies us: like objects in a scientific experiment, it may return an unpredictable "answer" to our "questions." The whole point of reading, for a critic like Iser, is that it brings us into deeper self-consciousness, catalyzes a more critical view of our own identities.[22]

Many of Socrates' interlocutors are nothing if not ideologically committed and therefore not open to the transformative power of dialectic. Most of the dialogues depict Socrates' dealings with those who think themselves wise but are not (*Apology*, 21b–22e). These interlocutors have adopted a way of life conducive to material comfort and advantage, they have a stake in the existing Athenian social structure, and they risk something when these are challenged. These interlocutors certainly can be called ideologically committed and are, for the most part, not positively transformed by dialectic. The

---

21. Cf. Gadamer (1997, 36): "'Hermeneutic' philosophy, as I envision it, does not understand itself as an 'absolute' position but as a path of experiencing. Its modesty consists in the fact that for it there is no higher principle than this: holding oneself open to conversation. This means, however, constantly recognizing in advance the possibility that your partner is right, even recognizing the possible superiority of your partner."

22. Eagleton (1983, 79).

ideologically committed reader is, likewise, not a good reader of the dialogues. She is not likely to question, much less revise, her beliefs. She will often identify with the interlocutors only insofar as she expresses her frustration with and loathing of Socrates. But for the reader who wants to see herself as different—not as stubborn, ignorant, dense, or arrogant as the interlocutor—such interlocutors serve as learning devices. Plato's dialogues, in imitation of Socratic dialectic, attempt to transform the reader and are therefore consistent with Iser's conception of the valuable work of literature.

The reader's identity becomes engaged by her reading of a text, just as the interlocutors' identities are engaged by Socratic dialectic. Beneath the questions explicitly posed in the various dialogues, there is one unifying yet suppressed question that Socratic dialectic compels the interlocutors to ask and Platonic dialectic compels the reader to ask: "Who am I?" This aspect of Socrates' questions is inextricably linked to the psychological dimension of dialectic that works on shame and on transformation of identity. As Alcibiades tells us, simply being with Socrates and permitting oneself to be caught up in the dialectic makes one vulnerable to self-examination of the most painful, but perhaps the most constructive, kind (*Symposium*, 216a–c). Plato's project compels the reader in much the same way. The reader of a Platonic dialogue also faces self-examination and possibly transformation. She asks herself many of the same explicit questions that Socrates poses in the dialogues, and in addition to these she asks whether she shares the conceits of the interlocutors, whether she holds the same inconsistent beliefs they do, or whether her life lives up to Socratic ideals. In responding to a Platonic dialogue in this way, the reader could transform herself in a manner consistent with the "deeper self-consciousness" and "more critical view of our own identities," which come from the valuable work of literature.

The dialogues in these various ways compel the reader to some activity that I believe Socrates would call philosophy. The reader of the dialogues is an agent, not a mere spectator or logical analyst; there is a moral dimension to the search for truth depicted in the dialogues that compels reader response. Readers of the dialogues can thus become philosophers. This activity can be likened to Iser's view of the reader's activity. Iser claims that the relationship between text and reader is a dialectic one. This means not only that there are potential connections that, when made, contribute to a meaningful literary experience, but that these connections can contribute to a meaningful moral and philosophical experience: the creation or transformation of the reader. The transformative power of reading is epitomized in the reader's relationship to the Platonic dialogue, whose function is to turn the reader to the philosophical life that is embodied in a lifelong commitment to dialectic or Socratic inquiry. Plato's dialogues help to awaken in the reader a critical and self-reflective enterprise through which the self can be shaped and formed. I should like to think not only that Iser's response theory describes well what happens when one reads a dialogue but that the theory itself can be called Socratic.

4. Only Readers?

We in the twentieth century experience the Platonic dialogues almost exclusively as readers. But there is another dimension to the dialogues that Plato's contemporaries might have experienced more properly as an audience. If we consider the dialogues not as literary texts but as aural and visual displays—as drama—then there is quite a bit more to be said about Plato's philosophical project and the means through which that project achieves success. In the next chapter, I take up the issue of the dialogues as drama, and I discuss the philosophical functions of the poetic and dramatic elements of the dialogues.

3

Drama

Content presents the task; form the solution.

Friedrich Hebbel, *Journals* (1838)

On the subject of Plato and the poets, what comes to mind most readily are the famous (or to some, infamous) passages in the *Republic* in which the poets are banished from the city and their art is transformed and co-opted by the philosopher kings in order to achieve their political ends. Because of these passages, Plato is reviled by many as the enemy of the poets. What does not—but should—come to mind when we think of Plato and poetry, I believe, is an entire corpus of work, conspicuously poetic itself. Plato is poet, dramatist, and philosopher, and the dramatic and poetic aspects of Plato's dialogues, far from being mere "form," are essentially linked to Plato's philosophical project.[1] That philosophical project depends necessarily for its success on the dramatic and poetic elements of the dialogues.

1. For the time being, I shall make little distinction between poetry and drama in the ancient sense of those words. A poem, ποίημα, might be considered the larger category,

I shall begin, in the first section of this chapter, with ancient sources, establishing that by ancient standards there is good cause for conceiving of Plato as a poet. My thesis then forces a reconsideration, in section 2, of the passages in Plato's *Republic* that criticize the role and function of poets and poetry. I show that the critique of poetry given by interlocutors in the dialogues is consistent with Plato's being a poet. In section 3, I examine Aristotle's functional definition of tragic poetry and what he took to be the six essential elements of tragic poetry. I formulate a parallel definition for a Socratic dialogue and show whether and how these six elements function in Plato's work. In the final section, I address five more general poetic and dramatic features of the dialogues and demonstrate how they are necessary to Plato's philosophy. Poets, dramatists, and drama critics have always been acutely aware of the significance of audience, performance, and reception. Unfortunately, many philosophers have hitherto remained, with some exceptions, unmoved by such considerations when it comes to Plato's dialogues. In contrast, I demonstrate just how the dramatic and poetic aspects of Plato's dialogues function philosophically with respect to the reader or audience and, consequently, how these aspects of the dialogues are necessary for Plato to achieve his philosophical aim.[2] Plato's philosophical aim, I argue, is to engage the reader in philosophical exchange, and ultimately to turn her toward the life of inquiry. Plato accomplishes this through, and cannot accomplish it without, the dramatic and poetic aspects of the dialogues.

1. Plato as Poet and Dramatist

One often hears that Aristotle described the dialogues of Plato as "midway between poetry and prose." This description actually comes from Diogenes Laertius who cites Aristotle in using it.[3] We do not, in fact, find this formula-

---

meaning literally something made, produced, or created. A drama, δραμα, more strictly speaking, denotes a performance or action represented on stage. I shall, later in this chapter, draw attention to the origins and meanings of these terms. Liddell and Scott (1985). Cf. Aristotle *Poetics*, I.1–14 (1447a) and III.4–5 (1448a).

    2. The status of Plato's dialogues as literal or oral phenomena is discussed by several authors: Havelock (1963); Ryle (1966); more recently by Hershbell (1995, 25–39); West (1995, 41–60); Waugh (1995, 61–77). Cf. Chapter 2, note 2.

    3. μεταξὺ ποιήματος . . . καὶ πεζοῦ λόγου, Diogenes (1991, III.37). Cited hereafter as *Lives*.

tion anywhere in Aristotle's *Poetics* or elsewhere in his work. There is a passage in Aristotle's *Poetics*, however, that might plausibly be construed as the source for Diogenes' claim and is at least consistent with it. The passage has the further virtue of making a strong case for considering Plato among the Greek poets.

Aristotle begins the *Poetics*, as he does other works, searching for both the essence, or first principle, of the subject at hand as well as its various species. He then presents a catalogue of the various species of mimesis.[4] He mentions epic, tragedy, comedy, dithyramb, flute-playing, harp-playing, and dancing as kinds of mimesis. Among these mimetic arts, some use language and rhythm, some use tune and rhythm but no language, and so on with various combinations.[5] Then Aristotle says,

> But the art which employs words either in bare prose or in meters, either in one kind of meter or combining several, happens up to the present day to have no name. For we can find no common term to apply to the mimes of Sophron and Xenarchus and to the Socratic dialogues.[6]

Although he does not say literally that Plato's dialogues are "midway between poetry and prose," Aristotle implies as much here since he says that the dialogues are like poetry insofar as they are a species of mimesis, but are also like prose insofar as they are not consistently written in meter. This is therefore a plausible source for Diogenes' claim, which he attributes to Aristotle.

But Aristotle's compelling point in these passages is this: it is not by virtue of any of these several elements—rhythm, meter, tune, language, and so on—that these works are all called poetry, but rather on account of their mimetic qualities. Since he introduces the notion of mimesis immediately after claiming to begin with the first principle of poetry, and since he concludes the section by attributing the differences he cites among the various

---

4. The discussion surrounding this one technical term employed by Aristotle in the *Poetics* could fill volumes. I do not wish to enter that discussion as it takes me far away from the focus of this chapter. I shall simply use the transliteration, "mimesis." As a starting point for understanding mimesis, see Havelock (1963), Kauffman (1979, esp. 36–40), Kosman (1992a), and Woodruff (1992). (The view of Plato I present here differs significantly from that presented by Woodruff.) Havelock refers to mimesis as "that most baffling of all words in [Plato's] philosophical vocabulary" (20).

5. *Poetics*, I.1–6 (1447a).

6. Ibid., I.7 (1447b).

mimetic arts to differences only in the *means* of representation, mimesis, it would seem, is the essence of the various poetic arts. While it is strongly implied in the opening paragraphs of the *Poetics* that mimesis is the essence of poetry, Aristotle states explicitly later that "[i]t is clear, then, from what we have said that the poet must be a 'maker' (ποιητὴν) not of verses, but of stories, since he is a poet in virtue of his 'representation' (μίμησίν)."[7] By Aristotle's own account, therefore, we would have to consider Plato's dialogues poetry by virtue of their clear mimetic quality, and we would have to consider Plato himself a poet "in virtue of his representation."

Diogenes Laertius's biography of Plato clearly assumes that Plato is a poet: Diogenes defines Plato's art of dialogue writing in explicitly poetical terms; he links Plato to distinctively poetic practices and activities; and he links Plato intellectually to two Sicilian poets. My argument, in examining these three aspects of Diogenes' text, is that we ought to take seriously his conspicuous attempts to link Plato to the poetic tradition, especially in light of the modern conception of Plato as the antipoetic champion of pure reason. Though many scholars consider the details of Diogenes' biographies specious or at least questionable, Diogenes nevertheless provides a framework for each life that he examines that cannot easily be overlooked. Diogenes' biography of Plato compels one to ask why he has placed this life, in particular, in a poetic framework. Examining these three distinct elements of Diogenes' biography of Plato reveals several reasons why we, too, ought to consider Plato a poet or, at the very least, a writer coming from the poetic tradition.

Diogenes claims that Plato ought to "be adjudged the prize for [the dialogue's] invention as well as for its embellishment" because he "brought this form of writing to perfection."[8] Diogenes defines the art form that Plato perfected in the following terms: "A dialogue is a discourse consisting of question and answer on some philosophical or political subject with due regard to the characters of the persons introduced (τῆς . . . ἠθοποιίας τῶν . . . προσώπων) and the choice of diction (τὴν λέξιν)." It is highly significant that the elements that Diogenes mentions as essential elements of Plato's dialogues

---

7. Ibid., IX.9 (1451b).
8. *Lives*, III.48. Diogenes first gives us two names for the possible inventor of the dialogue: Zeno of Elea and Alexamenus of Styra. Immediately after citing these two names, however, he offers his own opinion, a third possibility, namely, Plato, for the reasons he gives in the passage cited. The attribution of the first dialogues to Zeno or Alexamenus is complex; Diogenes cites Favorinus, who cites Aristotle's lost dialogue, *On Poets*. It is significant for my thesis, in any case, that a dialogue by Aristotle titled *On Poets* would contain the reference for the first writer of the *dialogue*.

are ones we would distinctly associate with poetry. Both character and diction are among the six necessary parts of tragic poetry Aristotle names in the *Poetics*.[9] Furthermore, the word translated in this version of Diogenes' text as "person" (πρόσωπον), is often translated as the dramatic term, "persona," and is also the technical term referring to the masks worn on the stage in Greek theater. Diogenes' definition of a dialogue, the form of writing brought to perfection in Plato's work, is therefore unmistakably poetic.[10]

Diogenes indicates a further connection between the dialogues and Greek poetry when he reports Thrasylus's claim that Plato's dialogues were published as tetralogies in the same manner as were the poems performed at the various festivals. Even more surprisingly, Diogenes reports that the dialogues actually competed at certain of the festivals.[11] Whether or not we trust Diogenes on this account, the testimony is nonetheless telling. To conceive of the dialogues in this manner is to conceive of them in relationship to the works of the great poets. Merely by taking up the issue of whether the dialogues were grouped in the traditional poetic manner as tetralogies or were performed at the great festivals, Diogenes' depiction of Plato on this matter seems really to be a portrait of Plato as poet.

We owe Diogenes also for the well-known tale of Plato as the young, aspiring Tragedian who burned all of his tragedies seemingly for the sake of philosophy.

9. *Poetics*, VI.9 (1450a) et passim. The six elements of tragedy are plot, character, diction, thought, spectacle, and song (μῦθος καὶ ἤθη καὶ λέξις καὶ διάνοια καὶ ὄψις καὶ μελοποιία). The fuller treatment of character appears in *Poetics* at XV.1ff. (1454a), and that of diction at XIX.7ff. (1456b). I shall discuss at length in section 3 of this chapter Aristotle's six elements of poetry and their relationship to elements of the Platonic dialogues.

10. One might object that Diogenes simply borrows terms and phraseology from Aristotle in his definition of "dialogue" and so is unoriginal here. But if that is the case, it strengthens not weakens my point. Diogenes, on that account, borrows from Aristotle's *Poetics* in order to define "dialogue." That is, Diogenes turned to the source he felt most likely to render aid in defining the essence of the Platonic dialogue, and he found that help in Aristotle's great work on poetry.

11. *Lives*, III.56. In particular, he mentions the festival Dionysia, the Lenaea, the Panathenaea, and Chytri. There seems to be no corroborating evidence on this point, and Diogenes' claim is improbable at best. Even so, one must wonder about the origin of such a "fact" and why Diogenes relies on it or creates it in relating the story of Plato's life and works. Cf. Schleiermacher on Diogenes' claims (1836, 20). Diogenes lists several possible groupings of the dialogues that make up the tetralogies. It is interesting to note that the groupings Diogenes gives do not correspond to contemporary perceptions of the order in which the dialogues were written. It appears that the attempt to order and group the dialogues is an activity that has occupied considerable time of scholars through the ages. There is little agreement about the ordering even among contemporary scholars. For an excellent, comprehensive treatment that lays out clearly and concisely all the various contemporary positions, see Nails (1992).

[W]hen he was about to compete for the prize with a tragedy, he listened to Socrates in front of the theater of Dionysus, and then consigned his poems to the flames, with the words: "Come hither, O fire-god, Plato now has need of thee." From that time onward, having reached his twentieth year (so it is said), he was the pupil of Socrates.[12]

It is at least likely that Plato did have aspirations to write tragedy, and perhaps he actually completed works. He certainly did not lack the talent to pursue such a course in life; the dialogues bear witness to his considerable talent for evoking the tragic. We will never know the tragedies Plato could have written or did write, but nevertheless one might argue, as I do here, that Plato did not dispense with poetry if and when he burned those tragedies. He found a way to be the pupil of Socrates, to live the philosophical life, and to continue to write poetry.

Finally, Diogenes recounts two specific occasions on which Plato gave public readings of his dialogues, thus providing evidence of the performative aspect of the dialogues.[13] One imagines Plato drawing an audience of young men who listen intently to the dialogues and go off to discuss them after the performance. These readings of Plato's dialogues, one also imagines, must have been done dramatically, with various tonal inflections and possibly even facial expression or physical movements intended to convey something about the characters, the action, the interaction between interlocutors, and so on. The dialogues thus share another important aspect of poetry insofar as they were performed. This scenario gains plausibility in large part because it is so *implausible* that readings of the dialogues would be done in some other manner, say, flatly and with no regard to voice, intonation, inflection, no attention to the different characters involved, no bodily or facial expression. It is difficult, therefore, to imagine the dialogues not rooted in the context of dramatic performance.

Apart from these more general poetic references to Plato's dialogues, Diogenes makes specific connections between Plato and two Sicilian comic

---

12. *Lives*, III.5–6.

13. The first is a mention of Plato's reading the *Lysis* and the second is of his reading *On The Soul*. See *Lives*, III.35 and III.37, respectively. About the reading of *On the Soul*, Diogenes reports that only Aristotle remained until the end; all others went away. Since in the Greek world when one read, one read aloud, there was no practice of reading to oneself silently as is widely practiced today. Therefore, readings of the dialogues would entail reading to someone, an audience, even if there were only a single reader reading to himself in solitude. We know also that other forms of poetry, for example epic, were performed publicly by a single reader or interpreter, the rhapsode. See Waugh (1995).

poets—Epicharmus and Sophron—in his treatment of Plato's life and works. Recall that Aristotle, too, evoked the name of Sophron in the same breath with the Socratic dialogues, thereby urging some connection between them.[14] I wish to argue that Plato's work fits nicely within this Sicilian poetic tradition and, furthermore, that the dialogues—qua writings—share with Epicharmus and Sophron a closer connection than they do with the writings of those whom we consider philosophers of Plato's time. Plato borrows from Epicharmus and Sophron their dramatic devices and style, and more importantly, these devices and style play a pivotal role in Plato's philosophical project.

Diogenes' discussion of the link between Epicharmus and Plato is relatively lengthy,[15] and an examination of Epicharmus's work shows good cause to link his dramas to Plato's dialogues. Epicharmus lived approximately between 550–460 B.C.E., and he composed his dramas in meter. His dramas fall into one of three categories: scenes and characters of everyday life, myth travesties, and comedies about philosophy or rhetoric.[16] Epicharmus employed names of characters significant to the character type, for example, a rough gymnastics teacher whose name, Kolaphos (Κόλαφος) means "fist" or "punch."[17] Epicharmus developed characters such as the rustic or country bumpkin, the gullible, superstitious woman, the snob, the social climber, the heavy drinker, the glutton, the sham hero, as well as characters who carried regional stereotypes, for example, the Sicilian, the Sybarite, the Corinthian. He depicted scenes and events such as banquets, religious rites, disputation between people, Odysseus as sham hero, and puzzles of language.[18] Epicharmus is twice named in Plato's dialogues, once in the *Theaetetus* (152e) and once in the *Gorgias* (505e). In the *Theaetetus* passage, Socrates names Epicharmus among the comic poets to whom we might ascribe a doctrine of becoming and constant flux. The *Gorgias* passage consists of a brief attribution of some fragment in passing. In addition to these explicit references to Epicharmus, there are many passages in the dialogues that seem to echo known fragments of Epicharmus. It is therefore certain that Plato was

---

14. *Poetics* I.7 (1447b) cited above in note 7. Cf. Klein (1989, 3, 18 et passim) who refers to the dialogues as mimes and Tejera (1984, 93–94 et passim), who refers to the dialogues as intellectual mimes and specifically links them to the works of Sophron and Epicharmus.

15. *Lives*, III.9–17. Diogenes draws heavily from the texts of Alcimus in these passages.

16. McDonald (1931, 77). The myth travesties were really "the comic transfer of scenes and characters of everyday life to the realm of gods and heroes" (ibid., 2).

17. Ibid., 5.

18. This is a small but representative sample. See McDonald's full discussion (1931, 5–74), as well as his tabular summaries (ibid., 75ff.).

familiar with Epicharmus, and probable that some passages in the dialogues are reminiscent of passages in Epicharmus.[19]

As his final piece of "evidence" that Epicharmus and Plato share a philosophical background, Diogenes cites Epicharmus's prophecy:

> [M]y words will some day be remembered; some one will take them and free them from the meter in which they are now set, nay, will give them instead a purple robe, embroidering it with fine phrases: and, being invincible, he will make every one else an easy prey.[20]

Diogenes' text makes it clear that he believes that that "some one" is Plato. Even if these are Epicharmus's words, they could hardly be taken as evidence of any intellectual reliance of Plato on Epicharmus's thought; Diogenes' anachronism is blatant. But they do underscore the strong connection Diogenes wishes to make between Plato and the poet, Epicharmus.

Sophron, living in Sicily after Epicharmus, flourished around 440–430 B.C.E., and fragments of his mimes still exist. Sophron's mimes were small dramatic pieces that depicted scenes from quotidian life and portrayed character types, although they were not written in meter but in a kind of rhythmic prose. Another difference between his mimes and Epicharmus's dramas was the element of plot.[21] Whereas Epicharmus's dramas apparently told some sort of completed story, Sophron's mimes were, for the most part, simply "scene delineation and character portrayal."[22] Sophron's mimes were divided into men-mimes and women-mimes depending upon the type of characters portrayed.[23] The names of Sophron's characters, like those of Epicharmus, were often puns indicative of their character-type. For example, there is Rhonka (Ρόγκα), a sluggish, stupid and half-awake girl whose name means "snore."[24] Or take Cothonias (Κωθωνόας), the son of a fisherman, whose name is a play on words that mean both "gudgeon," a kind of fish, and a kind of drinking cup, marking him as a drinker and carouser.[25] Among

19. For full discussion of the evidence, see McDonald (1931, 119–28).
20. *Lives*, III.17.
21. Aristotle attributes the invention of plot-making to Epicharmus, *Poetics*, V.5–6 (1449b), although there is a difficulty with Aristotle's text at this very point. See also Aristotle's mention at *Poetics*, III.5.
22. McDonald (1931, 80). See also Haslam (1972).
23. It is unclear whether this division originated with Sophron or with later critics. See McDonald (1931, 80–81, 134–36).
24. Ibid., 90.
25. Ibid., 102.

his cast of characters were the seamstress, the poor speech maker, the mother-in-law, the glutton, the courtesan, the old man, someone suffering a head cold, the spendthrift, and the messenger.[26] Sophron's mimes depict such scenes as old men discussing old age, the buying and selling of goods, attending religious festivals, an argument between a fisherman and a farmer, women sharing gossip, and wine drinking. Sophron's mimes portrayed ordinary people engaged in everyday activities, and relied on nonmetered, everyday dialogue to make the characterization vivid.

About Sophron, Diogenes tells us that Plato was the first to bring his heretofore neglected mimes to Athens, and to draw characters in the style of Sophron's mimes. Diogenes claims that "a copy of the mimes . . . was actually found under [Plato's] pillow."[27] The story of Plato sleeping upon the works of Sophron might be apocryphal, but the connection between Sophron and Plato is probable. There is no explicit reference to Sophron in Plato's dialogues, but there is mention of "men-drama" in the *Republic* (451c) and a reference to some clever man, a teller of tales, perhaps some Sicilian or Italian in the *Gorgias* (493a). Both of these passages have been taken by some to be references to Sophron and indications of his direct influence on Plato.[28]

While the evidence is not conclusive and the debates are highly speculative, hinging on small fragments, historical evidence does point to the probability of a connection between Plato and Sophron. Plato spent time in Syracuse and was known to study the works of many literary figures. There is at the very least reason to believe that Plato was familiar with the mimes of Sophron, and it is not unlikely that he was influenced by having read or seen Sophron's mimes performed. His character development is reminiscent of and perhaps influenced by Sophron's style. There is an especially strong connection between Plato's dialogues and the mimes' rich character portrayal and their depiction of common dialogue.[29]

---

26. Again, this is a small but representative sampling. See McDonald's full discussion (1931, 79–113) as well as his tabular summaries (114ff.).

27. *Lives*, III.18. Similar testimony on the connection between Plato and Sophron that predates Diogenes is attributed to Duris (c. 340–270 B.C.E.), *Athenaeus,* Book XI, Chapter III, 504b; Timon of Phlius (c. 320–230 B.C.E.), in John Tzetzes, *Chiliades*, X. 806–10; Balerius Maximus (first half of first century A.D.), *Facta et Dicta Memorabilia*, VIII.7.3; Quintilian (c. 35–95 A.D.), *Institutio Oratiora*, I.x.17. Of course, it is likely that each of these sources relies on those preceding itself, so the number of them should not be taken to be stronger evidence than it is. For a discussion of the reliability and trustworthiness of this testimony—especially that of Duris and Timon—see McDonald (1931, 129–34).

28. McDonald (1931, 134, notes 27–31).

29. For full treatment and discussion, see ibid., 129–41.

In terms of his writing style, Plato has more in common with these Sicilian comic poets—Epicharmus and Sophron—than with philosophical writers of his time. Plato wrote detailed dialogues between people set in their everyday surroundings, and through these means he portrayed rich characters. The conversations that Plato constructs between his interlocutors are complex. These conversations reflect the age, sophistication, dialect, and prejudices appropriate to the character speaking the lines. The dialogues are set in Athens and its nearby surroundings, in places commonly frequented by Athenians. The dialogues are occasioned by banquets, religious festivals, court proceedings, public lectures, and the like.[30]

Plato also uses interlocutors' names that are tightly bound to their character types, just as Epicharmus and Sophron did.[31] For example, there is Euthyphro, the "straight thinker" whose arguments, ironically, keep going around in circles only to end just where they began; there is Erixymachus who must "hold back" or "fight off" Aristophanes' hiccups in the *Symposium*[32]; there is Polus the young, eager colt who comes loping into the argument in the Gorgias; and there is the "daring operator," Thrasymachus, who proves his "boldness in battle" in the early scenes in the *Republic*.[33] As with Epicharmus and Sophron, Plato's treatment of many characters has a light comic touch. These qualities of Plato's dialogues, accompanied by the high likelihood that Plato was influenced by them, indicate that his dialogues follow in Epicharmus's and Sophron's tradition of dramatic dialogue and character portrayal.

Plato's dialogues, while dealing with Eleatic and Heraclitean philosophical ideas,[34] bear little resemblance to the writings of those figures, nor to any of

30. McDonald (1931, 382–84) also notes important differences between Plato and these two comic writers, summarizing, "Plato's characters are almost altogether masculine, urban, of the leisured or professional class or at least prosperous employers of labor . . . people who do not work with their hands, educated" (384).

31. Cf. *Cratylus* for a discussion of whether names have a natural or only conventional connection to their referents. See also Tejera (1984, 273ff.).

32. This example was suggested to me by Drew Hyland.

33. Some of these are probably historical characters, but this need not undermine my point here. Plato uses their names in crafting his characters. Thrasymachus, for example, is most likely a historical character. It is unclear, however, whether "historical" testimony about his character—a character who is portrayed in a manner consistent with the meaning of his name—is accurate or is taken from Plato's portrayal of him in the *Republic*, in which case the confirmation would be circular. See Aristotle, *Rhetoric*, II.23.29, where Aristotle refers to Thrasymachus in discussing the topic (τοπος), which uses the meaning of a name. See a discussion of the historical person as well as ancient sources that mention him in Guthrie (1956, 294–98).

34. The dialogues deal also with Pythagorean ideas, but my point here is to contrast writing styles, which cannot be done in that case since Pythagoras left no writings and we associate no particular writing style with the Pythagorean school.

the sophists' writing, another intellectual current of fifth- and fourth-century Athens.[35] These thinkers were themselves innovators in their writing styles, each choosing a particular style that complemented and advanced his ideas. There is little similarity between Plato and Heraclitus's work, for example. The ancient Riddler wrote in cryptic aphorisms, consistent with his view that one could know many things and yet not understand the logos. Parmenides, arguing against the evidence of sense perception, claimed to have received his controversial *Truth* directly from the goddess (who speaks in her own person), and he composed the work in meter. Zeno carried on the Eleatic tradition but argued in his rigorous, *reductio* fashion, producing his now famous paradoxes. And while it is clear that Plato could easily imitate the eristic, debating style of the sophists, as well as their grandiloquent speech-making, he spends considerable time in the dialogues undermining the value of such discourse. If we were to place Plato in some literary tradition, it would clearly not be with any of these philosophers. Dressing him in the literary tradition of the Sicilian comic poets, Epicharmus and Sophron, is a much better fit.[36] Plato chose a dramatic medium using prose dialogue to depict people's lives; he dealt with the most serious of human subjects with the most subtle comic touches. McDonald ventures to call Plato's dialogues "philosophical mimes" because "the philosophical arguments are interwoven with the character-traits, interests, and daily activities of varied types of men."[37] By these standards, Plato is surely a poet.[38]

35. Kerferd (1981, 94) places at least Gorgias "within the main stream of the history of philosophy" since his work directly addresses Parmenidean ontological issues. Regardless of whether or not we expand the boundaries to include any, some, or all sophists as philosophers, they represent a group of Greek thinkers and writers in whose writing tradition Plato cannot be well placed.

36. I must address the question of Aristophanes' role in the historical scenario I describe and his possible influence on Plato. Aristophanes is certainly better known to modern audiences and closer in time and geographical vicinity to Plato than either Epicharmus or Sophron. Plato may certainly have also been influenced by Aristophanes, which would support the view that Plato belongs in the poetic tradition. We have the explicit reference to Aristophanes in the *Apology* (19b–c), when Socrates attributes his poor reputation among the Athenians to Aristophanes' comedy, not mentioned by name, but obviously *The Clouds*. Plato's *Symposium* also portrays Aristophanes in great detail, subtly and comically. For a discussion of the possibility of Epicharmus's and Sophron's influence on Aristophanes, see McDonald (1931, 135 notes 35ff.). If Aristophanes were influenced by either of these two poets it would undermine Diogenes Laertius's claim that Plato was the first to introduce Sophron's mimes to Athens.

37. McDonald (1931, 143). Cf. Klein (1989, 3, 18) and Tejera (1984).

38. Another important question, although beyond the scope of this work, is what kind of poetry Plato wrote. Should we consider the dialogues to be comedy, tragedy, or some other form of Greek poetry? Although I use comic sources here to draw parallels in the use of literary styles and devices, I believe ultimately that Plato's dialogues, while fitting into no category neatly, do exhibit both tragic and comic qualities. For fuller discussions of the mingling of both

2. Plato's Works Reconsidered: Criticizing Poetry

If what I have argued so far is to carry any weight, something needs to be said about passages in Plato's dialogues in which interlocutors criticize poetry and poets. I shall make the case that despite these passages, it is consistent to consider Plato himself a poet. I will focus on the passages in the *Republic* since these are the most thorough-going, well-known, and complete criticisms of poetry to be found in the dialogues.[39]

In painting their picture of the advantages of living the unjust life, Glaucon and Adeimantus rely almost exclusively on the poets, citing them repeatedly (Homer: 363a–b, 364d; Hesiod: 363a–b; 364d; Aeschylus: 361b; Musaeus: 363c; Archilochus: 365c; Orpheus: 364e). It is clear that their case for living the unjust life would be significantly impoverished and lacking in vivid illustration without the poets on their side. These scenes from the *Republic* thus portray dramatically how the poets and their art can be used for ill purpose. This scene, in which Glaucon and Adeimantus put the poets and poetry to use in favor of injustice, is what leads Socrates to his explicit consideration of the kinds of poetry to be allowed into the just city. It seems right to infer, therefore, that Socrates' critique of poetry stems from these particular examples of poetry that portray the unjust life as desirable and rewarding. That being the case, one need not interpret Socrates' criticisms to be a wholesale rejection of poetry.

In fact, despite his critique of and restrictions on poetry, Socrates makes clear that he is not making a wholesale rejection of the poets and poetry. The introduction Socrates gives to the first explicit discussion of poetry tells us

---

tragic and comic elements in the dialogues, see Hyland (1968); Hyland (1995), esp. chap. 5; and Seeskin (1984).

Nussbaum (1988, 122–35) argues, on the contrary, that Plato's dialogues are a kind of theater meant to supplant tragedy as the paradigm of ethical teaching. In order to distinguish the dialogues from tragedy, Nussbaum argues that, whereas tragedy causes us to interact with it and involves our emotions and feelings, the dialogues engage only our wit and intellect. I find her argument odd for two reasons. First, the Platonic dialogues certainly do engage us emotionally (e.g., through shame, humor, feelings of superiority and humility, and so on) and, as this project shows, they certainly compel us to interact with them. Second, Greek tragedy seems also to engage the wit and intellect and so is not distinct from the dialogues on these grounds either; Nussbaum's own writings on Greek tragedy bear witness to that!

39. This dialogue, and these passages in particular, have been studied in depth by many scholars. I wish only to explain them briefly in light of my thesis that Plato ought to be considered a poet. For a variety of detailed and thorough treatments, see Bloom (1968); Elias (1984); Hyland (1995); Nussbaum (1986); Partee (1981); Rosen (1988). See my further discussion of image-making in the *Republic*, Chapter 6.

that the city will keep the noble stories that the poets create and get rid of only the bad ones (377b–c). What follows throughout the remainder of Book III is a critique of particular aspects of poetry, not poetry itself. When asked specifically why most of the existing stories must be gotten rid of Socrates tells Adeimantus that, "one ought first and chiefly to blame" cases in which "anyone images (εἰκάζῃ) badly in his speech the true nature of gods and heroes" (377d–e).[40] Socrates gives specific guidelines for how the gods are to be spoken and written about (379a–393a); he lays out the proper type of mimesis which the city's poetry ought to exhibit (393b–397b); he then discusses the regulation of poetry's rhythm, harmony, and meter (397b–402a). Socrates tells us that the guardians "may not be bred among images (εἰκόσι) of evil" in order to prevent collecting "a huge mass of evil in their own souls" (401b–c).[41] That great evil from which the guardians must be protected is *bad* poetry, not poetry itself. Bad poetry, when ingested regularly can result in the corruption of the soul, the greatest evil to befall anyone. Rather, the guardians must be exposed to artists who feed them true beauty and whose poetry is beneficial. Then perhaps "something of the fine works will strike their vision or their hearing, like a breeze bringing health from good places" (401c–d).[42] These could hardly be the objections to poetry of someone who despised it entirely and essentially as a literary form.

There are indications that Socrates might be making a more universal critique of poetry when the discussion of whether to allow poetry and poets into the city is resumed in Book X (595–608a). Socrates seems to be saying there that mimesis itself is problematic since it is far away from the truth and since it appeals to the emotions (603a–b, 605a–b). That bad poetry is capable of the worst of evils resonates in Book X when Socrates says that mimesis has the "power to corrupt, with rare exceptions, even the better sort" of person, and that "is surely the chief cause for alarm" (605c). Through a series of analogies Socrates makes the case that the tragic poet, as imitator, imitates good and bad things of which he has no true knowledge. Moreover, tragic poetry both portrays and gives vent to feelings and emotions that we would—and should—be ashamed to display outside of the theater. But even

40. For reasons that will become clear in Chapter 6, I note the use of a verb form of the Greek root meaning "image."
41. Shorey translates εἰκόσι as "symbols." Again, in the interest of issues that I develop later, I render this term as "images." On the topic of proper beliefs about the gods, see *Euthyphro* (6a–b), where Socrates claims that he is being prosecuted because he refuses to believe bad stories about the gods.
42. Translation by Bloom (1968).

at the end of this second consideration of the matter, however, there is hope for the redemption of poetry. Socrates welcomes any argument that could be given to prove that poetry has a place in the well governed city; recognizing its powerful charm, he invites the champions of poetry to speak in prose on its behalf showing it to be not only pleasurable for men but useful for the city (607c–e). So, despite its potential for harming the souls—which we have already witnessed in the young men's use of it to defend the unjust life— poetry can serve the interests of the city and presumably the individual souls in that city. Socrates reasons in the *Crito* that what is capable of the greatest evil is also capable of the greatest good (44d).[43] By Socratic reasoning, since it is capable of the greatest evil, poetry can also, therefore, be the source of greatest benefit to the human soul. Socrates' restrictions on poetry are testimony to its great power, and we can rightly infer that poetry, by virtue of its great power, is capable of the greatest good and the greatest evil. The difficult task is then to find poetry that is both beneficial and beautiful (607e–608d). Plato's dialogues are that poetry—capable of the greatest good—and in the following two sections I shall explore and explain in just what manner they might edify the soul and thus be of the greatest benefit.[44]

3. Plato's Works and Aristotle's *Poetics*

If we are to consider Plato a poet and his works poetic, it makes sense to consult a contemporaneous and authoritative work on Greek poetry to see what it might tell us about Plato's dialogues insofar as they are poetry. In the *Poetics*, Aristotle begins with a definition of tragic poetry from which he derives and enumerates six necessary elements.[45] In his definition of tragic poetry, he states that

43. In the *Crito* passage, Socrates wants to downplay the majority's power in putting him to death. To die, he wants to convince Crito, is not the greatest evil that can befall a man. Socrates diminishes the power of the majority by claiming that they are not capable of inflicting the greatest evils, for if they were, they would also be capable of inflicting the greatest good. Presumably, the greatest evil would be not death, but the corruption of his soul; the greatest good, its improvement and edification. See also *Phaedo*, 107d: "For the soul takes with it to the other world nothing but its education and nurture, and these are said *to benefit or injure* the departed greatly from the very beginning of his journey thither."

44. I discuss *Republic* further in Chapter 6 in regard to images, vision, and their role in philosophy.

45. I am aware of some problems with using Aristotle's *Poetics*. The text moves back and forth between normative and descriptive treatments of tragic poetry, and it comes some years after the composition of Plato's dialogues. But it likewise comes considerably later than much of

[t]ragedy is, then, a representation of an action which is heroic and complete and of a certain magnitude—by means of language enriched with all kinds of ornament, each used separately in different parts of the play: it represents men in action and does not use narrative, and through pity and fear it effects relief to these and similar emotions.[46]

This compact definition, which is functional in nature, explicates the object of tragic poetry's mimesis, its medium, its form, and its effects. Its object is heroic action; its medium is language; its form is dramatic rather than narrative; and its effect is to give relief to the emotions.[47] From this definition, Aristotle goes on to derive the elements essential for tragedy to be what it is. "Necessarily then every tragedy has six constituent parts, and on these its quality depends. These are plot, character, diction, thought, spectacle, and song."[48]

As the extant text of Aristotle's *Poetics*—let's call it *Poetics I*—deals with tragic poetry, and a putative *Poetics II* would likely have dealt with comic poetry, so I wish to consider what a *Poetics III*, an examination of Socratic dialogue, might look like.[49] A functional definition of Socratic dialogue as a genre of poetry, as well as a comparison of the elements of Socratic dialogues with the six essential elements of tragic poetry, helps not only to point out similarities and differences between tragic poetry and the dialogues, but opens the door to our investigation of the philosophical function of poetry in Plato's dialogues. Following Aristotle's definition as an example, we might define Socratic dialogue's mimetic object and its medium, form, and effect in the following manner:

Socratic dialogue is an imitation of philosophical activity which by means of language represents dialogue that aims at turning one toward the philosophical life.

the poetry it analyzes. My primary aim in looking to Aristotle's text is threefold: it is relatively contemporaneous with Plato's dialogues; it is a reasonable representative of Greek views regarding poetry; and since it has been heavily relied on by dramatists and critics for thousands of years it remains a credible frame of reference for the scholarly treatment of drama and poetry. Overall, I believe that the benefits of using the *Poetics* in this capacity outweigh these difficulties.

46. *Poetics*, VI.2 (1449b).

47. Louis Mackey points out to me that this definition also refers to all the Aristotelian causes: efficient cause = heroic action, material cause = language, formal cause = drama, and final cause = catharsis.

48. *Poetics*, VI.9 (1450a), μῦθος καὶ ἤθη καὶ λέξις καὶ διάνοια καὶ ὄψις καὶ μελοποιία.

49. This particular framework for the ideas presented in this section of the paper was suggested to me by Charles Young.

Its object of mimesis is philosophical conversation; its medium is language; its form is dialogue; and its effect is to turn one to the philosophical life. The necessary elements of such poetry would be thought, character, plot, diction, and spectacle.

Aristotle believes plot (μῦθος) carries primary significance among the six constituent elements of tragic poetry. Character has secondary importance. In describing the fundamental importance of plot and its relation to character, Aristotle tells us that

> [t]he most important of these [six constituent parts] is the arrangement of the incidents [i.e., plot], for tragedy is not a representation of men but of a piece of action, of life, of happiness and unhappiness, which come under the head of action, and the end aimed at is the representation not of qualities of character but of some action; and while character makes men what they are, it is their actions and experiences that make them happy or the opposite. They do not therefore act to represent character, but character-study is included for the sake of the action.[50]

Aristotle sees human life in terms of actions. An individual's happiness resides, for the most part, in his or her actions, and tragedy—the depiction of human happiness and misery—depends essentially therefore on the portrayal of human action. The primacy Aristotle accords to plot compels him to say that there could be tragedy without character-study, but there could not be tragedy without action (as portrayed through plot).[51] Aristotle tells us, further, that the plot is that end at which tragedy aims,[52] and tragedy thus aims most of all to tell a story through human action. Plot is thus the "soul" of the tragic poem,[53] and character follows from plot. The reverse would seem to be true of Platonic dialogues: We could not have a dialogue without character study, but we could (and do) have them without much action.

Aristotle tells us that thought "appears whenever in the dialogue [the characters] put forward an argument or deliver an opinion."[54] As I have defined

---

50. *Poetics*, VI.12–13 (1450a).
51. Ibid., VI.14 (1450a).
52. τέλος, ibid., VI.13 (1450a). The arousal of pity and fear, which could also be considered an end of sorts, is described by Aristotle as the object to be "aimed at . . . in the construction of plot" (Ὧν δὲ δεῖ στοχάζεσθαι . . . συνιστάντας τοὺς μύθους), XIII.1 (1452b).
53. Ibid., VI.19–21 (1450a–b).
54. Ibid., VI.8 (1450a).

the Socratic dialogue, thought (διάνοια) is given primacy in the manner that plot is given primacy for Aristotle in tragic poetry. Thought for Plato bears the relationship to character that Aristotle believes holds between plot and character in tragic poetry: in the Platonic dialogues, thought is primary, and character emerges through it. In Plato's dialogues, the characters are portrayed for the most part through their thoughts, arguments, and beliefs (more so than their actions) all of which would fall under the rubric of thought as Aristotle defines it. What is remarkable and artful about Plato's dialogues are the characters of the interlocutors as expressed through their thoughts, ideas, beliefs, stories, and arguments. The dialogues are often subtle character studies, portraying with great acuity the psychological complexity and depth of the characters involved. The series of actions which they depict, while certainly significant, seem to follow from their characters and beliefs rather more than the plot seems to dictate literary control over these elements.[55] When the dialogues do depict significant actions of the interlocutors, their actions *reflect* their characters, and their characters are the result of what they believe and how they think. The dialogues show that what we believe and how we think determine the life we live and the types of characters we develop.

This difference between Plato and Aristotle regarding the relative importance of thought, character, and plot is worth investigating further. This difference between the ontological precedence of plot over character in Aristotle's (normative) conception of tragic poetry and the lesser role of plot in Plato's dialogues is reflective of the difference between their conceptions of the best human life.

For Aristotle, ethics reside firmly in actions. These actions can be inculcated through training and practice. We come to live the good human life in great part, with the addition of the necessary external goods, through the repetition of good actions and through learning to derive pleasure from their performance.[56] This contrasts sharply with the picture we get from Plato's dialogues. Ethics, the good human life, emerge from beliefs and ideas which reside in the soul, and from a good soul, good actions follow. Through dialectic examination we test our beliefs—our very selves—and thus edify the soul. This would account for the heavy emphasis on thought and character,

---

55. I do not want to disregard plot or action. The Platonic dialogues could not do without plot. What I aim to show in my comparison here is the relationship of plot to other parts of poetry, that is, which elements of poetry are ontologically prior to or dependent upon other elements.

56. *Nicomachean Ethics*.

relative to plot or action, that we find in Plato's dialogues. We come to know and judge the characters by what they believe and how they think. Each dialogue contains key insights into the characters of the interlocutors, and furthermore, compels the reader to concentrate on character, her own as well as that of the interlocutors. The reader focuses on the characters as they express their ideas and their beliefs; she then considers her own beliefs, her reasons for holding them, and the state of her soul as a result. So, while Attic tragedy compels the audience primarily through the story it tells, the actions it depicts, Plato's dialogues work on the reader more strongly through thought and character development. The difference we might observe regarding the relative importance of plot and character between Aristotle's ideal tragic poetry and what is presented through Plato's dialogues is, therefore, a manifestation of their different perspectives on how to achieve the good in human life.[57]

Despite the relative function and import of plot to other elements of the dialogues, I do not deny the fundamental significance of action in the dialogues. In fact, what action there is in the dialogues is essential to their philosophical impact, since the dramatic elements are philosophically necessary for Plato, and the dramatic resides essentially in action.[58] A more detailed examination of Aristotle's account of action in tragedy sheds further light on the role and function of action in the Platonic dialogues as well. I wish to focus attention on not one, but two levels of action with respect to the Platonic text: there is the action depicted within the dialogue, that is, the plot, and there is the inter-action between the reader and the dialogue. Both levels of action in Plato's dialogues bear on his philosophical aim of turning souls toward the life of inquiry.

Two of the most important features of the actions contained in plot, according to Aristotle, are what he calls "reversal" and "discovery," and these features play a significant part on both levels of action in Plato's dialogues. A reversal is formally defined as a "change of the situation into the opposite,"[59] and refers most likely to Aristotle's earlier claim in the *Poetics* that the proper length of a tragedy is such that it "admits of a change from bad

---

57. Cf. Gadamer (1986, 60–62), who wants to undermine the polarization of Aristotle and Plato in their ethical approaches—Plato's intellectualization and Aristotle's focus on habituation. I agree with Gadamer's argument in general, as my comments below on action and doing in Plato's dialogues demonstrate, but I maintain that there are palpable differences between Attic tragedy and Platonic dialogue with regard to thought and action.

58. Drama comes from the root verb δράω, "I do." See definition of drama above, note 1.

59. *Poetics*, X.11.1 (1452a).

fortune to good or from good fortune to bad."[60] So we can take reversal to be that aspect of plot in which there is a change in fortune. Aristotle defines discovery as "a change from ignorance to knowledge, producing either friendship or hatred in those who are destined for good fortune or ill. A discovery is most effective when it coincides with reversals."[61]

The conjoined reversal and discovery found in Sophocles' *Oedipus the King* epitomize these poetic devices for Aristotle. At the beginning of the drama, King Oedipus believes that he has escaped the terrible prophecy that has darkened his life, namely, that he would kill his father and marry his mother. By all appearances he stands in good fortune. Later in the drama, information from a messenger meant to reassure Oedipus of his good fortune ironically reverses his fortune. Oedipus discovers from the messenger that the parents he thought to be his own were not, and that he has indeed fulfilled the dreaded prophecy by killing Laius and marrying Jocasta (*Oedipus the King*, 950–1185). Oedipus's reversal of fortune coincides with his newfound discovery, moving from ignorance to knowledge about his life and identity.

We do not see explicitly depicted in Plato's dialogues the reversal from good fortune to bad fortune in the manner Oedipus experienced these, but reversals are at work in the dialogues for all those interlocutors who seem to be wise, wealthy, prominent, and powerful, but whose real fate, Socratically speaking—that is, the fate of their souls—is not what they anticipate for themselves. Clear examples of this type of reversal of fortune in the dialogues are implied in the lives of Alcibiades in the *Symposium*, Anytus in the *Meno*, and Meletus in the *Apology*. These reversals are not depicted dramatically within the dialogues; rather they are implied and rely on an attentive reader to bring out their full implications. Consequently, a significant difference between Platonic reversals and those about which Aristotle speaks is that, in addition to being left for the reader or audience to discover, they remain for the most part undiscovered by the interlocutors or *dramatic personae* themselves.[62]

Thinking of good and bad fortune in the most Socratic of terms, the dialogues do depict reversals for Socrates himself. We might think, for example, of Socrates' own fortune or misfortune. His death was thought of by his accusers, his jurors, and some of his friends, as the worst misfortune to

---

60. Ibid., VII.7.12 (1451a).
61. Ibid., XI.4 (1452a).
62. Cf. *Poetics*, XI.8 (1452b).

befall any man. But the *Apology*, the *Crito*, and the *Phaedo*, dramatically speaking, reverse his fate of death as the worst misfortune to befall a man, and reflect Socrates' own view that it is one's soul, and therefore the quality of one's life, that matters rather than one's simply living or dying. The seeming misfortune of Socrates' impending death is thus reversed in these dramas. Socrates knows not what awaits him beyond his execution, but he might be off to a better fate and, in any case, death is not to be feared.[63] In the *Phaedo*, Socrates is slightly more dogmatic that good fortune awaits him after death, but nearly all of the dialogues celebrate the life of Socrates, heralding its richness and happiness, despite his impending death which lurks in the background of many of them. Socrates also makes clear in the dialogues that no ill fortune can befall a good man. This highly significant point sets the dialogues far apart from Attic tragedy which, according to Aristotle, is tragic for the very reason that it depicts the fall of good men.[64]

The examples Aristotle uses to illustrate discovery do not represent just any kind of knowledge; they represent knowledge gained in the discovery of identity. Again, Oedipus serves as a paradigm. The dramatic turning point at which his fortune is reversed is occasioned by the new-found knowledge of his, Jocasta's and Laius's true identities. The discovery one finds in Plato's dialogues is likewise a discovery of identity, and it plays a pivotal philosophical role in the dialogues. We can distinguish three kinds of discovery in the dialogues. There is (1) an interlocutor's discovery of his own identity; (2) the reader's discovery of an interlocutor's identity; and (3) the reader's discovery of her own identity.[65]

Regarding the first type of discovery, which takes place wholly within the text, confident, reputedly wise characters fall into bumbling confusion and vexation in the face of Socrates' questions. While there is always hope that the interlocutors will discover their own ignorance in this process, seldom does an interlocutor move successfully from ignorance to knowledge about himself. This, despite Socrates' sometimes blatant attempts to aid the interlocutor in discovering his own identity. Euthyphro provides perhaps the clearest example of the interlocutor who tenaciously clings to his self-image as an expert,[66] and who fails to catch on to Socrates' jabs and criticisms. One

63. *Apology*, 38e–42a; *Crito*, 48b; *Phaedo* in its entirety, but especially 115c–118.

64. *Poetics*, III.4 (1448a); XIII.2–13 (1452b–1453a).

65. I note that the first type of discovery takes place on the first level of action described above, wholly within the dialogue; the second and third types of discovery take place on the second level of action, between text and reader.

66. *Euthyphro*, 3c, 4e–5a et passim.

might expect such an outcome since the *Apology* tells us that the consequences of Socrates' quest to prove the oracle wrong were to show that those
who were thought by others to be wise and who thought themselves wise
were not so at all and did not realize it.[67] There are occasions, however, where
the interlocutor's self discovery is depicted in the dialogue, for example,
Alcibiades in the *Symposium*, Hippocrates in *Protagoras*, Meno in *Meno*,
and Theaetetus in *Theaetetus*.

But the reader *does* often discover the explicit portrayal of a seemingly
wise and powerful man to be false; this constitutes the second type of discovery, and it takes place in the inter-action between text and reader. It does
not take long, for example, to discover that Gorgias, the great sophist, is
neutralized quite easily when challenged by Socratic dialectic.[68] Euthyphro is
again perhaps the most transparent of the interlocutors in this regard.
Although he is a self-proclaimed expert on piety and all religious matters,
the reader sees quickly that Euthyphro is deluded about his identity in this
regard and he knows little about piety. The same is true of Ion, the rhapsode
and self-proclaimed expert on the poetry of Homer. Ion's desire to perform
and expound for Socrates is thwarted by Socrates' questions that reveal not
only that the rhapsode's art does not comprise real knowledge but also that
Ion is himself only a medium through which the divine works. If the reader
comes to see the shortcomings of the interlocutors in this way—to discover
their true identities—there is hope that she can take the next step and use her
interaction with the dialogues to discover important truths about herself
and her own life. Most significantly, therefore, the dialogues are about self-
discovery, the third type of discovery.

Ideally, the reader discovers her own identity from the Platonic dialogues.
The reader comes to see how interlocutors' thinking they know what they do
not know prevents them from improving their souls, how their arrogance
keeps them from engaging in real inquiry. In the best cases, the reader is then
compelled to see the same weaknesses in herself and to rectify them, ultimately
turning toward the philosophical life. There will, of course, be cases when the
self-discovery does not occur, even cases in which the reader becomes vexed
at Socrates and frustrated in the same manner as the interlocutor.

We cannot say, strictly speaking, that Socratic or Platonic discovery is a
movement from ignorance to knowledge. Rather we and the interlocutors
move from ignorance accompanied by the illusion of having knowledge to a

67. *Apology* 21b–23c
68. *Gorgias* 448a–461a.

state of recognition of our ignorance. Altogether the movement from illusion to recognition is still real discovery, though, since it is a depiction of emerging cognitive awareness. Finally, by Aristotle's own standards, the discovery experienced by a reader of a Platonic dialogue is discovery of the best kind, that is, it is accompanied by a reversal—the change of the reader's bad fortune to her good fortune. The dialogues provide the opportunity for the reader to move from misplaced confidence in her apparent knowledge to discovery that she can instead be turned toward a life of inquiry and thus improve her soul. The new awareness, which stems from a discovery of identity, constitutes the beginning of good fortune as the reader embarks on her new life of inquiry.

Such is the useful manner in which Aristotle's poetic elements of plot, character, and thought can be held alongside Plato's dialogues in order to shed light on Plato's project and the manner in which Plato utilizes these poetic devices. In both tragic and dialogic poetry these three elements are most significant, although their relative order of importance differs due to the different function and aim of each form of poetry. But there are other elements common to both forms of poetry and significant to the Platonic project.

The manner in which the characters express thought is itself an important art in Plato's dialogues and is also essential to his philosophical project. I move therefore to diction (λέξις). Aristotle defines diction twice, once more broadly than the other. He first tells us that by diction he means "the metrical arrangement of words."[69] This is the more narrow definition and does not apply to Plato's dialogues since they are not composed in meter. But Aristotle says later that "under the head of Diction one subject of inquiry is the various modes of speech, the knowledge of which is proper to elocution."[70] Plato is able to capture through dialogue the modes of speech and elocution appropriate to the characters he portrays. The dialogues are filled with speeches given in the manner of well known Greeks. The *Symposium* is perhaps the single dialogue that demonstrates this ability of Plato's most clearly. Each of the individual speeches in it contains different vocabulary, style of speech, and sensibility that reflect the character of the interlocutor giving the speech. As a result, each speech evokes quite different moods, from the subtly comic to the tragic, from the abstractly philosophical to the farcical. Or take, for example, the *Phaedrus*, which demonstrates Plato's

---

69. *Poetics*, VI.6 (1449b).

70. Ibid., XIX.7 (1456b). What follows this definition of diction is a lengthy and detailed treatment of various ideas which come closest to what we might call grammar. Their immediate connection to poetics is unclear. For discussion of these passages, see Bywater (1945, 68ff.).

mastery of the style of the Attic orator, Lysias. The *Protagoras* more than any other single dialogue shows off Plato's flair for stylizing the banter and speech-making popularized by the sophists; in that single dialogue we meet the dense Hippias, pedantic Prodicus, cagey Protagoras, and of course in Socrates' poetry analysis he "out-sophists" the sophists.

But the mastery of these discourses, that is, the poetic element of lexis, is not merely a technical skill that Plato acquired. It serves his philosophical aim as well. Plato's work underscores repeatedly the importance of discourse and expression in inquiry and therefore in forming character. Beliefs, remember, form character, but it is important not just what we believe, but by what method we have come to hold our beliefs and by what method they can be defended and tested. In *Phaedo*, Socrates admonishes Crito about speaking properly, in particular, about using the proper words and expression: "For, dear Crito, you may be sure that such wrong words are not only undesirable in themselves, but they infect the soul with evil" (115e). In *Phaedrus*, Socrates prefaces his tale of the locusts' song, saying, "Then that is clear to all, that writing speeches is not in itself a disgrace. . . . But the disgrace, I fancy, consists in speaking or writing not well, but disgracefully and badly (αἰσχρῶς τε καὶ κακῶς)" (258d). Dialectical discourse is encouraged throughout the dialogues as being the source of well-tested beliefs and the good soul; other manners of discourse are disparaged if they do not conduce to edification of the soul and if they encourage one to cling to untenable or harmful beliefs.[71] So, the dialogues show that the manner in which we speak and carry out discourse with others has important bearing on the development of our souls. Plato's developed facility with lexis or diction is therefore linked both to his detailed and subtle character portrayal as well as to his philosophical emphasis on modes of discourse as important to the development of the soul.

Aristotle tells us that song-making (μελοποιία) is the most important element to "enrich" tragedy,[72] but it is not shared by Platonic dialogues so has little relevance here. In the same breath with song making, Aristotle addresses spectacle (ὄψις). Although he introduces all six elements, saying they are necessary,[73] Aristotle later says: "Spectacle, while highly effective, is yet quite foreign to the art and has nothing to do with poetry. Indeed the

71. These themes pervade the entire corpus, but see, for example, *Meno* 75b–d, 76b–c; *Protagoras* all; *Phaedrus* 242d ff., 258c, 259–end; *Theaetetus* 172c–173b.
72. Literally, "sweeten" it (ἡδυσμένον, τῶν ἡδυσμάτων), *Poetics*, VI.3 and VI.27 (1449b and 1450b).
73. At *Poetics* VI.5, he specifically calls spectacle and song necessary (ἀνάγκης), and at VI.9 he tells us that every tragic poem necessarily (ἀνάγκη) has these six constituent parts.

effect of tragedy does not depend on its performance by actors."[74] Still later, Aristotle tells us that spectacle and music "make the pleasure all the more vivid; and this vividness (τὸ ἐναργὲς) can be felt whether it is read or acted."[75] These are two surprising claims for Aristotle to be making about a cultural art form that would seem to depend on public performance. The first claim states straightforwardly that tragedy does not depend on spectacle for its effect. The latter, which testifies to the impact of spectacle in poetry whether or not it is performed, implies that visual imagination must play an important role in the reading of dramatic texts. The imagination of the reader or audience is the only plausible site for the spectacle, which is a part of poetry "whether it is read or acted." The drama is brought to life in the imagination of the reader or audience; a reader creates spectacle in the imagination.

These last statements have strong bearing on whether Plato's dialogues ought to be considered poetry since they imply that aside from any given performance, the engaged reader or audience of a dramatic work imagines the setting, character, action, and so on, and thus contributes to her own dramatic experience. Plato's dialogues convey the vividness of poetry through their many dramatic devices. I shall have the opportunity in Chapter 6 to discuss in more detail the role that vision might have in philosophical activity as a consequence of the role that images and image-making have in Plato's dialogues. In any case, spectacle remains a part of the dialogue through the reader's imagination, which can be stirred by a dramatic reading. The reader's own experience, therefore, is an essential component of how Plato achieves his philosophical aim.

4. Plato's Works: Making and Doing

The Greek terms for poetry and drama, as well as their English cognates, come respectively from Greek root verbs "to make" and "to do." The poem is something made or created by the artist, and the drama is a representation of action, a doing. In this literal fashion, Plato's dialogues are unquestionably both poetic and dramatic. But making and doing have further significance for my purposes. In carrying out my investigation of Plato as poet and dramatist, I want to ask of Plato's work What does it make? and What does it do?

74. Ibid., VI.28 (1450b)
75. Ibid., XXVI.10–12 (1462a–b), τῇ ἀναγνώσει . . . τῶν ἔργων.

Plato achieves his aim of turning souls toward the life of inquiry, by *making* us into philosophers, by getting us to *do* philosophy. Plato attempts to accomplish his aim through the dramatic elements of the dialogues, and not without them. This amounts to what I call "Plato's philosophy." It is not a doctrine; it is not a system; it is a making and a doing. The dialogues, by virtue of their poetic and dramatic elements, attempt to make us into philosophers, and we become engaged in doing philosophy through them. In what follows I describe some of the ways in which the dialogues make us into philosophers and the manner in which we do philosophy with the dialogues, none of which would be accomplished independently of the dramatic and poetic aspects of the dialogues.

I begin with what I take to be the most obvious feature of the dialogues, which is ironically often overlooked: Plato nowhere writes directly and in his own voice. All the words, ideas, jokes, foibles, hypotheses, stories, myths, and arguments are voiced by dramatic characters. Even Aristotle views this poetic device as a sign of superior poetry—when the author breaks from mere narrative, relating the incidents himself, and moves toward letting the characters speak in their own voices.[76] This feature of the dialogues, conspicuously true of drama, drives a wedge between reader and author, and speaks against looking in the dialogues for Plato's own thoughts on the subject. Plato's writing thus precludes the activity of examining what we might call "Plato's thought." Plato's thought remains hidden from us; he refuses to be an authority.

Consequently, the reader must turn inward for answers to the questions the dialogues pose, to rely on herself and the text in order to bring some meaning to the dialogues. Alan C. Bowen describes the difficulty we have as readers. When we read a Platonic dialogue, we engage in two activities. The first is an interpretive act regarding the meaning of the dialogue, the second is a philosophical act of thinking with the text as our guide and, according to Bowen, "[n]either involves interpreting Plato's philosophical thought."[77] Bowen goes on to underscore the notion that Plato's texts cannot serve as sources of a certain kind of knowledge, namely, knowledge of Plato as authority. Bowen explains that when a reader interacts with a Platonic dialogue

> he thinks for himself; he does not discover what Plato thinks. Unlike the works of Aristotle and later philosophers, Plato's text does not

76. Ibid., XXIV.13–14 (1460a).
77. Bowen (1988, 59–60). Cf. Hyland (1968).

require the reader to sit in Plato's school and learn his philosophy; it demands instead that the reader become a philosopher in his own right.[78]

The dialogues are instruments of the kind of learning in which the individual and text interact, the reader philosophizes along with the text. Plato's deliberate authorial distance, created by his use of the dramatic form, compels the reader to search beyond the text itself for answers to the very queries which the text proposes, and in so doing, the reader participates in doing philosophy.

Second, the dialogues draw the reader into serious consideration of the nature of character by their portrayal of rich dramatic characters. As I have discussed above in regard to Plato's connection to the poets, Epicharmus and Sophron, one of Plato's finest literary faculties is his ability to draw detailed, subtle, rich, and often poignant characters. He also provides clues for the reader and audience about the personalities and habits of his characters by his clever use of descriptive names. The focus on dramatic character provides the impetus for reflection on moral character. Each of the dialogues draws the reader's attention to the character of some interlocutor as that character is portrayed through thoughts, ideas, and speech. The reader then often compares that character to Socrates' as well as to her own. The reader thus turns from text to self. As my discussion of Aristotle's account of the device of "discovery" shows, the dialogues are about discovering the true characters of the interlocutors and, ultimately, about self-discovery. Many of the interlocutors consistently exhibit characters that are arrogant, unwilling to engage in dialectic, inflated or egotistical, and lacking in most virtues. The reader, in her desire to compare favorably to these characters, must face difficult self-examination, asking whether she holds the same beliefs as the characters portrayed in the dialogues, whether she holds her beliefs dogmatically and without examination, in sum whether she exhibits the same character traits as the interlocutors. The example of Socrates looms large in the dialogues, and his character provides the reader with an example of the virtues of the examined human life. The Socratic move toward self-knowledge works on the reader, in part therefore, through Plato's use of character portrayal. In the final summation, the dialogues are about coming to know who we are and who we might become through living the examined life. The vehicle for much of the movement in this direction is Plato's dramatic character development.[79]

78. Bowen (1988, 62).
79. Chapter 4 addresses the literary device of character development in detail.

Third, the dialogues invite the reader to play a role in the dialogues. As Bowen describes, the reader is compelled to take on the positions of the interlocutors, to weigh them, to evaluate them, and ultimately to take a position of her own.[80] Bowen's view of the reader of the Platonic dialogue sounds nearly identical to Iser's description of the perspectival aspect of the wandering viewpoint. Adopting a role in the dialogue is part of the doing or acting that a reader does when engaged by a dialogue. With each reading, a dialogue takes on an additional *dramatic persona*. The cast of characters grows by one when the reader enters the agora, the paleastra, or the banquet, thinks through her own answers to Socrates' queries, and evaluates the responses of the interlocutors. The reader can become the respondent to Socrates' questions, she can question the interlocutors further, she can improve upon the interlocutors' responses, and most importantly, she can come to act out the role of philosopher beyond the reading of the dialogue.

Through her participation in the drama of the dialogue, the reader is, fourth, afforded a lived human experience. Drew Hyland describes the manner in which the dialogues provide the reader an opportunity to experience philosophical activity first hand.[81] What is significant for Hyland is that the dialogues convey much more than the logoi or arguments of philosophy. Since they represent real philosophical conversations, what they convey to the reader is philosophical experience. Plato chose the dialogue form of writing because it was the only medium through which he could convey to the reader his experience of philosophy.

> It is for this reason that the traditional dichotomy between Plato the philosopher (the arguments presented and the analysis thereof) and Plato the artist (the portrayal of personalities, dramatic situations, myths, etc.) simply will not do; because Plato is denying the very conception of philosophy as "arguments" (a series of propositions) which allows the dichotomy. The concrete portrayal of the experience of philosophy is at least as important an aspect of his "doctrine" as the arguments presented.[82]

The dialogues are in this way enactments of the philosophic life,[83] and thus their dramatic aspects prove to be necessary to Plato's philosophical project.

80. Bowen (1988).
81. Hyland (1968).
82. Ibid., 42–43.
83. See Press (1995b).

Through the dialogues' unique dramatic qualities, Plato provides the reader with philosophical experience, and Hyland's view takes him well beyond any notion of *vicarious* experience; the dialogues provide direct, concrete philosophical experience. We do philosophy with the dialogues. Aristotle claims that with tragic poetry the audience experiences pity and fear directly, but this is not quite analogous to Hyland's position. I understand Hyland's position to be that just what the interlocutors are portrayed as experiencing, the reader/audience is likely to experience. Comparatively, Aristotle's description of the audience's experience of pity and fear are due to a more vicarious interaction with the drama.[84] Oedipus himself does not experience pity and fear over his plight, although the audience watching the unfolding drama of his life is experiencing those emotions. The audience of the Platonic dialogues, to the contrary, are experiencing philosophy just as are the interlocutors, and their experience could include the entire range of experiences we see portrayed among the interlocutors: anger, frustration, arrogance, antipathy toward Socrates, voyeuristic intrigue, genuine desire to be engaged, intellectual stimulation, turning.

The concrete experience of doing philosophy comes directly from the "doing" which is the essence of drama. As Hyland implies, the philosophic and the dramatic cannot be separated without misunderstanding Plato's work. Moreover, the concrete experience provided by the dramas helps Plato convey further that philosophy is rooted firmly in human life and experience, not abstracted from them. Beyond a method, a procedure, or an argument, we see enacted before us—and we participate in—human life, which is the proper setting for philosophy.

And finally, the dialogues as poetry or drama offer us ambiguity, and their very ambiguity starts the reader on the task of doing philosophy. The "meaning" of a dialogue is certainly never univocally expressed and is never clearly manifest. The dialogues consist of several characters' viewpoints; they place the reader in aporia; they offer contradictions; they offer inconsistencies; they challenge us to understand them. Even some of the seemingly straightforward speeches of the character, Socrates, are offered in a dramatic context which is far from straightforward—often mysterious, paradoxical, perplexing—and therefore the reader is compelled to do some work in an effort to understand the meaning of those speeches within their dramatic contexts.[85] Hence the need for interpretation, as well as the possibility for different interpretations.

84. Cf. Aristotle, *Poetics*, XIII.1–XIV.19 (1452b–1454a).
85. Such a view is apparently not shared by those who write about the historical Socrates and draw "his philosophy" from the Platonic dialogues. See, for example, Vlastos (1991) and

The poetic feature of ambiguity, therefore, stirs the reader to hermeneutic activity—at least a starting point on the path toward inquiry. This hermeneutic activity is another doing occasioned by the dialogues.

Our conception of Plato as poet and dramatist, in sum, shows there to be two levels of making and doing. As a poet Plato not only creates or makes dialogues, but he attempts to make us into philosophers. And in their dramatic capacity the dialogues not only represent a doing among Socrates and the interlocutors, but occasion a doing on the part of the reader while reading the dialogue and, one hopes, beyond it. Plato's task of making philosophers again underscores the connection between dialectic and identity. His dialectic engagement through poetic device contributes to the creation, or making, of better identities.

In conclusion I would like to return to Friedrich Hebbel whose journal entry opened this chapter. Hebbel was a German poet, dramatist, literary critic, and novelist of the nineteenth century (1813–63). His cryptic journal entry, "Content presents the task; form the solution," is packed with significance for Platonic project.[86] While Hebbel's journal entry relies on an intellectual abstraction that separates form and content from one another, the meaning of the entry conjoins form and content by linking their *function* in the dramatic construct. Form and content together provide task and solution, neither one having purpose or sensible function without the other. In Plato's case, the dialogues' content presents the task of living our lives in such a way that our souls are edified, that is, improved by reason, dialectic, and virtue. The solution offered by the form of the dialogues provides the means to achieve our task. If the form of the dialogues presents the solution, then the dramatic form compels us to *do* certain things: to inquire, to believe, to think on our own, to question, to confront our true selves. The solution lies in earnest philosophical doings.

5. Making Characters

In this broad context of making and doing, Plato attempts to make his audience into philosophers, he induces them to engage in philosophical activities.

Benson (1992). Cf. Gadamer (1980, 111): "Multiple valences of meaning . . . contain a *productive* ambiguity."

86. Hebbel was a student of the Platonic dialogues. One of Hebbel's dramatic works was "Gyges and His Ring" (written in 1854), a play based on the myth of Gyges as it is related in

In the next chapter, I look at one dramatic device in detail, that of character development. In double fashion, Plato works on the development of the character: as a writer he develops characters in the course of a given dialogue, so he "makes" his fictive creations; and he contributes to the "making" of the characters of his audience insofar as his dialogues have transformative power. I examine next the double "making" of character.

Plato's *Republic*. This journal entry is not, however, made in reference to Plato or the dialogues, but is rather a general remark about playwrighting.

4

Character

Character is that which reveals choice, shows what
sort of thing a man chooses or avoids in circumstances where the choice is not obvious. . . .

Aristotle, *Poetics*, VI.24

Commonly, "character" can denote at least two things: a persona in a drama
or a work of literature, and a moral personality. This semantic ambiguity in
the English word "character" is mirrored in Greek terms with similar meanings in both the moral and the dramatic sphere.[1] I wish to rely on this
semantic ambiguity so as to link the dramatic and the moral spheres in
Plato's work.

Questions about whether virtue can be taught, such as Meno's question
that opens the dialogue named for him, can be construed as questions about
moral character. Since the *Meno* explicitly addresses a question about

---

1. "Éthicos" (ἠθικός) describes that pertaining to morals, moral character, or ethics;
"éthos" (ἦθος) refers to a dramatic persona, and both terms share roots with substantives and
verbs that mean, respectively, a habit or a custom and to be in the habit or to be accustomed
(ἔθος, ἔθω).

whether character can be affected or changed for the better, it seems quite natural in examining it to focus on the literary device of character development and how it functions philosophically in the dialogue. The dialogue itself answers Meno's question, "Is virtue teachable?" through its presentation of his character. In the course of this dialogue, Meno's character changes,[2] and that change comes from an engagement in dialectic. While ultimately the dialogue indicates that virtue cannot be *taught*, it shows on another level that it can be induced by other means: it is dialectic engagement that is at work here in Meno's transformation. But Plato creates characters in two ways that correspond to the ambiguous denotation of the term. Plato creates dramatic characters and, through them, he creates the possibility for a transformation in the moral character of the reader of the dialogue. So, Meno's is not the only transformation at stake here.

The change in Meno's character can best be illustrated by dividing the dialogue into three parts. In the first part of the dialogue (approximately 70–80d), Socrates begins with a detailed description of Meno's initial character traits, and Meno's speech and actions in this first part accurately reinforce Socrates' description. In the second part of the dialogue (approximately 81–86c), Socrates introduces the story of recollection and conducts the demonstration with Meno's slave. This represents a turning point in the dialogue, and there is evidence in this second part that the very traits characteristic of Meno introduced in the first part of the dialogue are ones that Socrates tries to change. Finally, in the third part of the dialogue (approximately 86d to the end), Meno's character does change for the better. After demonstrating the change in Meno's character, I explore the moral implications of that change and how the moral character of the reader of this dialogue might be affected by the portrayed change in Meno's character.

Unlike other chapters in this work, this chapter focuses on a single dialogue and offers an interpretation of its meaning and philosophical significance. The chapter's aim, however, coincides with the others insofar as it attempts to show that (and how) Plato carries out his philosophical project through what is considered a literary device, in this case, character portrayal and

---

2. I have found only two other references to such a view, but neither is developed. The first can be found in Brumbaugh (1975, 112), and even Brumbaugh comments on the fact that few accept this idea, saying, "Even the best commentators . . . miss the full impact of this dramatic development." But Brumbaugh does not develop his view in the manner that I think it can and should be developed. Rather, he devotes little more than a paragraph to Meno's character change. Second, there is a brief mention in Seeskin (1987, 125). As counterexamples, see Guthrie (1956, 11) and Klein (1989, 184), who deny explicitly that Meno's character changes.

development. The further implications of this chapter, therefore, go beyond the dialogue at hand. I would not necessarily argue that other dialogues depict the particular transformation I argue occurs in the *Meno*; character transformation is germane to this dialogues in ways it is not to others. Other dialogues, however, do provide evidence that Plato's masterful creation of character, character change, and character development—even character intransigence—serve the philosophical ends that I describe here.

1. Introducing Meno's Character

"Can you tell me, Socrates, is virtue teachable? Or is it not taught, but something acquired by practice? Or is it neither something acquired by practice nor learned but accrues to humans by nature or by some other means?"

Commentators on this dialogue have had much to say about Meno's opening question (and I shall venture my own view later in the chapter), but little to say about Socrates' response to that question.[3] It is such an odd response, in fact, that it demands our attention. Socrates replies in a manner that seems like a *non sequitur*, but I want to show that, on the contrary, his reply is the key to understanding Meno's character. It is, therefore, also the key to understanding what follows in the rest of dialogue and what I believe to be clearly central to it: the transformation of Meno's character.

Socrates' response to Meno's opening question does not sound much like a direct response to the question "Is virtue teachable?"

> Meno, before now, the Thessalians were well reputed among the Greeks and they were marveled at both for horsemanship and for riches; but now, as it seems to me, they are also reputed for wisdom, and not least the fellow citizens of your companion, Aristippus of Larissa. And Gorgias is responsible for this reputation of yours.

---

3. Brumbaugh (1975, 111) is, again, a refreshing exception. Grote (1888, 232) does not say anything about this passage, and in fact, it is as though it did not exist. In his commentary, he has Meno open the dialogue, "Can you tell me, Sokrates, whether virtue is teachable—or acquirable by exercise—or whether it comes by nature—or in what other manner it comes?" Socrates answers immediately, saying only, "I cannot answer your question. I am ashamed to say that I do not even know what virtue is." Klein (1989, 41) does treat Socrates' response, but seems more concerned with the historical references in this passage than any personal bearing on Meno. Arieti (1991, 202) summarizes this passage, noting that Socrates' response is "surprising" but he does not explain its role or significance in the dialogue.

Having come to the city, he was wooed by those who court wisdom—
the preeminent among the Aleuadae, one of whom is your lover
Aristippus—and by all the other Thessalians. And he [Gorgias]
especially accustomed you to this habit: to answer fearlessly and
magnificently whenever someone asks something, just as an expert
would probably do. And likewise he submitted himself to questioning by any Greeks who wanted to ask questions. And no one was
not answered by him. But here [in Athens] my dear Meno, it turns
out to be quite the opposite. As if there were a drought of wisdom,
wisdom probably left here and went there to you. If you want to ask
someone here that kind of question, everyone would laugh and say,
"Oh Foreigner, I must seem to you to be quite fortunate if I know
whether virtue is teachable or by what means it comes about. But I
am so far from knowing whether it is teachable or not teachable that
neither do I know at all what virtue itself is."

And I am this way, too, Meno. Along with my fellow citizens, I
am lacking in these matters, and I blame myself for not knowing at
all what virtue is. For not knowing what something is, how could I
know the sort of thing it is? Does it seem possible to you to know
whether Meno is beautiful, or wealthy, or well-born or the opposite
of these things, not knowing at all who Meno is? (70–71b)

Socrates raises the question explicitly of who Meno is at the end of this
passage, and ironically, he has just given a detailed description of him.
Meno introduced the dialogue by asking a question about character, and
Socrates' response tells us about character—about Meno's character.[4] It also
sets up the first part of the drama in which Meno enacts the character traits
ascribed to him in Socrates' response.

Socrates' response tells us that Meno, along with other Thessalians, has
gained a reputation for wisdom. Meno's behavior will later show that he,
too, believes that he is wise, and he shows great interest in keeping and per-
petuating his reputation. We learn most importantly from Socrates' response
that Meno has come under the influence of the sophist Gorgias, and we
learn from Socrates' response that Meno's character traits stem from habits
that Gorgias has instilled in him.[5] Significantly, whereas some of the sophists

4. Klein (1989, 199–202) argues also, but not in reference to Socrates' introduction, that
the dialogue presents us with an answer to the question, "Who is Meno?"
5. τὸ ἔθος ὑμᾶς εἴθικεν . . . (70b).

claimed to teach virtue, Gorgias was a conspicuous exception among them. He publicly denied that he taught virtue.[6] So Meno is under the tutelage of— and acquired the habits, ethos, or character of—a man who presumably denies that he teaches virtue. The sophists are portrayed in the dialogues, moreover, as having competitive attitudes toward discourse, making grand speeches, and having the general ability to create entertaining spectacles with their art of discourse. In keeping with his attraction to the sophists, Meno is described as one who gives answers, and specifically confident and grand answers. The first part of the dialogue illustrates Meno's confidence in giving answers as well as the deterioration of that confidence. Gorgias serves as an odd type of authority figure in the early passages of the dialogue, an authority figure who, although absent from the scene of the drama, is strongly present through Meno's references to and reliance on him. Meno will often resort to what Gorgias says, what Gorgias has told him, and what Gorgias believes (71c, 71d, 76b, 76c).

All of the character traits that Socrates attributes to Meno in this opening passage, and which he will act out, make him a poor learner: His belief that he has earned his reputation for wisdom (and his concern for reputation in general), his sophistic attitude toward discourse and all that it entails, his tendency toward giving magnificent answers and being confident in giving them, and his reliance on external authority, all conspire to thwart learning. All of these character traits conflict with certain Socratic—that is, dialectic—ideals presented in the second part of the dialogue that tend toward learning and virtue. The first part of the dialogue will thus depict Meno exhibiting these poor traits.

The drama establishes first that Meno is one concerned with reputation and apparent wisdom. When Socrates admits that he cannot discuss the qualities of virtue (i.e., whether it is teachable or not) until he knows what virtue is, but that he does not know what virtue is, Meno's response is consistent with Socrates' description of his character. "But Socrates, do you truly not know what virtue is? Shall we tell the folks back home these things

---

6. Guthrie (1971, 20) claims that Gorgias "laugh[ed] at the professed teachers of civic virtue. The art of clever speaking, he said, was all that any ambitious man needed to learn." But later, Guthrie conjectures that Gorgias's claim might have been disingenuous, that he provided his pupils with the same skills that Protagoras did while claiming to provide civic virtue (44). We must be cautious in relying on Guthrie as a purely historical source, however, since many of his primary sources of information about the life and practices of Gorgias are Plato's dialogues. Therefore what seems to be "confirmation" about Gorgias is in reality circular. In any case, it is clear that Plato conceived of Gorgias in this way, and in Plato's work, *Gorgias*, the sophist is clearly associated with a disclaimer about teaching virtue.

about you?" (71b–c). Meno expects that Socrates should be embarrassed not only about admitting his ignorance here but about others knowing of it as well. Meno's dismay and mild threat to tell others of Socrates' ignorance demonstrate his concern with reputation, in general, and his concern with guarding a reputation for knowing, in particular.

When the investigation of virtue begins Meno is quite confident in giving answers. "But it's not difficult to say, Socrates. First, if you want the virtue of a man, that's easy. . . . And if you want the virtue of a woman, that's not hard to go through. . . . And there are many other virtues, so one can not be at a loss (ἀπορία) to say what virtue is" (71e–72a). For Meno the answers come more quickly and easily than they should. But the ease with which Meno answers Socrates' questions soon shows itself to be illusory. As he realizes more clearly that he does not know the answers, and he answers less and less confidently, he grows more and more frustrated.

As one might imagine, being confounded in giving answers is not something a person with a reputation for wisdom—and an interest in fostering that reputation—relishes. Meno experiences an incongruity between his self-image and his performance here with Socrates; it is not fitting that he should be at a loss, given his wisdom. He becomes an angry man, digging his heels in, trying to subvert the discussion in many ways in order to avoid more confusion and frustration. At any point in the dialogue Meno could simply have said, "Socrates, I guess I don't know what virtue is," and this would have changed the entire complexion of their conversation. But it would be out of character at this point for Meno to do so because he sees himself as one reputed for wisdom, because he truly believes he deserves that reputation, and because he delights in the opportunity to give a speech on virtue.

A struggle ensues between the two in which Meno continually attempts to avoid answering Socrates' questions, and Socrates continually attempts to draw him into dialectic. Meno balks three times at proceeding with the dialectic, getting Socrates to define "shape" twice and "color" once (75b, 75c, 76a). Meno's contentiousness in argument marks in him sophistic attitudes toward discourse and an inability to engage in dialectic with Socrates, character traits inspired perhaps by Gorgias's influence. Meno responds with such things as, "No, Socrates, *you* say what [virtue] is" (75b). Socrates provides Meno with an example of how to give definitions by giving two definitions of "shape" on the condition that after Socrates defines it, Meno will begin dialectic engagement by saying what virtue is. Socrates first defines "shape" as "the only existing thing which always follows color" (75b) and then, more succinctly as "the limit of a solid" (76a). But Meno pushes

Socrates' indulgence even further. He is not satisfied with the first definition. Meno objects that one could not be satisfied with such a definition of shape, which uses the term "color" in it, if one did not know what color was.

Socrates reprimands Meno for his improper behavior and takes the opportunity to speak about the art of dialectic, to explain and defend his method of dialectic in contrast to Meno's more sophistic approach (75c–e). There is a proper way to engage in dialectic, Socrates gently chides; each participant has a particular role, and each follows the rules accordingly. Once someone has answered a question for an argumentative and contentious questioner, it is the task of the questioner to refute the argument given. But if they are friends—and here Socrates is gently encouraging Meno to take a less adversarial approach to their conversation—it is necessary to answer more gently and in a manner more fitting for dialectic. This means not only answering truthfully, but also speaking in terms that the one answering agrees that he knows. Socrates conveys to Meno some necessary ingredients of proper dialectic: truthful answers (ones that truly reflect one's own beliefs), a reciprocal willingness to give and take in questions and answers, and an elimination of the adversarial stance.

Still, Meno shows his affinity for sophistic discourse. He resists further, saying, "When you tell me [what color is], I'll tell you [what virtue is], Socrates" (76b). Socrates asks Meno whether he should tell him what color is after the manner of Gorgias, which of course, Meno will follow best (76c).[7] But what does Socrates mean when he says that he will answer after the manner of Gorgias? What most characterizes Socrates' answer is its relative complexity and its phony, esoteric sound. Color, it turns out, is the out-flowing from shapes fitted for or suited to sight and which is perceived. From Socrates' description of the out-flowings and the channels along which they travel, Meno can easily infer that sound is the out-flowing suited to ears and is heard, and likewise, smell is the out-flowing suited to the nose and is smelled (76c–e). To anyone else this definition might sound humorous. It seems an overly complex and convoluted way of defining "color," especially compared to Socrates' previous definitions of "shape" which were particularly concise. Meno is infatuated with grandiloquence, becoming enthralled with the Empedoclean definition of color that Socrates gives him. Socrates frames his presentation of Empedocles' definition in a manner that further establishes Meno's character. We are told explicitly that this is the kind of stuff that Meno likes and follows, and that it resembles what he is accustomed

7. Βούλει οὖν σοι κατὰ Γοργίαν ἀποκρίνωμαι, ᾗ ἂν σὺ μάλιστα ἀκολουθήσαις.

to hearing from Gorgias. Consistent with Socrates' initial response to Meno's opening question, it is implied here that Socrates knows and understands Meno's character, that he is capable of knowing what Meno wants to hear and of giving it to him in a suitable fashion. In addition, the palpable shift in the tone of the definition, from simple and succinct to elaborate and showy, implies, although more obliquely, Socrates' understanding of Meno's character.

Meno prefers this flashy definition, and he has a real flair for the theatrical at the expense of substance. Socrates tries to tell Meno that really the definition of shape was a much better one, the more simple and accurate one that he gave earlier, but Meno is unconvinced (76e). In fact, Socrates has left him hungry for more such drivel. Meno forgoes initiation into the mysteries to hear more. "But I'll stay around, Socrates, if you'd tell me many such things" (76e). His enthusiasm for this type of definition shows his habit of favoring the superficially theatrical over the dialectical, perhaps the same character trait that attracts him to sophistic speeches rather than to Socratic dialectic in the first place.

There is an interesting choice of words in the course of this Empedoclean definition. The channels of which Socrates speaks are "poroi" and the effluences or out-flowings themselves are "aporrai." The first of these terms shares a common root with the word "aporia," a pivotal term in this dialogue and in Socratic dialectic generally, meaning to be at a loss or to have a difficulty, to have no way out. That common root, "poros," denotes literally a means of passing a river, a ford; a narrow sea, a strait, passage or channel; a way out. The term for the effluences, "aporrai," comes from the prefix "apo" and the verb "reo," meaning to flow or run or stream out. The sounds of these two terms are remarkably similar, and the frequency of these words seems too high to be merely coincidental. In eight lines (76c–d) "poros" occurs three times and "aporrai" occurs four times.[8] Plato would seem to be relying on the repetition of the sounds of these words for effect and emphasis. Taking seriously the oral culture that was the backdrop of the dialogues, as well as the performative nature of the dialogues, the repetitive sound of these words would indeed have had an impact on Plato's audience. Perhaps these terms are being used to emphasize the importance of aporia and to underscore Socrates' attempts to bring Meno to this state, the beginning point of learning, a starting point Meno has already denied (71e–72a). Meno must come to embrace aporia if he is going to learn and if his character is going to change.

8. Klein (1989, 79) also briefly notes the frequency of this word and its cognates.

In retrospect, we can understand Meno's opening question in a different light now.[9] Socrates' opening remarks pointed out Gorgias's sophistic influence in Meno's life, and among the things Gorgias taught Meno were to answer and to speak confidently, and to love spectacle. Meno's opening question, along with Socrates' description of him as entrenched in the Gorgianic view of discourse, indicate that he has asked his question in order either to hear Socrates give a speech on the topic of teaching virtue, or to give one himself. It is quite literally a rhetorical question. Meno's opening question in the dialogue is posed as an invitation, or even a challenge, to speak on a topic on which the sophists and their followers commonly elaborated. Moreover, it portends the conception of learning with which Meno begins the dialogue. As Samuel Scolnicov so succinctly puts it: "'Can you tell me, Socrates?' Meno's very first words summarize his conception of learning; he wants to be told."[10]

Wanting to be told is the mark of someone used to relying on authority. We have already observed Meno's tendency to rely mostly on Gorgias (71c, 71d, 76b, 76c), but we see Meno's desire to appeal to authority in other ways as well. While Meno is enthralled by Empedocles' definition of color, beyond his desire to be entertained by such fancy stuff, Meno perhaps likes the definition simply because it is Empedocles' view—which Socrates offers while citing Pindar, another authority. And, of course, Meno has relied on Socrates as authority in this conversation as well.

In contrast, Socrates dismisses the authority of Gorgias. He does not remember whether Gorgias seemed to him to know what virtue is.[11] He cannot remember the testimony of the external authority to which Meno wants to appeal, and in casting off authority by an appeal to lack of memory, Socrates thus opposes recollection (ἀνάμνησις) to authority. In this way Socrates introduces the inseparable themes of recollection and independent learning. Socrates wants to cast Gorgias away for now and to focus on Meno himself (αὐτός, 71d), laying stress on Meno's own thoughts without any appeal to authority. In contrast to authority, which Socrates forgets, the

---

9. Just as Iser's conception of the temporal aspect of the wandering viewpoint tells us, the reader moves forward and backward within the text in the construction of meaning. See Chapter 2, page 44.

10. Scolnicov (1988, 51). It also appears that Meno's early responses to Socrates' questions are themselves the beginnings of speeches that Meno is eager to make, for example, "It is not hard to tell you, Socrates. First . . ." (71e–72a). On the sophistic background behind the opening question, see Guthrie (1971), Kerferd (1981, 131–38), and Arieti (1991, 202).

11. Οὐ πάνυ εἰμὶ μνήμων. . . (71c).

dialogue distinctly espouses things remembered, things which come from oneself.[12] This early dramatic detail about learning and memory thus ushers in concepts that will become pivotal in the second part of the dialogue.

There are further indictments of Meno's character in the first part of the dialogue, and they come directly from Socrates in the form of teasing that at times borders on insult. During the first part of the dialogue, Socrates makes fun of Meno, implying among other things that he is vain, that he is disrespectful, that he is uncooperative, and that he is essentially handsome but stupid. Socrates attributes Meno's brazen attitude to his youth and good looks, which put Socrates, who is less than beautiful, at a distinct disadvantage (76b–c). This exchange, while mocking in tone, points a finger at Meno's reluctance to participate equally and fairly in their search for what virtue is.

Whereas in the early scenes of the dialogue Meno may have viewed Socrates' question, "What is virtue?" as an occasion for giving a speech, for expounding his views, or perhaps more likely, those views he has assimilated from Gorgias, by the end of the first section of the dialogue Meno is experiencing the sting of Socrates' questions, and he does not like it (just like many of Socrates' interlocutors). What has happened between then and now? Unfortunately for Meno, Socrates' questions do not occasion great speeches, and consequently do not cater to inflated egos. Rather they require his interlocutors to put forth their views honestly, clearly, and succinctly, and then submit them to scrutiny. Meno is coming to realize this, and he is not pleased. It may bring his reputation for wisdom and for answering fearlessly, quite literally, into question.

At this point in the dialogue (79e–80b), Meno does his best to subvert the discussion by introducing his challenge (ἐριστικὸν λόγον, 80e) to Socrates. His challenge to Socrates is: How can one search for something? If one already knows it then there is no need to search for it. If one does not yet know it, then how will he know it when he comes upon it? The dilemma

12. Cf. Bowen (1988, 62): "[The reader] thinks for himself; he does not discover what Plato thinks."

MacIntyre believes that the separation of authority from reason, especially with respect to ethical matters, is purely a modern phenomenon, beginning in Kierkegaard's *Either/Or*: "The notion of authority and the notion of reason are not . . . intimately connected, but are in fact mutually exclusive. Yet this concept of authority as excluding reason is, as I have already noticed, itself a peculiarly, even if not exclusively, modern concept, fashioned in a culture to which the notion of authority is alien and repugnant, so that appeals to authority appear irrational" (MacIntyre [1981, 41]). On the contrary, this is an ancient notion with Socratic roots. It is a major Socratic motif, although it certainly seems plausible and fitting that this distinctly Socratic theme re-emerges in Kierkegaard's works that explicitly pay tribute to the Socratic approach. Cf. Nietzsche (1966, aphorism 191).

that Meno introduces attempts not only to end their discussion of virtue—what it is and whether it is teachable—but it challenges Socrates on the deepest level, making the claim that learning is not possible. This dilemma threatens Meno's inquiry with Socrates, currently under view by the reader, and it threatens inquiry in general. Because this challenge is so subversive, it indicates the height of Meno's frustration and the extreme manifestation of his unsuitability for learning. He doesn't even think learning is possible.

2. Interlude

I turn now to the demonstration with Meno's slave to show how it is a pivotal point in the dialogue, and how it signals the coming change in Meno's character. I wish to discuss the demonstration in two respects: first, the meaning of the demonstration and its philosophical significance as a scene within the drama and, second, the dramatic structure of this passage and how it fits in with the overall structure of the dialogue.

The demonstration comes immediately after Meno has presented his challenge to inquiry. Meno has up to now shown himself incapable of learning so, consistent with that character, he claims that learning is not possible. As stated earlier, the purpose of the demonstration with the slave is to answer Meno's challenge to inquiry: to show *that* learning is possible and, furthermore, to show *how* learning is possible. Simply speaking, the demonstration shows that learning is possible because the slave does experience his ascent and comes to know how one derives the area of a square based on the diagonal. The demonstration shows how learning is possible in more subtle ways. Recall that Socrates demonstrates with Meno's slave that learning is possible, first of all, only from a position of ignorance.[13] The slave must realize that he does not know geometry in order to go forward and to learn what he does not know. Second, the individual learns through self-examination; the answers are recalled from within. Third, the learning takes place through questions and answers. And finally, learning does not take place from an external authority.

All of these qualities, which the demonstration shows are necessary for learning, stand in stark opposition to Meno's character as it was introduced and as it has been shown to us so far in the dialogue. Meno is working from

13. See discussion in Chapter 1, pages 35ff.

an inaccurate self-image as a wise person, and he therefore resists any admission that he is truly ignorant. He has relied on Gorgias, Empedocles, Pindar, and Socrates as external authorities rather than thinking on his own. He is not at a loss when he should be, and he is reluctant to engage in the question and answer necessary for dialectic learning, being much more enthusiastic for giving and hearing speeches.

Meno never does admit his own ignorance explicitly, but through the demonstration with the slave Socrates creates the situation that allows him not to have to do so—a sign that Socrates adjusts his method to suit the character of his interlocutor. This is a man, remember, who puts much stock in his reputation for being wise. For Meno to admit that the slave is made better off by admitting his (the slave's) own ignorance is enough to satisfy Socrates that Meno has made a connection between himself and his slave.[14] If Meno were not able independently to recognize himself in the image of his slave, Socrates makes it vividly clear to him. It is fortunate for the slave, says Socrates, that he, in all his confusion on geometrical topics, has been saved from giving many fine speeches to large audiences on those topics. Meno made a similar boast earlier in the dialogue about his own experience giving speeches on the topic of virtue. Both Meno and his slave are ignorant and both are benefited by admitting it. Meno is shamed by having to be instructed by his own, admittedly uneducated, slave and for being compared to him (and unfavorably, at that!) in Socrates' subtle way. The content of the slave demonstration shows clearly what the impetus is for Meno's character to change. The shame that Meno feels here plays a role in his future participation in the dialogue and his overall change of character. There is even further reason to believe that there will be such a change in Meno's character when we move from the content of the slave demonstration to its dramatic structure.

Structurally, the demonstration with the slave could roughly be divided into three parts. In the first part, Socrates brings the slave to the point at which he realizes his ignorance regarding the geometrical properties of a square. The second part is an interlude in which Socrates turns away from the slave momentarily to talk to Meno. And finally, the slave ascends to knowledge[15] from a point of ignorance with the aid of Socrates' questions.

As I have suggested, the dialogue as a whole can also be roughly divided into three parts. The dialogue begins with Meno in a state of unrecognized

---

14. See Miller on "mimetic irony" (1986, 4–5). Miller describes the philosophical protagonist of Plato's dialogues as putting "the interlocutor on stage before himself" (5).

15. ἐπιστήσεται; ἐπιστήμην, 85d.

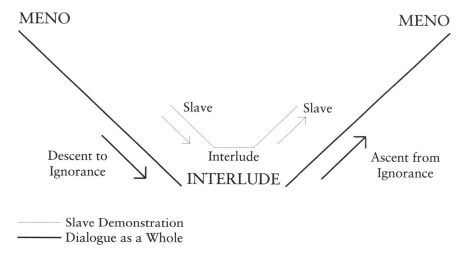

Slave Demonstration
Dialogue as a Whole

Fig. 4.1

ignorance, feeling knowledgeable and confident about himself. Through Socrates' questions he is brought down closer and closer to an awareness of his ignorance, to a point of frustration, at which point he presents his challenging dilemma to Socrates. The drama is then interrupted by an interlude comprising the story of recollection and the demonstration with Meno's slave. After the interlude with Meno's slave there is the third part, which thus far has escaped analysis, and really stands at the crux of what I wish to argue here. I argue that we see a rising up in the third part of the dialogue parallel to, although not identical to, that experienced by the slave. Meno begins his ascent here on his way to becoming a better learner. The basic dialectic movement is thus portrayed doubly in this dialogue. Both part and whole reflect in their structure the proper movement of learning—first a breakdown to an awareness of one's ignorance, then a building up through the art of questioning.

On the basis of this parallel dramatic structure, I argue that the dialogue as a whole mimics the demonstration with the slave, or more properly speaking, that the demonstration with the slave is a microcosm for the rest of the dialogue. If one were to accept such a hypothesis, that the demonstration with Meno's slave is a microcosm for the dialogue as a whole, then there are certain conclusions that naturally follow from it. In particular, I am interested in the fact that the slave experiences an ascent from ignorance in the third part of the demonstration. What follows is that there should be some kind of analogous ascent for Meno as well. I accept the microcosm hypothesis, including its implications for a change in Meno's literary character in the third part of the dialogue. As naturally as this kind of conclusion seems to follow if one is to make an analogy between the two dramatic scenes, there seems to be a resistance to accepting those conclusions.

Commentators on the *Meno* have unwittingly implied the microcosm thesis I offer here, but have neglected an examination of the implications for the dialogue as a whole. For example, Teloh argues that there are two parts to Socrates' dialectic,[16] a negative aspect (elenchus) and a positive aspect (psychagogia). The former consists of using questions to cross-examine the interlocutor and to reveal inconsistencies or other problems in his beliefs. The latter consists of using questions, after the elenchus has occurred, to lead the soul of the interlocutor toward various beliefs that are better than his original beliefs insofar as they have better withstood the test of dialectic.

Teloh then uses this conception of Socratic dialectic to explain the two parts of the slave demonstration (separated by the interlude with Meno) and therefore the two parts of the dialogue as a whole (Meno before the slave demonstration and Meno after the slave demonstration).[17] Once the slave has been shown, through elenchus, that his beliefs about the area of the square figure are wrong, he can then be led to better beliefs in the latter part of the demonstration. The connection that Teloh does not make explicit, even though he is willing to admit that the slave demonstration mimics the dialogue as a whole, is that Socrates does a similar thing with Meno and Meno's beliefs. Rather, Teloh maintains what seems to be a contradiction: that Meno is unaffected by Socrates' dialectic and, at the same time, that the slave demonstration is a microcosm for the dialogue as a whole. In this way, Teloh's view leads to an insoluble dilemma: if Meno is unaffected by the elenchus, then there is no analogy between the slave demonstration and the dialogue as a whole; but if there is an analogy between the interlude and the larger drama, then Meno must be affected by elenchus in a manner at least similar to his slave. Another way to describe the difficulty, using Teloh's own conclusions, is that if Meno were unaffected by Socrates' elenchus, as Teloh claims, then Socrates would have no reason to move on to the second phase of dialectic, i.e., soul-leading, and we have little explanation of the last third of the dialogue.

16. Teloh (1986).
17. Ibid., 155–59.

I argue, to the contrary, that what Teloh calls the "elenchus" has been effective, and Meno is now ready for soul-leading and that the third part of the dialogue parallels the slave's ascent to knowledge. Meno's increasingly disagreeable character during the first part of the dialogue shows that what Teloh calls "elenchus" has been effective. That effectiveness is marked by Meno's clearly experiencing aporia, when he began the dialogue claiming he could not be at a loss for words. Socrates resourcefully plays to Meno's character (the major thesis of Teloh's book)—a vain one concerned with reputation for wisdom—by inducing shame in him and thus preparing him for the positive aspect of dialectic which follows the slave demonstration. Meno successfully makes the connection between the slave's ignorance and his own. The interlude not only provides a solution to the dilemma Meno has introduced—and thus clears the way for inquiry to proceed—it also shows Meno an image of someone who is ignorant, who recognizes and admits his ignorance, and who is then able to learn once he has recognized this ignorance. Insofar as Socrates gets Meno's assent that the slave is better off for all that, the soul leading has already begun.

Teloh claims that the latter portion of the dialogue must be aporetic rather than positive. I agree that overall it is aporetic, that is no "answers" are found. Teloh defines psychagogia in terms of having new beliefs replace old ones, and clearly Meno still does not know what virtue is. But as much as any other interlocutor, Meno has been compelled to confront several new beliefs: dialectic interaction should not be contentious; the debater's argument is not a good one, and we ought not believe it because it makes us lazy in inquiry; it is beneficial to recognize one's ignorance; it is shameful to speak knowingly about things of which one is truly ignorant. So, the dialogue is positive with respect to Meno's character, and Teloh is therefore wrong to assume that the positive and the aporetic are exclusive of one another.[18]

To experience aporia is, furthermore, just the incentive an interlocutor might need to be encouraged to ask questions. In other words, aporia is really a necessary component of the positive aspect of dialectic. One can only build up or be edified by asking questions when he feels the need to ask

18. In a similar manner, several aporetic dialogues still have what I would consider positive results. For example, although Theaetetus never receives an answer to the question "What is knowledge?" in *Theaetetus*, he is shown the difficulties, both epistemologically and morally, of relativism; although the *Protagoras* never answers the question whether virtue is teachable, Socrates shows Protagoras that contentious debate and sophistry are not appropriate vehicles for human inquiry nor for the good human life; although the *Euthyphro* never answers the question "What is piety?," it does offer a compelling critique of Greek polytheism and effectively undermines Euthyphro's self-professed expertise.

questions, and aporia leaves one with such a need. Remember Meno's claim when giving his first definition. He could hardly be at a loss (aporia). But being at a loss is just what Socrates wants to occur in Meno. It is the beginning of philosophical inquiry.

In a more obvious case of neglecting the implications pointing to the change in Meno's character, Jerome Eckstein says that after the demonstration with the slave, the format of the discussion between Socrates and Meno changes radically—again, a view consistent with my own thesis. But strangely, in explaining that radical change in format, Eckstein says that "[n]ow, however, Meno *either unexplainedly acquiesces or is obligingly oblivious*" (my emphasis).[19] But why should we assume that Meno is either oblivious or that his actions are inexplicable? Such an assumption carries with it further assumptions about Plato as author that I am unwilling to accept, specifically about his (in)ability to draw a coherent character. In any case, I prefer a plausible explanation to none, and it is plausible, if not probable, that the format of their discussion has changed because Meno is now willing to be a better participant in dialectic and to proceed with his and Socrates' inquiry into the nature of virtue.

Teloh implies and Eckstein explicitly recognizes that there is a change in Meno in the latter part of the dialogue, and both accept some form of what I call the microcosm hypothesis, but both refuse to go as far as that hypothesis should carry them. They seem to ignore the implications of their own interpretations. That Meno does change in character is consistent with their interpretations, and assuming so goes the further step to explain the third part of the dialogue in a manner which their analyses cannot.

3. Transformation

We can now move on to the third part of the dialogue to see just how the changes in Meno's character become manifest. Meno's improved participation is apparent in several instances in the dialogue after the slave demonstration. He no longer answers questions quickly and assuredly, and he is therefore answering them better than he did before. Overall, Meno is more agreeable in conversation from here on out. He becomes more tentative in his answers, begins participating in dialectic, and becomes a cooperative

19. Eckstein (1968, 54).

partner for Socrates. For example, he asks, "Yes, but does it seem to you that there are teachers of virtue?" (89e). And he responds tentatively to a question about whether the sophists teach virtue, "I can't say, Socrates. Just like many people, sometimes they seem so to me, but at other times not" (95c). None of these answers could be considered "confident and grand," as Socrates originally describes Meno's Gorgianic style of answering questions.[20]

It is also in this third part of the dialogue that Meno asks his first philosophical question: "So I wonder, Socrates, whether there are any good men, or in what manner good men might come to be" (96d). Upon first glance this might seem to be the same question that opens the dialogue. While the question here seems to be asking how virtue is acquired, in a manner similar to the opening question, the two questions are different in the responses that they elicit. The opening question, as I have argued, is one meant to occasion a speech—either from Meno (who claims to have given such speeches before) or from Socrates. In the opening question, Meno is much more contentious, saying literally, "Are you able to tell me, Socrates?" This later question seems really to elicit from Socrates what he thinks about the issue, and it moves the conversation along smoothly, keeping it to the philosophical issues. The two types of questions can also be distinguished by the epistemic position from which they are asked. Unlike the question that opens the dialogue, the question as it appears in the third part of the dialogue begins with a sense of wonder (θαυμάζω), and as Socrates makes explicitly clear in *Theaetetus*, philosophy begins in wonder.[21] This kind of wonder stems from aporia, from a real position of ignorance. Soon after his first philosophical question, Meno asks another one, again from this same position of wonder. "So I wonder, Socrates, this being the case, why knowledge is valued so much more than correct opinion, and since they are different, what the difference is between them" (97c–d). Meno stands here as evidence against his own challenge to inquiry. Meno shows that inquiry is possible by engaging in it.

We also get from Meno two instances that come as close to an admission of ignorance as we could expect from him. Twice he asks Socrates to explain something to him that he does not understand, saying, "How do you mean this, Socrates?" (96e and 97a). These requests that Socrates explain or elaborate can be fruitfully distinguished from Meno's earlier demands that Socrates show him how to give a proper definition by defining "shape" and "color." In the earlier instances, Meno's questions distinctly steered their conversation away from the difficult topic at hand. In both of these later instances, Meno's request for clarity and understanding serve to advance their conversation, not circumvent it.

Finally, all poking fun at Meno's character stops in the last part of the dialogue. Guthrie, who argues that Meno's character is "sustained through-out the dialogue," claims in the same sentence that Socrates teases him about that character.[22] But the teasing stops, and at a critical juncture. No longer does Socrates make comments about Meno's good looks or his manipulation of an old and ugly man in discourse. After the demonstration with Meno's slave, all personal references to Meno stop—his looks, his character, his youth. That Meno is treated better by Socrates is an indication that he has become a more worthy partner in dialectic. Both Teloh and Eckstein agree in general that Socrates' treatment of his interlocutors varies according to their personalities.[23] In Teloh's case it is the thesis around which his book centers. It is what he calls the "Phaedrus principle," and it defines, in part, the Socratic method of dialectic for him. Socrates' earlier comments implied that Meno, although beautiful, lacked what was necessary to engage in dialectic and to learn. We see Meno begin to change those very aspects of his character which were preventing him from engaging properly with Socrates in their search and, at the same time, Socrates' teasing comments stop. If we accept the notion that Socrates gears his rhetoric to the character with whom he speaks, and he chides that character early in the dialogue, it seems significant that this chiding stops in the latter third of the dialogue. Socrates is quite patient and mild with Meno from here on out, consistent with Meno's changed character.

All we need do now is look back at Meno at the beginning of the dialogue to see that at this point we are dealing with a significantly changed character. The first part of the dialogue depicts Meno as he is described in Socrates' opening words: he thinks he is wise and gives confident and grand answers to what is asked, he is concerned with reputation and others' opinions, he relies on authority figures for knowledge and learning, he is contentious and disputatious in argument, and he denies the possibility of inquiry. In contrast, the interlude with Meno's slave demonstrates the possibility for inquiry and defends it in terms strongly opposed to Meno's early character: in inquiry one must admit one's ignorance, one must examine oneself and one's own beliefs in order to recall what one knew, one cannot rely on authorities, and one

22. Guthrie (1956, 11).
23. Teloh (1986, vii, 1–23); Eckstein (1968, 24)

must participate honestly in question and answer. The confrontation between these two starkly opposed images of discourse has an effect on Meno. By being shown his own ridiculousness, he is compelled to recognize the benefits of admitting one's ignorance, the perniciousness of the debater's dilemma he has proposed, and the benefits of real inquiry. The result is a changed character in the third part of the dialogue—a character who asks questions, a character who is tenuous when he does not know the answers to questions, a character who asks questions that demand deeper explanation and thereby further the present inquiry, a character who actually experiences wonder!

4. Character Transformation and Plato's Project

These changes in Meno's literary character have immediate bearing on the meaning and substance of this dialogue. This dialogue's central concerns are virtue, learning, teaching, and the dialectic method. The dialogue dramatizes a solution to the riddle—that virtue is knowledge, but it cannot be taught— by displaying the power to transform one's character through dialectic engagement, a process which is not teaching but results in a kind of knowledge. Dramatically speaking, the scene with the slave (a drama within the drama) refutes Meno's challenge to the possibility of learning and reaffirms the fundamental importance of dialectic by reproducing its movement in its structure: a movement toward recognizing one's ignorance followed by an upward ascent toward knowledge. All of this takes place within a dialogue that begins as an investigation of virtue and character. Meno's character change in the drama is a depiction of the kind of transformation that could come about from dialectic engagement, and thus Meno's character change is a dramatic manifestation of the philosophical questions asked in the dialogue. Virtue is not teachable, if teaching is construed as telling; virtue can be brought about by dialectic engagement, which constitutes a special kind of (self-)knowledge.

One of Plato's concerns as a philosopher, as well as one of his strengths as a writer, is his nuanced and vivid character development. Recall the ambiguity of "character," which denotes both a literary persona as well as a kind of moral personality. Consistent with that ambiguity, Plato's dialogues can be said to work on character in two ways: the content of Plato's dialogues works on moral character development in the reader or audience, and they attempt to accomplish this through a medium that works on character development as a literary device. Readers become dialectically engaged by the character portrayal, and there is hope that they may see the value in the life devoted to inquiry and turn toward it.

Plato's detailed and vivid portraiture draws the reader into relationship with the interlocutors, and the subject matter being discussed by the interlocutors aids in focusing the reader's attention to particular aspects of the characters being portrayed. In the case of Meno, the reader pays particular attention to his virtue or his lack of virtue. In addition, the dialogue turns the reader's attention to Meno's conceptions of learning and teaching and how these might conduce to or inhibit the acquisition of virtue. Then the interplay between Socrates and the interlocutors contributes to the character portrait, making some characters appear to be lacking in fundamental ways, to be pathetic or ridiculous, other characters to be ominous or threatening, and some even to be laudable. From this position, the reader then forms judgments of the characters she sees. But the dialogues also complicate the reader's judgment of the characters before her, and here is where character portraiture acts as a medium for turning the reader toward the philosophical life.

Just at the point where Meno is meant to judge himself and his actions in light of the slave demonstration (which mirrors his own actions in important ways and reflects something different altogether in other ways), just at the point where Meno needs to see himself from Socrates' critical perspective, so the reader must do the same—not only see Meno in this light, but see herself, too. This dialogue asks who Meno is, both explicitly and implicitly,[24] and the dialogues more generally pose the implicit question, "Who am I?" to the interlocutors;[25] The effect of character portrayal in Plato's dialogues is to force that very question upon the reader as well. Who am I? At a crucial point in the dialogue, Meno serves to admonish the reader in a manner parallel to his slave's serving to admonish him, and the reader is compelled to judge her own character by the standards she uses to judge the interlocutors.

We see explicit manifestations of Plato's concern for moral character and moral character development in the *Republic* and *Phaedrus*,[26] and implicit concern in most other dialogues. The *Republic* concludes with a discussion of the types of souls that correspond to the types of polis, and the dialogue makes clear that our characters and the character of those with whom we

---

24. Cf. note 4 above.
25. See Chapter 1, pages 29–30.
26. *Republic*, 544d–592b and 617e–619b; *Phaedrus*, 271a–c. Cf. McDonald (1931, 368ff.)

choose to associate are of the utmost importance; our souls are at peril otherwise. The *Phaedrus* introduces the notion that speech must be suited to the
soul of him who hears it if it is to improve his soul. The best speech maker,
that is, the one who knows the soul of his interlocutor, must be a careful
student of character. Certainly the dialogues show that one's mode of discourse and one's beliefs are emblematic of one's character. Because moral
character is an integral concern for Plato philosophically, his medium for
expressing this philosophical concern must focus on character portraiture
and development. Plato's technique of sometimes using the name of an interlocutor to signal that interlocutor's character-type serves, too, as an impetus
for the reader or audience to begin pondering that nature of that character
and the implications of that character's beliefs, thoughts, and actions for the
good human life. Plato's literary character portraiture links him strongly to
other Greek poets who share this art.[27] This art was practiced and refined
not only by the Attic tragic and comic poets, but by Epicharmus, Sophron,
and Theophrastus. Even Aristotle's *Nicomachean Ethics* is full of character
portraits.[28]

Socrates' closing remarks in the dialogue are telling with regard to
Meno's character change and the meaning of the dialogue. Socrates says,
"But now it is time for me to go somewhere. And you [Meno], persuade this
foreigner, Anytus, of what you have been persuaded[29] in order that he be
more even tempered. If you persuade him, you will bring a benefit to the
people of Athens" (100b). Note that Socrates does not talk about teaching
or learning—that is, he does not urge Meno to teach Anytus nor does he
refer to what Meno has learned—the matter with which the two have been
preoccupied up until now. Meno has denied that learning is possible, and
Socrates has denied that teaching is possible. Of what, exactly, has Meno
been persuaded? If we deem this dialogue aporetic, then he has not been persuaded of concrete or explicit answers to the questions, "What is virtue?"
and "Is virtue teachable?" What Meno has been persuaded of is the way of
dialectic, and it is this persuasion that is responsible for his character change.
If only the character of Anytus, one of the men directly responsible for
Socrates indictment, conviction, and execution, could be similarly turned
around, there would be a great benefit to the people of Athens.

27. See Chapter 3, pages 72–73.
28. Although they are not dramatic or dialogic. See McDonald's discussion of this point
(1931, 365ff.).
29. σὺ δὲ ταῦτα ἅπερ αὐτὸς πέπεισαι πεῖθε καὶ τὸν ξένον τόνδε. . . (100b).

In this dialogue, however, the character of Anytus is marked by having strong opinions about things of which he has no experience or understanding. Though he appears only briefly in the dialogue, Anytus makes his impact when he vilifies sophists and sophistry without knowing anything about them (92b–d). Recall that this is the very practice Socrates avoids in the earliest lines of the dialogue; he refuses to discuss the qualities of virtue without first knowing what virtue is (71b). When Anytus engages in that practice, Socrates mocks him and chides him for doing so. It is crucial at this juncture in the dialogue to remember that the charges brought against Socrates by Anytus and his compatriots were similar to charges brought against sophists, and so one infers that Anytus's indictment of Socrates stems from malign ignorance. If Meno were able to persuade Anytus of the value of dialectic and the philosophical life, the benefit would therefore certainly be profound, and the benefit that comes first to the minds of Plato's audiences is Socrates' salvation.

This drama, however, ends not in resolution but in quandary. More than the questions of virtue and its means of acquisition are left dangling in front of us: Meno himself is suspended somewhere between Socrates and Anytus.[30] As Socrates leaves the scene, Meno remains with Anytus to try to persuade him of what he himself has been persuaded. The audience is then left in a state of tension or agitation, wondering which of the two possibilities Meno (the literary character) will chose: the life of philosophical inquiry, on the one hand, or the unexamined life of treachery and political opportunism on the other. This choice will determine Meno's character—both his literary character and his moral character. Aristotle, too, understood the twofold nature of character. In his great ethical work he insists that moral character ultimately resides in choice,[31] and he knew, as the epigram for this chapter indicates, that a literary character is also understood through its choices. Treating Meno as simply a literary character, the dialogue named for him never reveals explicitly which choice he makes.

But if I am to address the effect of this dialogue on an audience, I must say something about the historical figure, Meno, for certainly he would be heavily on the minds of Plato's original audience.[32] Plato's original audience, knowing the life and fate of the historical Meno,[33] might experience this

30. Gorgias also represents another choice for Meno to follow.
31. *Nicomachean Ethics*, II.vi.15.
32. Several of the ideas in this paragraph were suggested to me by Louis Mackey.
33. Perhaps the best description of Meno's treacherous deeds and his gruesome end can be found in Xenophon's *Anabasis*, II.vi.21–30.

dialogue as an enactment of the possibilities that await those who escape the seduction of the vicious life and who allow themselves instead to be seduced by the life of philosophy. The end of the dialogue is dark indeed when viewed from this perspective, for the possibility of (the historical) Meno choosing the examined life must forever remain an unrealized one. Moreover, the powerful consequences of Anytus's not having been persuaded to choose the philosophical life would be profoundly felt by Plato's audiences, especially those who knew and loved Socrates.

I do not want to argue that this change in Meno's character will necessarily extend beyond the action depicted in the dialogue. In fact, if compelled to conjecture beyond the scope of this dialogue, I think that Meno would probably revert to his old ways. Nor am I arguing that we can conclude anything about the historical Meno in light of my argument about this dialogue; I am speaking after all about a fictive creation of Plato's. My entire project focuses on that fictive creation. The speculation I engage in about the future of the literary character, Meno, is akin to any speculation we might make about other literary characters and what they might do under hypothetical circumstances based on our knowledge of their character. That this character, Meno, might revert to his old ways does not change what has taken place within the scope of this dialogue. We need only be reminded of Alcibiades' moving speech in the *Symposium* (215e–216c) in order to understand Meno in this context. Alcibiades describes a reaction common among those who came in contact with Socrates: while in Socrates' presence, he is ashamed and realizes that he must act differently and better, but as soon as he leaves Socrates' company, he reverts to his old ways. Many might succeed momentarily in doing what Socrates urges them to do by his example and his dialectic, but in the end, the Socratic life is difficult to sustain. Even Socrates himself describes the fate of those young men who take leave of his midwifery services sooner than they ought to do so and then miscarry.[34]

Real virtue, one might contend, is stable or enduring and perhaps the result of lifelong habituation (Socratically speaking, I would accept the former, but not necessarily the latter), and so what goes on here in this brief dialogue has no implications for the acquisition of real virtue; Meno is only temporarily taking on seemingly virtuous behavior. But the dialogue as a drama stands as a response to such an objection, having rather important implications for virtue, our attempts to gain it, and our limitations in gaining it. Regardless of whether the character, Meno, has changed in stable and

34. *Theaetetus* 150e–151b.

enduring ways, the dialogue has the double function of *poesis* or making. Meno's literary character is a creation of Plato's making; this poetic device can, in turn, shape or make the moral character of the reader or audience. When Plato's work is successful, the reader or audience of the dialogue sees the virtue of dialectic engagement, and in any case wants not to identify with the Meno of the early part of the dialogue nor with any hypothetical Meno beyond the scope of the dialogue who might revert to ignorant sophistry or worse.

This dialogue introduces itself to us asking a question about character. It demands in its quiet way that we ask questions about character in reading the dialogue—that we look at how literary character is used in the drama and that we examine our own moral characters. We often discuss literary works in such contexts, believing them to be informative for our own lives in some way because we believe them to be representations of human moral lives. As such, the dialogue, through its representation of the change in Meno's character, therefore represents that same transformation as it can and ought to take place within ourselves.

5. Beyond Character Development

Just as moral and epistemic concerns are intertwined in Meno's character development, so other literary devices work similarly on self-realization and transformation. Irony is another such device that operates on the cognition of the interlocutor and the reader with far-reaching moral consequences. As with character development, irony in the dialogues is masterfully created and controlled to function doubly: in and among the interlocutors and between the text and audience. In the next chapter, I take up the issue of Socratic irony, working toward a definition that captures its full complexity. I examine the interlocutors' epistemic relationship to Socrates' irony within the dramatic context, asking why and to what extent interlocutors understand when Socrates is being ironic. The reader's epistemic relationship to the irony is quite different, however, so I then compare the interlocutors' relationship with Socratic irony to the relationship that Plato creates between the reader and irony. The comparison between the interlocutors' and the reader's relationship to irony illuminates the philosophical effect that the dialogues can have. Like Plato's double development of literary and moral characters, his irony functions doubly to turn souls toward philosophy.

5

Irony

I am not yet able, as the Delphic inscription has it,
to know myself; so it seems to be ridiculous, when I
do not yet know that, to investigate irrelevant
things. And so . . . I investigate not these things, but
myself, to know whether I am a monster more
complicated and more furious than Typhon or a
gentler and simpler creature, to whom a divine and
quiet lot is given by nature.

Phaedrus, 230a

I wish to return to a scene in the *Meno* that I have already considered, albeit
in another context.[1] Recall that at a point not long after Anytus appears in
that dialogue, we learn two things: [1] that the sons of virtuous men are
nevertheless vicious, despite their fathers' (failed) attempts to pass their
virtue on to their sons (91a–95a), and [2] that public affairs in Athens
proceed through the ignorance of the population and its elected leaders
(96d–99d). Before these conclusions are reached, however, Socrates introduces Anytus by saying that he is someone worth sharing their (Socrates'

Portions of this chapter were published as "Against Vlastos on Complex Irony," *Classical Quarterly* 46, no. 1 (May 1996).
1. In the earlier context, I explored the reader's forward and backward movement within the text. See Chapter 2, page 51.

and Meno's) conversation with because he is the son of a good father who has done his best to assure Anytus's education and because the Athenians seem to have high regard for him since they have elected him to high office (89e–90b). This seems to be a clear case of Socratic irony but, surprisingly, this ironic moment in *Meno*, would not be included in some accounts and definitions of irony.

Gregory Vlastos's work on "complex irony" has come to be the definitive word on Socratic irony for many Plato scholars in recent years,[2] and yet it fails to capture many types of irony, including that in the example above. Vlastos's notion of "complex irony" fails to recognize the dramatic context in which Socratic irony is situated. I want to examine the shortcomings of Vlastos's treatment of complex irony as a jumping off point for formulating a richer and more inclusive conception of irony in the dialogues, one that takes into account the dramatic context of the irony and which thereby provides insight into the philosophical function of irony in Plato's dialogues. Drew Hyland claims, and I agree, that most scholarly accounts of irony in the dialogues share a common defect "of stopping short of an explanation that attributes genuine philosophic intentions and significance to Plato's use of irony."[3] I hope to delineate that philosophic significance, specifically how irony functions to bring about greater self-knowledge in interlocutors and readers, and ultimately to turn them toward the philosophical life.

1. The Definition of Socratic Irony

Vlastos begins his work with a conception of simple irony against which he will position his own view of Socratic irony:

> "Irony," says Quintilian, is that figure of speech or trope "in which something contrary to what is said is to be understood" (*contrarium ei quod dicitur intelligendum est*). His formula has stood the test of time. It passes intact in Dr. Johnson's dictionary ("mode of speech in which the meaning is contrary to the words" [1755]) and survives

2. First published as, "Socratic Irony," *Classical Quarterly* 37, i (1987): 79–96; later published as chap. 1 in Vlastos (1991). All references contained here are to Professor Vlastos's book.
3. Hyland (1995, 92). Although my account of irony in the Platonic dialogues differs from Hyland's account, I believe that, like Hyland's account, it overcomes this defect.

virtually intact in ours: "Irony is the use of words to express something other than, and especially the opposite of, [their] literal meaning." (*Webster's*)[4]

Vlastos refers to these conceptions of irony as "simple" and then moves to redefine Socratic irony as "complex" irony. He says, "In 'simple' irony what is said is simply not what is meant. In 'complex' irony what is said both is and isn't what is meant."[5] Vlastos's definition does capture many cases of Socratic irony, and it improves upon the oversimplified definitions he begins with, but even his definition is too simple to tell the entire story.

One of the main weaknesses of Vlastos's definition is that it views irony as limited to language proper, that is, "things said," as opposed to, for example, how something is said or by whom or in what context. This truncated view of Socratic irony neglects the entire picture that we get in the dialogues. Most of the time, what we perceive as ironic, on Socrates' part, is so in the context of complex drama: we know the characters involved, we know what actions and discussions have preceded or will follow the remark or incident, we know the topic at hand, we know historical and social background, and so on. I would like to redefine a kind of irony that encompasses all of these things and so incorporates elements of what I will come to describe as dramatic irony.

Following Vlastos's example, I too will begin by looking at a dictionary definition of irony just as a starting point in our examination of Socratic irony.

1: a pretense of ignorance and of willingness to learn from another assumed in order to make the other's false conceptions conspicuous by adroit questioning—called also Socratic irony. 2 a: the use of words to express something other than and esp. the opposite of the literal meaning. b: a usu. humorous or sardonic literary style or form characterized by irony. c: an ironic expression or utterance. 3 a (1): incongruity between the actual result of a sequence of events and the normal or expected result (2): an event or result marked by such incongruity. b: incongruity between a situation developed in a drama and the accompanying words or actions that is understood by the audience but not by the characters in the play—called also

4. Vlastos (1991, 21).
5. Ibid., 31.

dramatic irony, tragic irony. 4: an attitude of detached awareness of incongruity.[6]

None of these definitions by itself captures the full range of Socratic irony for various reasons, but the ideas introduced in definition 3, oddly omitted from Vlastos's account of the Webster entry, will prove enormously helpful in gaining a fuller understanding of Socratic irony. Since Vlastos's argument begins by soundly disqualifying definition 2a of Socratic irony, I shall begin there as well.[7] Saying one thing in order to express its opposite meaning (the concept of simple irony that Vlastos rejects), does describe, for example, when Socrates calls an obviously ignorant and obstinate interlocutor "wise." But this conception is too limited, and Vlastos's definition shows clearly how and why it is too limited a definition of Socratic irony. Socrates is sometimes most ironic when he makes assertions that we are meant to take as truthful at least on one semantic level.

Vlastos's rejection of simple irony helps to underscore at least one manner in which definition 1 is also not acceptable. The first definition evokes Socrates' name, but Socrates' claims of ignorance are not unambiguously pretended, and Vlastos and I would agree in rejecting this definition of Socratic irony for that reason. Vlastos preserves the ambiguity of Socrates' claims to ignorance; these claims are meant and not meant. He recognizes that to resolve the paradox of Socratic ignorance by saying that it is merely pretense is to oversimplify the case and does not do justice to Socratic ignorance. Best known are perhaps Socrates' claims to ignorance in the *Apology*, and in that context we get enough of an explanation from Socrates to understand the seriousness of his claims (21a–22e). He is only wise insofar as he recognizes his ignorance, so we must take his professed ignorance seriously. Certainly there are beliefs to which Socrates is committed, and he is most often far ahead of his interlocutors in their investigations. But the entire way of life described in the *Apology* and lived by the character in Plato's dialogues would be something quite different if there weren't a genuine aspect to the ignorance Socrates avows. All of the dialogues underscore the importance of

---

6. *Webster's New Collegiate Dictionary* (Springfield, Mass., 1980), 606. Vlastos gives a less detailed entry from the dictionary, one that highlights the simple definition he wishes to discredit—2(a)—but that excludes the relevant introduction of dramatic context into the notion of irony as in 3(a) and 3(b). I shall have more to say about the significance of that omission in what follows.

7. Definitions falling under 2(b) and 2(c) depend upon how we end up defining "irony" since they include "irony" in the definition, so I omit discussion of them.

Socrates' professed ignorance as the starting point for the life of inquiry. Socratic ignorance is an epistemic, moral, and pedagogical stance that must be taken seriously. This first dictionary definition of irony, even though it invokes the name of Socrates, is therefore unsatisfactory because Socrates' ignorance, while ironic, is not simply pretended.

While Vlastos and I would agree in rejecting this first definition of irony on account of its lack of ambiguity, I would reject it for yet another reason for which Vlastos would not. I reject a conception of Socratic irony that accepts knowledge disavowal as constitutive of that irony, a conception that Socratic irony is paradigmatically about knowledge (and teaching) disavowals. Vlastos implicitly accepts such a conception of Socratic irony insofar as he has it in mind to explain what he takes to be the core of Socratic philosophy, namely, Socrates' disavowal of knowledge and of teaching.[8] The examples that Vlastos gives are all consistent with this conception of irony. Muecke also implies such a conception of Socratic irony when, in referring to several types of irony, he enumerates among them "the self-disparaging irony of a Socrates."[9] The wording here implies that Socratic irony, among many types of irony, is essentially self-disparaging, and while Socrates does engage in self-disparaging behavior often, he does so most famously in his disavowals of knowledge. The first of the dictionary definitions shows how commonly accepted this conception of Socratic irony as knowledge disavowal is, but Socratic irony is much more widespread in the dialogues than occurrences of knowledge disavowals so, for me, the first definition fails as a definition of Socratic irony on account of its narrow focus as well. While I would certainly include knowledge disavowals and other self-disparaging remarks among Socratic ironies, Socratic irony comprises much more than these instances. While Vlastos's complex irony provides a better framework for understanding Socrates' knowledge disavowals as meant on one level and not meant on another, it needlessly narrows our focus on what constitutes Socratic irony. I shall widen that focus through examples that follow.

The shortcomings of Vlastos's conception of complex irony become evident when we consider the third dictionary definition, 3a. The third

---

8. Vlastos (1991, 3) claims that his focus will be upon "Socrates' central paradox, his profession of ignorance." Vlastos also rejects Xenophon as an authentic historical source for the philosophical doctrine of the historical Socrates because Xenophon's work does not contain the kind of complex ironies embodied in disavowals of knowledge and teaching (31–32).

9. Muecke (1969, 44). See Gooch (1987, esp. 193), who also works from this conception of Socratic irony.

definition gets at an important element in Socratic irony—the dramatic element.[10] Given that his focus was to be Plato's dialogues, it is strange that Vlastos, while citing *Webster's Dictionary* at the beginning of his own work on irony, neglects to cite any entry that specifically mentions dramatic irony. Yet the dramatic context of Socratic irony would seem to be significant, if not essential, in order to get a full understanding of Socratic irony. I want to sketch a working definition:[11] Socratic irony is an incongruity between phenomena within the dramatic context of the dialogue. The incongruity can be between things said, between actions taken, between words and actions, between what is said and how it is said or to whom or on what occasion, between what one says and what one looks like, between one's actions and the meaning of one's name, and so on. I choose incongruity because it allows the latitude necessary for understanding irony in a more complex and subtle manner than either (a) saying one thing but meaning its opposite or (b) both meaning and not meaning what is said. Charles Griswold defines irony similarly. In irony,

> a doubling of meaning occurs, which is made visible by a tension, incongruity, or contradiction between aspects of a discourse, between the context and the discourse (e.g., between the deeds and words), or between different views expressed by the same person. Irony is a way of speaking (or writing) which is meant to point to what is not spoken (or written), to what is silent and is kept in reserve, as it were, by its originator.[12]

10. I mean here dramatic in its broadest sense: occurring within the context of drama and understood in that context. Often dramatic irony is synonymous with tragic irony, and I do not necessarily mean to limit myself to that understanding of dramatic irony. For fuller discussions of the history of such forms of irony and the word εἰρωνεία, see Muecke (1969, 47ff.) and Vlastos (1991). Muecke holds the representative view of εἰρωνεία as "deception," which Vlastos seeks to modify in his work.

11. I shall make the same kinds of disclaimers that many make who write about irony: to attempt an exhaustive definition is nearly an impossible task. For example, Muecke (1969, 3) opens his book with the words: "Getting to grips with irony seems to have something in common with gathering the mist; there is plenty to take hold of if only one could." Booth (1974, 1) admits that "the problem of definition is by no means a simple one," and notes several of the best attempts. Booth uses as an epigram to his first chapter Muecke's quip: "Since . . . Erich Heller, in his *Ironic German*, has already quite adequately not defined irony, there would be little point in not defining it all over again."

12. Griswold (1987, 78–79). Parenthetical qualifications are Griswold's. See also Griswold (1986, 13–16). Cf. Muecke (1969, 5): "Irony is the art of saying something without really saying it."

Actions, behavior, modes of expression, thoughts, and words can all be incongruous. But only "things said" are encompassed by the descriptions of simple and complex irony. Socratic irony must comprise sayings and *doings*, since it is embedded within drama. Vlastos's redefinition of Socratic irony as "complex" therefore still turns a blind eye to that irony's dramatic context.

I should like to examine a few representative examples for which Vlastos's definition of complex irony is insufficient, examples that in fact undermine his definition of complex irony, but that fit my broader definition because they include elements of incongruity understood within a dramatic context. These examples will help to illustrate the definition and therefore better characterize Socratic irony. Let us return to the example from the *Meno* that opens this chapter. The dramatic context is indispensable here if we are to understand this scene as ironic. This seemingly complimentary introduction of Anytus becomes ironic only in light of the later discussions of whether good men can pass their virtue on to their own sons and what the difference is between knowledge and true opinion, especially with regard to Athenian public affairs. Only with these discussions as background (or foreground) can we see the irony of praising Anytus's father and saying that Anytus is popular as a statesman. There is an incongruity in such praise which is revealed only by the dramatic context.

Vlastos's definition would require him to make the case that Socrates means and does not mean that Anthemion is a good man or that Socrates both means and does not mean that Anytus is a popular statesman. It seems wrong headed to claim that Socrates would not mean that Anthemion was a good man. It is essential for the point Socrates later makes—and for the irony to be expressed—that Anthemion be a good man, unequivocally. The passage is ironic because of the dramatic incongruity between praising someone's father and then pursuing a line of argument in the abstract, which establishes that even the best fathers have failed to make their sons virtuous men. The source of the irony lies in the incongruity between Socrates' seemingly deferential introduction of Anytus and the conclusion of their later discussion.

The same is true of the claim that Anytus is popular among Athenian citizens. It undermines Socrates' irony to say that on some level he does not mean this. Anytus simply is popularly elected by Athenians. In a manner similar to Socrates' claim that Anthemion is a good man, the claim that Anytus is popular must be understood unambiguously. The passage is ironic because of the dramatic incongruity between praising someone's popularity and then pursuing a line of argument that those to whom one owes one's popularity are ignorant. Furthermore, the ideas are pursued with a man who is known to Plato's audiences to be at least partially responsible for Socrates' execution at the hands of the Athenian state. In what manner could we say that Socrates does *and does not* mean that Anthemion is a good man or does *and does not* mean that Anytus is popular? In order for these passages to be ironic these thoughts must be unequivocally expressed by Socrates, so Vlastos's definition proves unsatisfactory.[13]

Let us take another example from the *Meno* that helps us to link irony to issues of identity and shame discussed earlier in the more general context of Socratic dialectic. The dialogue initially portrays a self-confident Meno who makes several attempts to define virtue. We know now that Socrates puts Meno to shame, and at the same time tries to induce him to engage in dialectic by using Meno's own words to great effect. Socrates claims that it is a good thing that the slave has realized his ignorance, since if he hadn't, he may have given many speeches before large audiences, lecturing that if we double the length of the side of a square, we thereby double its area (84b–c). What makes this claim ironic is its dramatic context, namely, what Meno has said in an earlier scene in this dialogue and what we know about Meno's character. Using nearly identical language, Meno made a claim earlier in the dialogue that he had given many fine speeches before many people about virtue (80b).[14]

The irony of this situation stems from the subtle way in which Socrates brings Meno's very own words back to him in a context that clearly makes Meno feel ashamed. The words Meno originally introduced as a boast are turned into an insult—an incongruity. There is also the incongruity of drawing a parallel between, or showing similarities between, an uneducated slave and the proud, arrogant Meno. When Vlastos says that on some level Socrates means an ironic statement, he implies that there is a sense in which the statement is true, we just have to figure out what that sense is. This claim about Meno's slave is ironic but, just as in the previous case, not according to Vlastos's definition. It is certainly not sufficient nor even accurate to describe this comment as ironic because Socrates both does and does not mean that the slave is fortunate to have been saved from giving such speeches. It is clear to us, and to Meno, that an uneducated Athenian slave would never have given such speeches, nor would he ever have had such an opportunity. The slave's social, personal, and historical circumstances

---

13. Cf. Tejera (1984, 32–36).
14. See Chapter 1, note 9, for a comparison of the Greek text in the two passages.

prevent this possibility. In what way, then, is it sufficient to explain the irony by saying that Socrates both means and does not mean that the slave would give many fine speeches? Clearly, in no way. Whereas Vlastos's definition fails to capture the earlier example because there is no sense in which Socrates could *not* mean what he said, it fails to capture this example of irony because there is no sense in which Socrates *could* mean what he said.[15]

Let us turn now to an example of irony from the *Protagoras*, an example that Vlastos's definition again fails to capture, but for yet another reason: this example represents an incongruity not between things said, but between what is said and how and in what context it is said. Sophistry and dialectic are juxtaposed throughout this dialogue; Protagoras practices, instructs, and even baits with the former, and Socrates continually attempts to cajole Protagoras into entering into dialectical question and answer, even giving him his choice of which role—questioner or answerer—he would like to take on. Protagoras eventually seems to accede to Socrates' wishes, taking on the role of questioner (338e). But what seems to begin as question and answer between Socrates and Protagoras turns out to be something quite different. In short order Socrates indulges Protagoras's challenge to engage in poetry analysis. After trying unsuccessfully for so long to get Protagoras to engage in dialectic, and then seeming to have succeeded, Socrates gives a grandiose demonstration of the sophists' art himself. For example, Socrates uses Prodicus's art—making pedantic distinctions with words—showing ironically that making distinction upon distinction in (mock) clarification can ultimately *obscure* meaning (340a ff.). Socrates beats Protagoras at his own game, and after all his interpretive gymnastics, he claims that none of what he has said is disputable anyway (347e). All along, and in strong language after his analysis (347b–348a), Socrates is pushing to get away from such eristic and to return to dialectic conversation, question and answer.

---

15. Socrates' claim here, ostensibly about the slave, is not really about him at all. Just as with so much of this dialogue, this statement is really about Meno—his identity, who he is. Socrates' claim glances off its seeming referent, the slave, and reflects back to its true referent, Meno. In that case, the statement is both ironic and didactic. It could almost be understood as a counterfactual: Meno, if you had recognized your ignorance about virtue, you could have been spared the shame of speaking on a topic about which you are ignorant. Cf. Miller (1986, 4–5) on what he calls mimetic irony: "[Socrates] holds back from giving explicit, authoritative criticism and instead puts the interlocutor on stage before himself." See also Griswold (1986, 222): "Plato's dialogues seem designed to function as mirrors of a peculiar sort, for they allow the reader who is unsuited to philosophy to see himself in the text (that is, to 'find' in the text only what he expects or wants to find), and the reader who is suited to philosophy to glimpse something that he has not yet achieved and that he desires (for example, self-knowledge)."

These passages are fraught with incongruity. Socrates' analysis of Simonides' poem is, therefore, heavily laden with irony, but Vlastos's definition will again fail to explain fully why. What makes this passage ironic is its dramatic context and *how* Socrates chooses to express himself. To begin with, Protagoras's seeming acquiescence to dialectic engagement gives way to the dialogue's longest sophistic speech, and it is given by, of all people, Socrates. Socrates insisted earlier that the conversation proceed dialectically and that they avoid long speeches; he even went so far as to claim that he did not have the skill to offer a long speech, yet he goes on at quite some length here, now employing the sophistic style himself. Moreover, Socrates uses the method Protagoras championed and seems to win the challenge of unraveling the poem only to demonstrate that both the method and the goal are useless. He ends his analysis by telling the gathering of sophists that there is no value in poetry analysis, and that it is an activity beneath any self-respecting men (καλοὶ κἀγαθοί, 347d). This long passage is ironic because of the manner in which Socrates chooses to speak, because of the incongruity between his consistent position against sophistic throughout the dialogue and his utter command of its use in this passage. We are no longer talking exclusively about content—about "things said"—but rather the mode of expression. We cannot say properly here that Socrates means and does not mean his sophistic mode of expression; it does not make sense.[16] What makes the passage ironic is not just what Socrates says but how he chooses to express it and in what dramatic context that expression occurs.

In our examination of the temporal and perspectival aspects of the act of reading we saw that a reader moves back and forth within the text in order to construct meaning in it. The reader recalls earlier passages, connects them to later ones, returns to the earlier passages with new understanding, sees passages from new and different perspectives, and so on. The reader contextualizes and recontextualizes during the act of reading. The examples I used to illustrate these reading phenomena serve doubly to illustrate the function of irony in Plato's dialogues, and they demonstrate, further, that the dramatic context of irony is essential to its meaning qua irony.

---

16. Although it would be plausible to argue that the content of what Socrates says about the poem on being and becoming is both meant and not meant, and therefore Vlastos's definition of complex irony would include this passage. Cf. Gordon (1991). That is not, however, the particular irony I wish to highlight here.

2. The Function of Socratic Irony

Definition 3b above speaks of dramatic irony as being something of which the audience is aware, but of which the players are not. I want to modify this understanding of irony when it is Socratic irony and, by that modification, illustrate Socratic irony's philosophical function. We must begin with Vlastos again. There is a historical component to his thesis regarding complex irony. Not only does Vlastos wish to redefine Socratic irony as complex irony, he also wants to argue that the historical Socrates is responsible for a shift in the meaning of εἰρωνεία. Before Socrates it means little more than "deception" and has largely a negative connotation. In the person of Socrates, Vlastos argues, εἰρωνεία becomes, more positively, something closer to our present understanding of "irony."[17] Paula Gottlieb, in her brief response to Vlastos, zeroes in on this issue. Contrary to Vlastos's historical thesis, she suggests that the meaning of εἰρωνεία did not, in fact, shift from "deception" to "irony" in the person of the historical Socrates, but rather that the phenomenon that Vlastos observes in Plato's dialogues can be explained in another manner.

While stressing the dramatic nature of the dialogues as I do, Gottlieb argues that there are outsiders and insiders involved as "audiences" to the dialogues. The insiders enjoy "the wit and humour of Socrates' remarks" but "for the outsider, however, irony remains as tricky and deceptive as it ever was." She concludes, "Irony has not changed. It is just that one's view of irony depends on whether or not one is its butt. In short, Socratic irony, like irony in general, is even more complex than Professor Vlastos allows." So, what is deception for the outsider is irony for the insider.[18]

For the most part I agree with Gottlieb's succinct criticism of Vlastos's position. But this type of definition (similar to 3b above), which relies on a distinction between insiders and outsiders, or players and audience, can be revised along Socratic lines. While dramatic irony is often at someone's expense, it need not exclude those within the dramatic setting—the players—from being or becoming insiders. There are some cases in which irony functions to change the cognition of its object—or "butt," as Gottlieb calls it—from outsider to insider, from not getting the irony to getting it. The

17. Vlastos (1991, 27–28).
18. Gottlieb (1992). Cf. Klein (1989, 5): "For a statement or a behavior to *be* ironical there must be *someone* capable of *understanding* that it is ironical" (Klein's emphasis). Also see Schleiermacher (1836, 18), who defines the esoteric and the exoteric aspects of the dialogues as depending upon insiders and outsiders, respectively, among Plato's hearers.

previous example of Meno and his "many fine speeches" illustrates that clearly. In that case, one function of Socratic irony is to get the interlocutor to come to some realization about himself. He is supposed to become aware of the irony if Socratic questioning and engagement are to do their work. The Socratic aim is thus to turn one from being outsider or butt to being an insider. While it is true that many a Socratic interlocutor is not aware of irony aimed at himself, the Socratic goal is ultimately for that interlocutor to become so aware. Socrates would love for his interlocutors to "get it." If and when they do, they are on their way toward a better self-conception (i.e., a more accurate sense of their identities) and on the path, one hopes, toward seeking wisdom.

We can take this reasoning one step further, beyond the action within the dialogue. The function of irony need not exclude the reader or audience of the drama. Another function of Socratic irony is to change the cognition of the reader. Through Socratic irony, Plato engages the reader in a manner that mimics Socratic irony's effects on the interlocutor, and he thus aims at turning them toward the life of philosophy or at least some deeper self-knowledge. Just as Socrates wanted Meno to question his identity, self-image, and beliefs by recognizing Socratic irony, so Plato constructs ironies that can act as vehicles for self-knowledge for the reader.[19] Irony, as Plato implements it, puts the reader in a dialectic relationship with the text. It is this dialectic relationship that eventually allows us to appreciate the irony and to learn more from the text. We would expect that Socratic irony is lost on many of the interlocutors since Socrates' quest is to find reputedly wise men who are actually ignorant and who are unaware of that ignorance.[20] The attentive reader, on the contrary, is really in something of a privileged position with respect to Socratic irony. Plato, as writer, creates the situation that makes it possible for the reader to be in that position. The reader can learn much about the characters—things they do not even know about themselves—from Socratic irony. But ultimately, Socratic irony can help the reader to come to know things about herself.

---

19. There are "two" ironists, Socrates the character and Plato the writer. On this issue, see Griswold (1987, 72, 78 et passim), who argues that Socratic and Platonic irony differ in their means: Socratic irony is delivered "orally" within the dramatic context of the dialogue; Platonic irony is expressed through "written" means outside the lived conversation depicted in the dialogues. Of course, Plato is certainly also the one who contrives Socratic irony. The conclusions I reach in this chapter are true for both Socratic and Platonic irony, as Griswold defines those.

20. *Apology*, 21b–22e.

The reader feels that she understands something the interlocutor does not and so has insider status vis-à-vis Socratic irony. So "getting it," on the part of the reader requires, at least at first, a distancing from, and a sense of superiority to, the interlocutor.[21] It requires that the reader occupy a position different from the interlocutor, a position from which the reader sees and understands what the interlocutor does not. But, if the reader maintains that distance from the interlocutor and falsely believes that she is essentially different in character from the interlocutor, and better than the interlocutor, then the joke is truly on her! Ironically, the reader must both distance herself from, and then identify with, the interlocutor in order *really* to get it, in order to see that she too can benefit from the Socratic lesson.[22] The reader must come to realize—and this might involve shame—that her identity is perhaps not as different as she would like to believe from the identities of the interlocutors, that she too might harbor a false (and smug?) self-image as knowledgeable. The move from outsider to insider—from not getting it to getting it—necessitates, for both the reader and the interlocutor, reassessing one's self-image. And if one recognizes oneself as the butt of such irony, then one might also experience shame in seeing one's identity as such. The shame might be followed by the desire to change one's character, to become the sort of person who is *not* the butt of such irony. Consistent with the fundamental movement of dialectic, we thus see the forces of shame and identity acting in concert through the literary device of irony.

In my alternative conception of dramatic irony, I have tried to preserve what I take to be one of the strengths of Vlastos's definition of complex irony, and what makes it superior to simple irony, namely, its embrace of ambiguity. Even in Vlastos's account we are at least suspended between two meanings or two levels of meaning. Socratic irony is in this way inherently unstable; there is no "resting place" for meaning when one is dealing with an ironist. Irony remains ironic, resonating among various meanings. If we erase the ambiguity or incongruity in some attempt to understand the irony simply, we erase the irony. One of the weaknesses of the notion of simple irony is that it reduces the original ambiguity or complexity of meaning in the irony to a single "real" or "true" meaning. Conceiving of irony as simple

21. Cf. Gadamer (1997, 32), who claims that just as Socrates uses irony to get his interlocutors to rid themselves of the "illusion of superiority," so "Plato through his art of dialogical poetry, robbed his reader of his assumed superiority."

22. Cf. Iser's example from Fielding's *Joseph Andrews*, see Chapter 2, pages 48–49. As Iser points out in his example, the reader must negotiate whether to identify with certain characters and in the process she must confront and weigh the personal costs of doing so.

irony, therefore, lays out the text's meaning once and for all before the reader, just like the traditional, objective theory of textual meaning. But the richness of irony is lost on this account and, consequently, any philosophical activity is thwarted.[23]

In addition to its function in changing the reader's and interlocutors' cognition, the instability of meaning characteristic of the irony in the dialogues is emblematic of the limitations of human knowledge. There are some things we just should not feel settled and comfortable about knowing once and for all. To do so is to stop dialectic and philosophical enterprise. Plato's irony tells the reader about meaning and answers in human inquiry. At the same time irony "teaches" a method for dealing with the limited knowledge and capacity for knowledge that human beings have. Irony must remain as something to be puzzled about in the text, to be questioned, to be engaged by the active reader. The ambiguity of irony stimulates us to philosophical activity. Embracing irony in all its ambiguity makes the dialectic relationship between text and reader clearly apparent. Because of this instability created by the incongruity, the reader must begin to philosophize. The reader is thrown back upon herself, irony providing the occasion in the text for constructing meaning, and therefore functioning as Iser's blanks do in the text.[24] Just as the reader might experience aporia and either turn away from the text or gain sensitivity to questions and questioning, so the reader might turn away in frustration from the ironic text or it might induce in her a sensitivity to irony. If the reader can realize that she is ignorant of the text's meaning, only then might she attempt to leave this state of ignorance in a quest to understand the ironic text. Unfortunately, though, just as some interlocutors react to Socrates, many readers will read the dialogues with no sensitivity whatsoever that something is afoot. They go happily about reading the dialogues, never attuned to Socratic irony. These readers don't get it. Others still might sense the irony, even sense that they are its object, and are moved to obstinacy. These readers refuse to get it.

But the fortunate reader will sense that there is perhaps more to the dialogues than just what Socrates is saying, even if she does not as yet know what that might be. The reader must now, in the absence of authority, in the

---

23. Cf. Booth's discussion of "stable irony" (1974, 507). Again, there are cases of "simple irony" in the dialogues, such as when Socrates tells an obviously ignorant interlocutor that he is wise, but there are other ironies as well.

24. See Chapter 2, page 46.

absence of univocal meaning, and in a state of aporia, turn inward, toward questioning herself, toward inquiry. Under these conditions the reader tries to understand the text and Socrates' ironic claims. Neither Plato the author, nor Socrates the character, tells her how to understand the text. This leaves the reader in the position of one who is engaging in the question and answer inherent in dialectic. The reader must ask questions of the text along the lines of: What could Socrates have meant by that? What philosophical insights emerge from this mysterious text? In what ways am I like these interlocutors? Why is it desirable to live the philosophical life? Could the joke be on me? and What is the joke, after all? By examining the dramatic context—the characters, the topic, the action, and so on—the reader might come upon some understanding of the complex meaning and incongruity of Socratic irony. Finally, by engaging a Platonic dialogue in this manner she might be moved to some insight about herself and even be turned toward the life of philosophy.

Such an account, philosophical or otherwise, of why and how Socrates would use irony seems to be an element lacking in Vlastos's account (as well as the traditional account of simple irony that he rejects). Vlastos never wonders or explains *why* Socrates expresses himself ambiguously. After all, Socrates is not ironic merely to mock his interlocutors. His mission is, quite to the contrary, their improvement. Likewise, Plato does not compose the irony in the dialogues simply to entertain or amuse his readers at the expense of the interlocutors. Moreover, in perhaps another case of irony as incongruity, Vlastos never seems even to hint at an answer why Socrates is an ironist *and* a moral philosopher, despite his book's title. Socrates is indeed both of these things, and an account of irony that did justice to Socrates would attempt to explain the connection between these two identities and what makes them both fundamentally Socratic. The account of irony I offer here as dramatic incongruity that has the philosophical function of changing the cognition of its audience is just such an attempt. If at the core of Socratic irony there is something that makes it Socratic, and possibly distinct from other forms of irony, it is this aim: the chiefly Socratic aim of turning souls around to a new awareness of self and circumstances—a turn toward philosophy. And as the epigram for this chapter from *Phaedrus* implies, self-knowledge—or at least the investigation of oneself—should precede and serve as the foundation for all other investigation.

I have focused considerable attention on what Vlastos's conceptualization of irony does not capture. This limited understanding of irony is a problem because irony is key to Plato's purposes. By neglecting certain instances of irony, one misses its function within the drama.[25] If we strip the drama away from the dialogues, we erase what Plato has contrived, his art(ifice): authorial distance, lived human drama, and a particularized relationship to some audience or reader created by such literary devices as irony. Understanding Socratic irony in its dramatic context helps us to understand how irony functions with respect to the interlocutor and, more importantly, with respect to the reader. With the dramatic context as a framework, we can do more than see the dialogues as mere vehicles for Plato's "theory."[26] They now become vehicles for real philosophical engagement.

I see irony as an incongruity within a dramatic context, and I see the function of irony being not only to draw interlocutors to realizations about themselves, but also to draw readers to realizations about the interlocutors' identities and their own identities and moral characters. A dramatic concept of irony enriches our reading of the dialogues and directs us to realize the significance of audience and reader. Socratic irony, even complex irony, is diminished when it is touted as the "height of urbanity, elegance, and good taste."[27] If we ignore the dramatic context of the irony situated in Plato's dialogues we ignore an essential aspect of the *function* of irony. Socratic irony is among the most powerful tools at Socrates' disposal for turning the lives of his interlocutors toward philosophy. And so for Plato and his readers.

3. Literary Devices and Plato's Metaphysics

So far, I have conceived of Plato qua writer, and have taken into consideration his philosophical project in relationship to his audience or reader. I have

---

25. It is worth mentioning a phenomenon among Plato scholars, but a full discussion of it would take me too far from my subject. There are cases in which difficult passages in dialogues are labeled as "ironic" when a scholar is trying to get at "Plato's view" or "Socrates' view" and faces problems of inconsistency or incoherence in doctrine or argument. That is, the offending passage must be ironic because it is inconsistent with other views deemed to be "Platonic" or "Socratic." Often these labels seem *ad hoc* when no explanation is given for why the irony occurs at the specific place that it does or how it functions in the dialogue at that particular moment. Irony in the dialogues serves a purpose, and we should be looking at it to see its purpose rather than looking at it as a means to deal with, that is, efface, difficult passages in which incongruity or outright contradiction might be located. Cf. Tigerstedt's discussion (1977, 19ff.) of "athetizing"—cutting out or removing so-called spurious texts and passages from the corpus—for similar reasons.

26. Or in Vlastos's case, "Socratic theory."

27. Vlastos (1991, 28).

therefore indicated that Plato's project does its primary philosophical work in this arena; Plato's project aims at the turning of souls toward the life of philosophy and it accomplishes this through what we have come to consider "literary devices." But this is not at all the usual view of Plato. More commonly, scholars derive from Plato's dialogues a great metaphysical system, a moral theory, or a political plan. By viewing Plato in his capacity as writer, and by paying special attention to his use of dramatic and literary devices that contribute to the ambiguity of the texts and that mitigate Plato's own philosophical authority, I hope, at the very least, to obscure in a general fashion whether we can in fact derive such moral theories, political blueprints, or metaphysical systems from his works or whether we are even meant to do so.

Plato's metaphysics, or what have come to be considered "Platonic metaphysics" are subject to scrutiny in the next chapter. Plato's use of images—certainly a practice considered by most to be at least extra-philosophical if not literary—undermines what has become an orthodox view of "Plato's metaphysics." I argue that Plato's artful creation of literary images belies any metaphysics, commonly imputed to him, which valorizes the invisible over the visible or devalues the image in relation to some higher reality. I argue, to the contrary, that the dialogues as a whole testify to the awesome power of images, to the role of the imagination in philosophy, and to the need for visual learning in turning souls toward the philosophical life.

6

Image

And a wolf is very like a dog, the wildest like the tamest of animals. But the cautious man must be especially on his guard in the matter of resemblances, for they are very slippery things.

Sophist, 231a

Next we must declare the most important benefit effected by [the eyes], for the sake of which god bestowed them upon us. Vision, in my view, is the cause of the greatest benefit to us, inasmuch as none of the accounts now given concerning the Universe would ever have been given if men had not seen the stars or the sun or the heaven. . . . From these we have procured philosophy in all its range, than which no greater boon ever has come or will come, by divine bestowal, unto the race of mortals.

Timaeus, 47a–b

Plato's images are among the most powerful and alluring ever contrived: the cave dwellers of the *Republic* sit in shackles before the shadows cast on the cave wall, prevented from turning their heads toward the real source of those images; the unruly, winged horse of the *Phaedrus* resists the bridled control of the charioteer and therefore fails to ascend to the heights; Socrates, the midwife in *Theaetetus*, aids in the birth of ideas and disposes of those ideas delivered stillborn or unfit; Aristophanes relates the story of our origins as double-sided humans in the *Symposium*—two joined as one, cart wheeling around with our other halves in erotic bliss; philosophy is depicted as medicine for the soul when it is in ill health; Alcibiades flaunts his striking and seductive beauty; and we might even say that Socrates flaunts his ugly visage. These images form so integral a part of the dialogues that the philosophical importance of Plato's image-making demands investigation.[1] And yet several dialogues contain passages in which interlocutors seem to throw into question the moral and epistemic value of image-making, and to denigrate what is visible in comparison to what is purely intelligible. If one wants to consider the significance of Plato's own use of images, one must therefore reckon with a deeply entrenched view of what has come to be considered "Platonic metaphysics."

It is widely accepted that Plato subscribes to some metaphysical system that involves two realms or kinds of being which are hierarchically arranged, and two kinds of apprehension or knowledge which correspond to the two kinds of being. The superior kind of being resides in the things-in-themselves, or forms, which are real and universal, as well as eternal and unchanging. Furthermore, the realm of the forms is the invisible realm, and so the forms must be known in some other manner than through the senses. They are known, if they can be known at all, through reason alone, that is, reason that operates independently of the senses or the emotions or the passions. Knowledge of the forms, which is purely rational, constitutes true philosophical enlightenment.

Inferior to the forms, in this same system of "Platonic metaphysics," are the phenomena of human experience. We apprehend the phenomena through our senses. They are in constant flux; they are created and perish. Sensation, passion, and emotion, which necessarily accompany human experience since we are embodied creatures, all hinder clear understanding. Furthermore, the phenomena are not wholly real but are imitations or mere images of the forms. When we grasp the phenomena, therefore, we perceive only

---

1. There are many ways to think of images. As the few brief examples cited in the opening paragraph indicate, some images in the dialogues are what we call metaphors; some are more properly considered analogies; some of them are woven into the fabric of what we consider myths or allegories. In addition, some are what we might call "fictional" stories, and in some cases these images take the form of plastic artifacts. The Platonic texts support the grouping of these various instances under the single heading "image," insofar as these several devices are referred to as εἰκών throughout the corpus and denote likenesses of one kind or another. Plato's language surrounding the use of images includes, as well, various cognates of image such as εἴδωλον and εἰκασία. I hope to point toward a link between images and the role of vision in Platonic metaphysics by drawing attention to the further connection to "that which is seen" and "form" (εἶδος). The semantic correlate to image would be παράδειγμα—the pattern or model after which a likeness may be produced. I shall cite the Greek terms being used in the many examples that follow in order to underscore the unity of the semantic field in which these terms are placed by Plato. There are even further links when one considers the term *mimesis* (μίμησις), which describes the relationship between an image and its original, between εἰκών and παραδειγμα.

images of reality. Our apprehension of these phenomena or images falls far short, at best, of philosophical wisdom. Finally, creating images of the phenomena, as an artist, writer, painter, or poet might do, is merely making images of images—still a further departure from the way of truth and wisdom.[2]

It is not hyperbole to consider Plato a master of image-making. If this two-realm metaphysics is an accurate depiction of Plato's metaphysical commitments and of his commitment to philosophy's residing in the realm of pure reason, then we might question why Plato did not himself maintain the level of discourse in his philosophical works by offering only rational argumentation for philosophical positions; why would he sully his own work with lowly, unphilosophical or antiphilosophical images? If to appeal to what is best philosophically is to appeal to what is purely rational, why didn't Plato just write arguments?

To the contrary, the dialogues never fail to appeal to our visual senses, forcing us to see and to create images in our minds in order to understand them. The dialogues draw from the phenomena of human experience over and over again, asking us to understand philosophical ideas through the finite, mutable objects of our experience. And beyond our sense experience, they rely on the fancy of our imagination to create other worlds and images. I shall argue that the dialogues are, therefore, paradigms of image-making as an avenue for philosophical insight and, further, that this traditional view of "Platonic metaphysics" needs slight re-vision.

My quarrel with the traditional view, and my reason for placing "Platonic metaphysics" in quotation marks, is twofold: First, there is a problem with imputing these views straightforwardly to Plato given the dialogue form, the variety of interlocutors who espouse them, and the complex dramatic circumstances that surround their utterance. Second, as I shall argue explicitly here, Plato's use of images makes these metaphysical claims, at the very least, worth a second look. While the dialogues are consistent with a commitment to the two-realm metaphysical view, they are not consistent with a view of philosophy as a purely rational enterprise. Plato's use of images and his implicit belief in their potential for good effect, as evidenced by his pervasive and artful use of them, are grounded, I believe, in epistemic commitments. We must, that is, understand human knowledge, and especially the limits of

---

2. For dialogues that are plausible sources for this view, see for example, *Phaedo,* 65a–67b, 66e, and 79a; *Republic,* 509c–511e, 514a–518b, and 597e–603b; *Sophist,* 234b–236e and 264c–266e.

human knowledge, in order to see why Plato chose to use images as he does and why they are such an effective tool for his project.[3]

1. The Evidence of the *Phaedo*

In order to understand their function and why Plato chose to work through images, I return to the story of recollection. The details of that story provide clues about human epistemological limitation and about the role images could play in philosophical enlightenment. I have already investigated in some detail the *Meno*, where the story of recollection is told. I turn now to the *Phaedo*, where Socrates also tells this story. In addition, the *Phaedo* happens to be one of the major sources for passages that seem to denigrate the senses in comparison to reason, and is therefore an appropriate locus for reopening the investigation of the traditional understanding of Plato's metaphysical commitments and just what role vision and images might actually play in philosophy. While *Phaedo*, on the surface, appears to support the traditional understanding of "Platonic metaphysics,"[4] it actually provides clear evidence that this understanding needs re-view and re-vision.

Set in Socrates' jail cell only hours before he drinks the hemlock, the dialogue, *Phaedo*, focuses appropriately on the immortality of the soul. Near the beginning of the dialogue, Socrates claims that the philosopher tries as far as is possible to live a life in which body and soul are separate. The philosopher is someone who shuns the so-called pleasures of the body such as eating, drinking, and sex. Moreover, such a man thinks little of personal adornment in clothes, shoes, and the like. In this way, the philosopher lives toward and desires death insofar as death is the separation of body and soul.

> "Altogether, then, you think that such a man would not devote himself to the body, but would, so far as he was able, turn away from the body and concern himself with the soul?"

---

3. My discussion of human limitation owes much to the work of Drew Hyland (1995).

4. In accordance with Mitchell Miller's notion of mimetic irony (1986, 4ff.), a reading of the *Phaedo* might argue plausibly that the dualism that pervades the dialogue is Socrates' attempt to mirror his interlocutors' own beliefs, specifically Pythagorean dualism. If so, then a reading of the dialogue that refuses to impute such dualism to Plato is even more plausible. For a thorough reading of *Phaedo* consistent in some respects to the one I offer here, see Ahrensdorf (1995).

"Yes."

"To begin with, then, it is clear that in such matters the philosopher, more than other men, separates the soul from communion with
the body?"

"It is." (64e–65a)

Socrates then reasons that anyone who shuns the body would have to shun
the senses as well, since the sense organs are bodily organs. This train of
reasoning sets up the epistemological dichotomy and its underlying ontology:
as body and soul are distinct, so then are the senses and reason, the appre-
hending faculties associated respectively with body and soul. Likewise, the
objects apprehended by these faculties become dichotomous—the objects of
human sense experience and things-in-themselves.

> "Would not that man do this [i.e., separate soul from body] most
> perfectly who approaches each thing, so far as possible, with the
> reason alone, not introducing sight into his reasoning nor dragging
> in any of the other senses along with his thinking, but who employs
> pure, absolute reason in his attempt to search out the pure, absolute
> essence of things, and who removes himself, so far as possible, from
> eyes and ears, and, in a word, from his whole body, because he feels
> that its companionship disturbs the soul and hinders it from attain-
> ing truth and wisdom? Is not this the man, Simmias, if anyone, to
> attain to the knowledge of reality?"
>
> "That is true as true can be, Socrates," said Simmias. (66a)

At this point in the dialogue Socrates has thus established the threefold
dichotomy: body and soul; senses and reason; objects of human experience
and things-in-themselves. As the traditional view of "Platonic metaphysics"
would have it, these pairs are wholly disjunctive, but when the story of
recollection is introduced, the dichotomies demand a closer look. The story
of recollection reveals remarkable means of connecting the two dichotomous elements, the two realms of being. I hope to show that it also contains
important clues about the role that images play in linking the two realms.

The story of recollection tells us that before the soul's embodiment or
birth, it knew the realities. Upon birth it forgets these truths, and if we are to
learn them at all, we must recollect them. Socrates tells us that various
things in our experience can remind us of other things. For example, seeing
the lyre can remind us of the one who plays it; seeing the cloak worn by a

lover can remind us of our lover; seeing a picture of Simmias can remind us
of Simmias.

> "All these examples show, then, that recollection is caused by like
> things and also by unlike things, do they not?"
> "Yes."
> "And when one has a recollection of anything caused by like
> things, will he not also inevitably consider whether this recollection
> offers a perfect likeness of the thing recollected, or not?"
> "Inevitably." (74a)

When we perceive one thing, it calls to our minds some other thing. The
item recalled can be different from or similar to, like or unlike, the item that
stimulated its recall. Furthermore, Socrates tells us, the individual who
recalls is then induced to analyze the recollection to see what relationship
obtains between the thing recalled and the item that brought it to mind. In
particular the subject evaluates the likeness or difference between the two.
Socrates continues his questioning:

> "Now see," said [Socrates], "if this is true. We say there is such a
> thing as equality. I do not mean one piece of wood equal to another,
> or one stone to another, or anything of that sort, but something
> beyond that—equality itself (αὐτὸ τὸ ἴσον).[5] Shall we say there is
> such a thing, or not?"
> "We shall say that there is," said Simmias, "most decidedly."
> "And do we know what it is?"
> "Certainly," said he.
> "Whence did we derive the knowledge of it? Is it not from the
> things we were just speaking of? Did we not, by seeing equal pieces
> of wood or stones or other things, derive from them a knowledge of
> abstract equality, which is another thing?. . .Then," said he, "those
> equals are not the same as equality itself."
> "Not at all, I should say, Socrates."
> "But from those equals," said he, "which are not the same as
> equality itself, you have nevertheless conceived and acquired knowl-
> edge of it?"

---

5. Fowler translates this phrase "equality in the abstract." I prefer the more literal
translation "equality itself," for my purposes here.

"Very true," he replied.
"And it is either like them or unlike them?"
"Certainly."
"It makes no difference," said he, "Whenever the sight of one thing brings you a perception of another, whether they be like or unlike, that must necessarily be recollection." (74a–d)

What makes this passage remarkable is its claim that we can come to know the abstract realities from the objects of human experience in the process called recollection! By using our senses—in this case, sight—we can come to know something of things-in-themselves. Socrates even claims that "it is impossible to gain this knowledge [of reality], except by sight or touch or some other of the senses" (75a). By perceiving, we are reminded of, and we recover, the realities our souls once knew. The objects of our experience and the things-in-themselves are both like and unlike, so we glimpse the realities insofar as they are similar to the images before us, and at the same time we recognize that the images before us are not the realities themselves, are unlike them in fundamental ways. Recollection thus provides the link between all three dichotomies: senses and reason are linked by recollection since we rely on our senses in order to grasp what we might later reason about, namely, the realities; objects of experience and things-in-themselves are linked by recollection since we recall the things-in-themselves through the objects of our experience; and body and soul are linked through recollection since the senses and the intelligence necessarily work together in that activity. This means, incidentally, that recollection is therefore what allows embodied souls to be integrated beings. Most importantly, what becomes clear when we take these aspects of recollection together, is that recollection is what makes philosophy possible. We *can* have access, and we can only have access, to the things-in-themselves through our dim images of them in this realm because of the links recollection makes possible.

The *Phaedo*, then, portrays philosophical investigation taking place *between* the realms of sense and intellect, and so the exclusivity of the two realms in the traditional "Platonic" metaphysical dualism needs to be reexamined. Socrates' explicit commitment to the study of the objects of human experience, and to the sensible faculties as a means for investigating the realities, i.e., as a means of philosophical investigation in the genuine learning process of recollection, remains incongruous with the traditional view. The two realms are necessarily linked, and philosophical inquiry into the nature of reality must necessarily take place within the realm of appearances. The reason why it must take place there is central to the *Phaedo*.

There is strong evidence in the *Phaedo*, and in other dialogues, as I shall show, that rather than being an escape from this embodied life, philosophy is a way of coping from within it. That is, philosophy is a way of addressing directly our human condition with courage and intelligence. The *Phaedo*, in this way, offers a radically different conception of philosophy than the traditional "Platonic" interpretation of it as purely rational activity carried out beyond the human realm. Within the two realm metaphysical scheme, the *Phaedo* places us squarely in one realm and outside the other. Socrates makes it clear that the human life is one of embodiment that necessarily limits the capacities of the soul, in particular the body limits the soul's access to things-in-themselves. We have not yet fully discovered the power of images as a way to philosophical truth, and the missing link to the story lies in what the *Phaedo* tells us about human limitation. The *Phaedo* offers a conception of philosophy as a human activity carried out within—and because of—our limitations, and images are a part of that philosophy.

Our first indication that philosophy might be the remedy for human limitation comes not from Socrates, but from Simmias. Simmias and Cebes each have objections to make in response to Socrates' three arguments for why they should believe that the soul is immortal. This is a critical juncture in the drama. Simmias and Cebes sit before a condemned man who will go to his death momentarily. He speaks of the immortality of the soul, literally on his deathbed, in response to the young men's challenge to the fearless manner in which he faces his fate (63a–b). The young men realize that to bring objections to Socrates' arguments will have frightful consequences if philosophy is not a match to meet those objections. If the issue cannot be settled as to the soul's immortality, then what Socrates' comrades in the jail cell will soon witness will be another event entirely. Simmias admits that both he and Cebes have wanted to ask a question, but were hesitant on account of Socrates' "present misfortune" (84d). Simmias therefore prefaces his objection with the following palliative:

> "I think, Socrates, as perhaps you do yourself, that it is either impossible or very difficult to acquire clear knowledge about these matters in this life. And yet he is a weakling who does not test in every way what is said about them and persevere until he is worn out by studying them on every side. For he must do one of two things; either he must learn or discover the truth about these matters, or if that is

impossible, he must take whatever human doctrine is best and hardest to disprove and, embarking upon it as upon a raft, sail upon it through life in the midst of dangers, unless he can sail upon some stronger vessel, some divine revelation, and make his voyage more safely and securely. And so now I am not ashamed to ask questions, since you encourage me to do so, and I shall not have to blame myself hereafter for not saying now what I think." (85c–d)

Simmias appropriately sets philosophy in the context of fundamental human limitation. Human life is carried out in rough waters where there is danger all around. We need beliefs and ideas to help us stay afloat, but it is difficult, if not impossible, to know which of those ideas are to be believed. We should cling to that vessel which serves us best, that belief which best stands the test of dialectic and, holding fast to it, make our way the best we can. To question, as Simmias is doing, is to take courage in this difficult situation, and philosophy is the means by which we test the worthiness of our own vessels and perhaps leave them behind when we have found sturdier craft. In any case, our plight is risky and uncertain, and philosophy provides the life raft. The *Phaedo* thus poignantly portrays the fundamental conflict between the limits of human knowledge and the human desire for answers. Both Socrates and Plato are confronted with the task of urging others to engage in philosophical inquiry when there is little probability that in this life we should find answers to our deepest questions.

Another passage that follows closely behind Simmias's previous statement reinforces the same profound difficulty, and again recommends philosophy as the courageous choice in the midst of uncertainty. Properly steeled up with philosophy on their side, Simmias and Cebes go ahead and make their objections, which appear to present formidable challenges to Socrates' arguments. Recalling what is at stake here for the condemned Socrates if the soul proves not to be immortal, it becomes clear that those witnessing the drama might experience anxiety with the introduction of these challenges to Socrates' arguments, and they need reassurance to assuage their anxiety.

[*Phaedo:*] Now all of us, as we remarked to one another afterwards, were very uncomfortable when we heard what [Cebes and Simmias] said; for we had been thoroughly convinced by the previous argument, and now they seemed to be throwing us again into confusion and distrust, not only in respect to the past discussion but also with regard to any future one. They made us fear that our judgment was worthless or that no certainty could be attained in these matters.

Echecrates: By the gods, Phaedo, I sympathize with you; for I myself after listening to you am inclined to ask myself: "What argument shall we believe henceforth? For the argument of Socrates was perfectly convincing, and now it has fallen to discredit. . . . So, for heaven's sake, tell how Socrates continued the discourse, and whether he also, as you say the rest of you did, showed any uneasiness, or calmly defended his argument. And did he defend it successfully? Tell us everything as accurately as you can.

Phaedo: Echecrates, I have often wondered at Socrates, but never did I admire him more than then. That he had an answer ready was perhaps to be expected; but what astonished me more about him was, first, the pleasant, gentle, and respectful manner in which he listened to the young men's criticisms, secondly his quick sense of the effect their words had upon us, and lastly, the skill with which he cured us, and as it were, recalled us from our flight and defeat and made us face about and follow him and join in his examination of the argument.

Echecrates: How did he do it?

Phaedo: I will tell you. . . . (88b–89b)

Notice that this passage marks an abrupt change of scene in the drama. Plato moves away from the jail cell momentarily, back to the original scene in which Phaedo is telling the story to Echecrates. Not only do those witnessing the action first hand in the jail cell need reassurance, but so does Echecrates who is hearing the story of Socrates' final hours from Phaedo's recounting. The reader is likewise provided with a respite from her anxiety by Plato's having created this interlude. The reader, who observes both of those scenes, suffers the same anxiety and benefits likewise from reassurance. We are all in need of reassurance because of the human anxiety suffered when our epistemological limitations confront our desire to know and to live by knowledge. In this case the knowing in question is mortally important. Plato and Socrates provide reassurance by way of a break from the pursuit at hand, a brief hiatus that provides time to restore our faith in philosophy.

But fear looms over this dialogue. Its context and setting would imply no less since it confronts death and human fate beyond death. In addition to the passage cited above in which fear and anxiety play a role, Socrates accuses the young men early on of having the "childish fear (δεδιέναι τὸ τῶν παίδων) that when the soul goes out from the body the wind will really blow it away and scatter it" (77d). Simmias distances himself from such fear by laughing and saying that while *they* are not afraid, perhaps some child within them might have such fears. Simmias's words seem to belie his real emotional state. He challenges Socrates to persuade the "child within" them "not to fear death as if it were a hobgoblin." Socrates replies that the solution is to "sing charms to [the child] until you charm away his fear" (77e–78a). Socrates eventually offers philosophy as the therapy for the unsettled soul. The soul that has been nurtured by philosophy "is not likely to fear that it will be torn asunder at its departure from the body" (84a–b).

These passages are reminiscent of those in the *Meno* in which, after Meno's introduction of the debater's argument, the future of all inquiry is threatened. In both cases the reader is faced with the possibility that inquiry is useless and that the philosophical life is not worthwhile. In the *Meno* passages Socrates offers dialectic and recollection as the antidote to any anxiety one might suffer at the thought that learning is not possible. The stakes are higher in *Phaedo*, since philosophical inquiry is needed to establish beliefs about the fate of our souls beyond death. The interlocutors in *Phaedo* are characters who desperately want to put their faith in philosophy. It means their (or at least Socrates') literal salvation at this point. Since courage is the antidote to fear, Socrates must steel up the courage of those present to combat the fear that is by now palpable in the jail cell. As Phaedo was just about to tell us, Socrates does cure the fears of his companions.

Socrates' cure for the anxiety of the interlocutors amounts to an admonition never to tire of the pursuit of an argument and, furthermore, when philosophy fails, never to blame the argument, but to see the failing in ourselves.

> "[L]et us guard against a danger. . . . The danger of becoming misologists or haters of argument," said he, "as people become misanthropists or haters of man; for no worse evil can happen to a man than to hate argument. Misology and misanthropy arise from similar causes. For misanthropy arises from trusting someone implicitly without sufficient knowledge. You think the man is perfectly true and sound and trustworthy, and afterwards you find him base and false. Then you have the same experience with another person. By the time this has happened to a man a good many times, especially if it happens among those whom he might regard as his nearest and dearest friends, he ends by being in continual quarrels and by hating everybody and

thinking there is nothing sound in anyone at all. . . . The similarity [between men and arguments] lies in this: when a man without proper knowledge concerning arguments has confidence in the truth of an argument and afterwards thinks that it is false, whether it really is so or not, and this happens again and again; then you know, those men especially who have spent their time in disputation come to believe that they are the wisest of men and that they alone have discovered that there is nothing sound or sure in anything, whether argument or anything else. . . . First then," said he, "let us be on our guard against this, and let us not admit into our souls the notion that there is no soundness in arguments at all. Let us far rather assume that we ourselves are not yet in sound condition and that we must strive manfully and eagerly to become so, you and the others for the sake of all your future life, and I because of my impending death." (89c–91a)

One might object that Socrates is saying exactly the opposite of what I want to establish, since he claims that our faith ought to remain in argument. True enough, but Socrates' view implies that arguments will necessarily fail us. What comes through strongly in these passages is again the fundamental limitation of human beings. Pure argumentation and pure reason are not viable avenues for philosophical enlightenment. Philosophical inquiry will sometimes disappoint us.[6] We ought not, nevertheless, let that deter us from the life of philosophy. Socrates' cure for anxiety, while assuring us that we ought to remain faithful to philosophy, at the same time warns us of our limitations.

The language used by the interlocutors in *Phaedo* clearly indicates that Socrates and the two young Thebans operate under the shared presumption of human limitation. The separation of body and soul practiced by the philosopher is always carried out "as far as he is able" and "so far as is possible." The philosopher, "if anyone" would be the one to ascend to the realities through reason alone. And Simmias's preface to his objection states explicitly that he and Socrates share the view that it is either impossible or very difficult to acquire clear knowledge.

Despite their conceptions of human limitation, all three of the participants in this dialogue, Simmias, Cebes, and Socrates, are committed to philosophical inquiry. If the *Phaedo* tells us to look to philosophy for preservation in

---

6. This or something like this seems to be the upshot of Socrates' "failed" investigation with Theaetetus.

the seas of uncertainty, it would seem to be important to look at how philosophy is carried out in this dialogue. In particular, it is worth inquiring whether philosophy is carried out by pure argumentation, that is, by an appeal to reason, separate from other faculties. Clearly this is not the case.

Near the beginning of the dialogue, Socrates describes his discussion of the soul and the afterlife as telling stories (μυθολογεῖν, 61e), and he prefaces his defense that he is right not to grieve at death by saying that he hopes (ἐλπίζω) to go to a good fate, "though I should not dare to assert this positively; but I would assert as positively as anything about such matters that I am going to gods who are good masters" (63c). The entire set up for Socrates' views on the immortality of the soul is therefore couched in non-conclusive, speculative terms. And, after having presented his views on the immortality of the soul, Socrates finds it necessary once again to attenuate: "There are still many subjects for doubt and many points open to attack, if anyone cares to discuss the matter thoroughly" (84c).

The largest portion of the dialogue contains what might be called "proofs" for the immortality of the soul and Socrates' response to objections. But even these proofs, objections, and responses are not enough, ultimately, to convey what Socrates says really lies at the heart of his belief that the soul is immortal, namely, the necessity of becoming "as good and wise as possible" (107d). Since the final justice meted out to good and bad souls appears to be as important, if not more important, than the mere immortality of the soul, Socrates completes the dialogue with a description of the journey of the soul in the afterlife and of the worlds it might come to inhabit (107b–115a). To demonstrate the importance of *how* we live our lives, the arguments for the immortality of the soul must be supplemented by more images and stories. Death can not simply be the separation of body and soul. If only that, death would be an escape and "a boon to the wicked" (107c). Regarding the truth of the story Socrates tells about the world and the fate of the soul, his last words on the subject are again about human risk and uncertainty:

> "Now it would not be fitting for a man of sense to maintain that all this is just as I have described it, but that this or something like it is true concerning our souls and their abodes, since the soul is shown to be (φαίνεται οὖσα) immortal, I think he may properly and worthily venture to believe; for the venture is well worthwhile." (114d)

None of what Socrates contributes to this dialogue would seem to be an appeal to pure reason or rational argumentation. He presents ancient stories and myths, and he presents them tenuously in keeping with his commitment to human limitation. What are the most likely candidates for pure argumentation in this dialogue—the "proofs" for the immortality of the soul—are flanked by disclaimers as to their demonstrative truth, and are in need of supplemental stories that supply essential elements of Socrates' view.

Furthermore, the objections made by the two young men each take the form of an image. Simmias likens the soul to a harmony and the body to a lyre. He asks why, if when the lyre is destroyed so is the harmony, would not the soul too be destroyed when the body is destroyed (85e–86d). Cebes uses the image of the weaver and his cloak. Perhaps, Cebes argues, the soul is long lived, but not immortal. Then, like the old weaver who has outlived several of his cloaks but dies and leaves one in particular behind him, the soul outlives several bodies, but degenerates continually, and one body is bound to be its last. The man would be foolish, therefore, who went to his death assured that his soul would live on (87b–88b). Plato draws our attention to the self-conscious use of images when he has Cebes say that, like Simmias, he too is in need of an image in order to express his objection (εἰκόνος γάρ τινος, ὡς ἔοικεν, κἀγὼ ὥσπερ Σιμμίας δέομαι, 87b). Simmias and Cebes are perhaps among the most intelligent, most earnest, and most philosophically inclined of all the interlocutors. Surely the manner in which they carry out their philosophical conversation is important.

The *Phaedo* presents clearly three points: that we must look to images of reality in order to learn about reality itself, that humans are fundamentally limited, and that we ought to maintain faith in philosophy. Moreover, that its three primary interlocutors make their most acute philosophical points through images has something important to say to us. The dialogue in its entirety encourages, through its telling of the story of recollection, the use of our senses in the service of philosophical inquiry. For human beings, learning just is looking to images. It is not a foolproof method; it will fail us at times, and it might lead us astray, but in the end it's all that we embodied, limited beings have. And, for the sake of our souls, now and ever after, the risk is worthwhile.

2. The Evidence of Other Dialogues

That human beings are inherently limited, that philosophy is the appropriate medium for human inquiry due to our limitations, and that philosophy needs therefore to be carried out to some extent through images, are pervasive ideas in the Platonic corpus. I do not intend here to give a full interpretation of any particular dialogue nor to provide an exhaustive treatment of all discussions about philosophy, human limitation, and the use of images; rather I mean to present enough evidence to establish that these ideas appear frequently and consistently in the dialogues and are fundamental to Plato's project.[7] In addition to the *Phaedo* there are equally powerful discussions of the limits of human reason and powerful suggestions that philosophy, working through images, is the best way to address those limitations.

The *Apology* provides testimony that human limitation is the bedrock of Plato's project insofar as it sets out in the clearest, most poignant fashion the meaning of Socratic ignorance. Socrates remains outstanding among other humans because he recognizes his ignorance while others do not recognize theirs. What makes Socratic ignorance "Socratic" therefore is nothing that mitigates the ignorance, but is instead the open and explicit recognition of the ignorance itself—the laying claim to that ignorance, which we know is a necessary propaedeutic for philosophy.[8] The two terms, "Socratic" and "ignorance," when put together, present both a universal human condition and a particularized human ideal: Socratic *ignorance* is emblematic of the universal human condition since all humans are alike in their ignorance, but *Socratic* ignorance is also representative of an ideal for humans who need to recognize and admit their ignorance and yet aspire to philosophize.

The *Symposium* addresses the human aspiration to philosophize, an aspiration driven by eros, and it portrays our limitations as humans. It can be read as a dialogue that attempts to bridge the gulf between human ignorance

7. Gadamer makes a similar case regarding the consistent message in the dialogues about human limitation and the role of vision. Gadamer (1980, 99–100ff.) enumerates and explains four means of communicating a thing, none of which guarantees that the thing will then be "known": the word or name of a thing (onoma); the explanation or conceptual determination of a thing (logos); the appearance, illustrative image, example, or figure of a thing (eidolon); and the knowledge or insight itself of that thing. Gadamer is then careful to warn us that we must not see these four ways as an ordered ascent, culminating in knowledge of the good. All attempts to see them as such "are completely mistaken" (111).

Ultimately, pure knowledge or the "life of pure theory" is not attainable for humans. Of the third means of communication, Gadamer says, "Examples, of course, are one of the necessary media in which true knowledge is presented" (115), and he further argues for the need for all four types: "For they all serve to make one more 'dialectical,' to educate one's vision for the thing itself" (122). Our human limitations are, according to Gadamer (1991, 4–5), "an essential characteristic of man's humanity" in light of which "Plato always sees man's existence . . . which means that he presents them as defined by the process of going beyond them. Man is a creature who transcends himself." Cf. Kosman (1992b) which has close links to this section.

8. See also, for example, *Meno*, 84a–b; *Theaetetus*, 210c.

and pure, enlightened wisdom. The language of Diotima's speech, for example, is filled with references to mediation, to finding a middle path, to navigating between two realms, and of the limited being who wants nonetheless to ascend to truth.[9] Our limitation implies that we cannot achieve pure rationality, nor need we remain flailing in the depths, but we can aspire to a middle path. Philosophy guides us in that middle path, steering away from ignorance, navigating toward wisdom, but forever remaining between the two. In one brief but telling passage Diotima responds to one of Socrates' questions:

> "Who then, Diotima," I asked, "are the lovers of wisdom, if they are neither the wise nor the ignorant?"
>
> "Why, a child could tell by this time," she answered, "that they are the intermediate sort, and amongst these also is Eros. For wisdom has to do with the fairest things, and Eros is a love directed to what is fair; so that Eros must needs be a friend of wisdom, and, as such, must be between wise and ignorant." (204a–b)[10]

Eros, in his capacity as lover of wisdom, that is, in his capacity as philosopher, is of the intermediate type between wisdom and ignorance. Socrates also loves wisdom and the beautiful but does not possess them, so he, too, is the intermediate type. Diotima portrays philosophy as the practice reserved for those who love wisdom and the beautiful, but who do not possess them, and she describes the ascent from the love of beautiful bodies to the love of the beautiful itself in language consistent with a view of humans as fundamentally limited. The final ascent to the beautiful itself is not accessible to Socrates, nor to any mortal. The lover who ascends to the highest level and glimpses the beautiful itself is not, Diotima tells us, "infected with the flesh and color of humanity" (211e). Her discussion of this highest rung of the ladder is clearly a counterfactual one that concludes on the note that if there were such a one, then he, if anyone, would be immortal (212a–b). Philosophy, then, is a mortal enterprise, fixed in that place but aspiring to the immortal.

We ought to take note that Diotima's method of teaching Socrates about eros is through an image: the ladder of ascent. "Beginning from obvious beauties [one] must for the sake of that highest beauty be ever climbing aloft, as

---

9. This position is argued in detail by Luce Irigiray (1994, 181–95).

10. I have translated φιλοσοφοῦντες as "lovers of wisdom" instead of Lamb's "followers of wisdom," and I have rendered Ἔρως as "Eros" rather than "Love."

on the rungs of a ladder. . ." (211c). She develops this metaphor in order to convey that there are different levels for various types of expression and objects of love: one perhaps begins by loving the beauty of a young boy's body; from there, one might come to love the beauty of many bodies; if one attempts to ascend to something higher, one could love those boys' beautiful souls; ultimately, one might even aspire to the love of the very essence of beauty. Philosophy, driven by eros, takes a similar path, aspiring in its ascent to what lies beyond the human. The wise Diotima knows many things, including the proper way for philosophy to be carried out. She therefore begins by engaging Socrates in question and answer (201e) and then she creates a beautiful image for him.[11]

An even more compelling image in the *Symposium* is drawn by the character, Aristophanes, and this image tells the story of human incompleteness (189c–191d). Long ago, we were beings that we would now consider "double," with four legs and four arms, two sets of genitals, and two faces, joined together back to back. Each such being exhibited great strength, vigor, and joy. We were, in that state, complete. These beings had such "lofty notions" that they "conspired against the gods," scheming to assault them in "high heaven." So, in anger the gods split these beings asunder, insuring that forever they would be doomed to seek their other halves for completeness. The drive behind seeking that completeness is erotic. Hyland argues that we can see both the humor and the tragedy of our fundamental incompleteness in Aristophanes' speech, that while the images conjured up by Aristophanes' story allow us to laugh at ourselves, on reflection, the details of the myth tell a different story:

> "First, all humans, from the first generation of split people on, are fated to our situation as erotic: incomplete and experiencing that incompleteness. That situation is not one we can control, nor is it something for which we are directly responsible: it is the consequence of the "original sin" of our forebears. Moreover, second, part of what we are fated to is that, as erotic beings, we are bound to strive to overcome the incompleteness we experience. That is precisely what the energy of eros is. Third, the nature of this erotic striving is such that it will never be finally successful."[12]

---

11. Socrates claims specifically at 201e that Diotima questioned him, and at 203b Diotima embarks on a long story (Μακρότερον μέν, ἔφη, διηγήσασθαι)
12. Hyland (1995, 118).

What Hyland refers to as our incompleteness is rooted in our limitations as humans. He argues that the comic and tragic elements of the *Symposium* portray human limitation through their depiction of Eros.[13] We lack the objects of our erotic impulse, one of which is wisdom.

The *Phaedrus* also tells the tale of erotic impulses toward wisdom. It is further linked to the *Symposium* insofar as it contains a myth that has many similarities to Diotima's ladder. The story and image of the charioteer, like Diotima's ladder, tell the tale of the lover ascending to the heights. Oddly enough, though, *Phaedrus* also relies on recollection and so has important links to the *Phaedo*. Socrates begins his story of the charioteer by saying that he cannot give a direct account of the nature of the soul, but will instead provide an image. He pays particular attention to the manner in which the soul can and should be discussed, claiming that it should not be through discourse, but through image:

> "Concerning the immortality of the soul this is enough; but about its form we must speak in the following manner. To tell what it really is would be a matter of utterly superhuman and long discourse (διηγήσεως), but it is within human power to describe it briefly in an image (ἔοικεν); let us therefore speak in that way." (246a)[14]

To make images is to do a human thing. The distinction between godly or superhuman discourse and human image-making serves as a frontispiece to the image of the charioteer and his team of horses which represents the human soul. Socrates implies that image-making is fundamental to human discourse—even philosophical discourse about the most important of issues.

Socrates persistently reaffirms the distinction between what is peculiarly human and what is superhuman through the images he creates in *Phaedrus*. The soul can sprout wings that help it to soar to the gods' dwelling place and to glimpse the realities there. While the gods clearly make the ascent to the realities and dwell there, seeing reality, the plight for humans is quite different. "Such is the life of the gods; but of the other souls, that which best follows after God and is most like (εἰκασμένη) him, raises the head of the charioteer up into the outer region and is carried round in the revolution, troubled by the horses and hardly beholding the realities" (248a). The

---

13. Ibid., 111–37.

14. Fowler translates ἔοικεν as "figure" but I have translated it as "image" in order to be consistent with all the translations of the same cognate elsewhere in this chapter.

description continues (through 248d) with language clearly stating that the charioteer will necessarily fail in his attempts to reach the realities. The image of the charioteer who is trying to control the two horses—one noble, the other troublesome—depicts a human attempt at ascent to the realities, entities that Socrates clearly demarcates as lying beyond human capacity. The horses continue to give humans trouble, even in the best of human circumstances, bound as we are beneath the gods. Thus the *Phaedrus* underscores our limitation.

But just when Socrates introduces human limitation into the myth of the afterlife in *Phaedrus*, he also introduces recollection, which provides a strong link to passages in the *Phaedo* that portray the importance of images for philosophy. An entire menagerie of souls are introduced into the myth of the afterlife in *Phaedrus*, differentiated and hierarchically arranged by the degree to which each soul has glimpsed the realities. Clearly there are several types of souls beyond any human, that is, embodied, souls (248a–c), but the best type of human soul is the soul of a philosopher or a lover of beauty, and all human souls glimpse what they once knew by means of recollection (249b).

> [I]t is not easy for all souls to gain from earthly things a recollection of those realities, either for those which had but a brief view of them at that earlier time, or for those which, after falling to earth, were so unfortunate as to be turned toward unrighteousness through some evil communications and to have forgotten the holy sights they once saw. Few then are left which retain an adequate recollection of them; but these when they see here any likeness (ὁμοίωμα) of the things of that other world, are stricken with amazement and can no longer control themselves; but they do not understand their condition, because they do not clearly perceive. Now in the earthly copies (ὁμοιώμασιν) of justice and temperance and the other ideas which are precious to souls there is no light, but only a few, approaching the images (εἰκόνας) through the darkling organs of sense, behold in them the nature of that which they imitate, and these few do this with difficulty. (250a–b)[15]

15. Griswold (1986, 144): "The gods of this myth do seem to be (among other things) idealized human types who serve the crucial purpose in the story of helping articulate the notion that we are imperfect in specific ways." Griswold also sees in *Phaedrus* "the possibility of reflection on its own status qua written work. This is in keeping with the view that the written word is an 'image' of the spoken (276a) and the assumption that the image is to be understood relative to its original" (219).

The earthly likenesses are dim compared to the realities, but are dim reminders nonetheless. Human access to the realities comes from things in this world that are images of the realities. What is needed is simply the right use of the aids of recollection (249c). Furthermore, the philosopher' vision— a vision of objects of human experience that reveals dim glimpses of reality, not direct vision of reality—will be difficult and rare. In this manner the *Phaedrus* echoes elements of *Phaedo* in which we learn that we gain understanding of things-in-themselves (e.g., the Equal) from objects of our experience (e.g., two sticks of equal length).

The *Sophist* treats images at length, and eventually points to their role in philosophical discourse. The Eleatic Stranger and young Theaetetus, in their complex and at times circuitous conversation, weave together a discussion of images (roughly 235b–236d; 239c–d; 264c ff.) and a discussion of the possibility of not-being (roughly 237c; 239d–264b). These two issues are, as one would expect, related. In particular, the formulation of the existence and ontological status of not-being that emerges from their conversation helps render philosophical discourse possible and delineates the role of images as part of that discourse.

Image-making, when done according to the true proportions of the thing imitated, is simply called "likeness-making" (εἰκαστικήν), and the Stranger and Theaetetus accept this kind of image-making as, at the very least, neutral, neither one of them making any disparaging remarks about this form of image-making (235d). But there is another category of image-making that produces appearances, not likenesses, that is called "fantastic art" (φανταστικήν) and contains an element of falsehood (236c).

> [T]he matter of appearing and seeming, but not being, and of saying things, but not true ones—all this is now and always has been very perplexing. You see, Theaetetus, it is extremely difficult to understand how a man is to say or think that falsehood really exists and in saying this not be involved in a contradiction. (236e–237a)

The Stranger and Theaetetus are confronted with the nature of negation and falsehood and the puzzle of what is not—something we conceive of and speak about in common discourse with little thought about it, but that presents difficulties when one attempts to examine its ontological status more closely. The two interlocutors are plagued by the sophistic claim that falsehood is utterly impossible since not-being could neither be conceived nor uttered since it has no part of being and is therefore nothing (260c–d).

The motivation for their search lies in the difficulty they face if they claim that the sophist deals with false discourse or creates false images. (Ironically, the discussion of the possibility of false language is rooted first in the possibility of false *images*. Framing the problem in this manner undermines contemporary treatments of this dialogue that cast the problem of not-being exclusively in terms of language, in terms of how false *propositions* can or cannot correspond to the world. Clearly it is not necessarily nor exclusively a problem of language that Plato is concerned with here since false images initiate the investigation.[16]) The two interlocutors therefore embark together on a mission the Stranger sets for himself: "I shall have to . . . contend forcibly that after a fashion not-being is and on the other hand in a sense being is not" (241d).

The larger aim here is to establish that discourse of all kinds—speech, opinion, conceptualization, and image-making—participates both in being and not-being. That is, discourse exists (participation in being) and yet there is such a thing as negative and false discourse (participation in not-being) which is distinguishable from positive or true assertion of being. Without that, discourse, at least meaningful discourse, is impossible. So the very existence of philosophical or any other type of meaningful discourse depends on the mixture of being and not-being, and it depends on the distinction between truth and falsity and the distinction that parallels it between true likenesses and fantastic appearances.

In establishing that discourse is necessarily a mingling of being and not being, the Stranger and Theaetetus have now allowed for the possibility of falsehood. So the position of the Stranger in *Sophist* is consistent with that espoused by Diotima in *Symposium* which places philosophy in the position of medium between two worlds. In the former case philosophy lies between being and not-being, and in the latter case between the fullness of divine reality and the poverty of human want. The possibility of falsehood that comes with the mingling of being and not-being, while it certainly brings with it the promise of philosophical discourse, carries with it significant consequences.

> Our object was to establish discourse (τὸν λόγον) as one of our classes of being. For if we were deprived of this, we should be

---

16. As an example of many such propositional treatments of these passages, see Wiggins (1978), Owen (1978), and even Rosen (1983). The dialogue contains clear statements that the falsehood under consideration is not only linguistic. See, for example, 235d ff., 260c.

deprived of philosophy, which would be the greatest calamity; moreover, we must at the present moment come to an agreement about the nature of discourse, and if we were robbed of it by its absolute nonexistence, we could no longer discourse; and we should be robbed of it if we agreed that there is no mixture of anything with anything. . . . But if falsehood exists, deceit exists. . . . And if deceit exists, all things must be henceforth full of images and likenesses and fancies. (εἰδώλων τε καὶ εἰκόνων ἤδη καὶ φαντασίας πάντα ἀνάγκη μεστὰ εἶναι Sophist, 260a–c)

This conception of philosophy precludes its dealing with pure being or with the realities directly, and roots philosophy firmly in a mixture of being and not-being. This brings with it an inherent risk characteristic of all human endeavors, and the risk here is deceit. The boon to mankind from the mingling of being and not-being is philosophical discourse, and the price we pay is the possibility of deceit. But somewhere between the benefit of philosophical discourse and the price of deceit lie images. Philosophy is described as mixing the realms of being and not-being, so it must contain images since it cannot contain the realities. Furthermore, by the very reasoning used by the Stranger, it would not be warranted to assume that since these images are not-real that they are therefore completely unreal. We know from several instances in this dialogue that there are two kinds of images, those that imitate reality and are called true images and those that do not imitate reality and are called false images.[17] It is more than plausible that the true images are those that point us, in comparing likeness and unlikeness, toward the realities and must therefore be a proper constituent of philosophical discourse.[18]

The *Timaeus* sets up the entire world of human experience as an image of some other world, specifically claiming that this world is a copy of some other world after which it is patterned.[19] Timaeus then plays on the etymological link between "likenesses" as an ontological entity and "likelihood" as an epistemological category, arguing that since humans must deal with an image or copy (εἰκων) we must accept that our knowledge will only be likely (εἰκότα).[20]

17. In addition to the passage cited above (236c), see 235d–f and 264c–267b.
18. As Rosen says (1983, 147, 152–53), the Stranger, unfortunately, never fully addresses the metaphysical status of the true images.
19. Cf. *Cratylus* 423, 43ff., in which words and language are discussed as imitations of reality.
20. Cf. Thayer (1977, 615–16) and Gadamer (1980, 120).

Again, if these premises be granted, it is wholly necessary that this Cosmos should be a Copy (εἰκόνα) of something. . . . Wherefore, Socrates, if in our treatment of a great host of matters regarding the Gods and the generation of the Universe we prove unable to give accounts that are always in all respects self-consistent and perfectly exact, be not thou surprised; rather we should be content if we can furnish accounts that are inferior to none in likelihood (εἰκότας), remembering that both I who speak and you who judge are but human creatures, so that it becomes us to accept the likely (εἰκότα) account of these matters and forbear to search beyond it. (29b–d)

Human limitation lies at the root of Timaeus's account in this passage, and he tells us that we must forever deal in images. We "are but human creatures," and as such we must accept our epistemological limitations.

Since what we experience as humans is an image of some other reality, then it would seem to be of paramount importance both to recognize that fact and to understand the difference between the images and the original. Two of the necessary conditions for turning toward the things-in-themselves is recognizing their existence and understanding (albeit in a limited capacity) their difference from what we sense and experience. These conditions would be satisfied through the activity of investigating likeness and unlikeness between image and reality, and to do that one must recognize the difference between image and reality. As limited beings we might use images to ascend to the realities, but we cannot confuse the two. We cannot change our finite, limited existence, but we must still be aware of and turned toward what lies beyond.

The *Euthyphro* (5d–e) *Laches* (190d–e), *Theaetetus* (146c–147c), and *Meno* (71d–72c) portray interlocutors who confuse giving examples with giving definitions. This amounts to confusing objects of human experience with the realities. The mistake of confusing examples and definitions that Euthyphro, Laches, Theaetetus, and Meno make is therefore akin to the confusion of the cave dwellers in the *Republic*. They too confuse what they sense and experience with the realities that cause them. Their bondage lies metaphorically in their chains, but points to their inability to be turned toward something of whose existence they are yet unaware.

The *Republic* is perhaps the dialogue singly most responsible for the condemnatory view of images and image-making imputed to Plato. Ironically, it is also the source of the most vivid and memorable images Plato created. In addition to its description of the cave and its unfortunate denizens, the dialogue in its entirety is predicated on an analogy between justice in the city and justice in the soul. And even further, this analogy is itself introduced by way of yet another image:

> "So, since we are not clever persons, I think we should employ the method of search that we should use if we, with not very keen vision, were bidden to read small letters from a distance, and then someone had observed that these same letters exist elsewhere larger and on a larger surface. We should have accounted it a godsend, I fancy, to be allowed to read those letters first, and then examine the smaller, if they are the same."
>
> "Quite so," said Adeimantus; "but what analogy to this do you detect in the inquiry about justice?"
>
> "I will tell you," I said: "there is a justice of one man, we say, and, I suppose, also of an entire city?. . . Is not the city larger than the man?. . . Then, perhaps there would be more justice in the larger object and more easy to apprehend." (368d–e)

The dim vision of the investigating party is emblematic of our human limitation or ignorance.[21] Our ignorance necessitates that we look to one image which is more easily seen or understood in order to understand another. The entire method of the *Republic*, in its effort to see justice in the soul by first seeing justice in the city, is based on looking at likenesses in order to learn about the object of inquiry.

The simile of the sun is likewise intended to help the interlocutors understand the form of the Good by way of another powerful image. Socrates puts off discussing the nature of the Good directly because he may not be able (μὴ οὐχ οἷός τ᾽ ἔσομαι) to explain the Good. Instead, he offers "what seems to be the offspring of the good and most nearly made in its image" (ὃς δὲ ἔκγονός τε τοῦ ἀγαθοῦ φαίνεται καὶ ὁμοιότατος ἐκείνῳ, 506e).[22] We are left to wonder whether Socrates, or any embodied being, would ever be able to explain the nature of the realities, and whether the image of the sun is therefore the most philosophically appropriate means for helping the young men understand the nature of the Good after all.

---

21. The *Republic* is read in its entirety by Drew Hyland (1995) as a treatment of human limitation and philosophy as the means to transcend that limitation. Hyland intends for his reading of the *Republic* to create a perspective for reading the entire Platonic corpus as well.

22. Shorey renders ἐκείνῳ as "likeness" but I have translated it as "image" for the sake of consistency in this chapter.

But images play a more important—even crucial—role in the *Republic*, philosophically speaking. As Socrates reveals in his conversation with Adeimantus, the primary activity of the philosopher, as depicted in the *Republic*, is to imitate noble images!

> "For surely, Adeimantus, the man whose mind is truly fixed on eternal realities has no leisure to turn his eyes downward upon the petty affairs of men, and so engaging in strife with them to be filled with envy and hate, but he fixes his gaze upon the things of the eternal and unchanging order, and seeing that they neither wrong nor are wronged by one another, but all abide in harmony as reason bids, he will endeavor to imitate (μιμεῖσθαί) them and, as far as may be, to fashion himself in their likeness and assimilate himself (ἀφομοιοῦσθαι) to them". . ."If then," I said, "some compulsion is laid upon him to practice stamping on the plastic matter of human nature in public and private patterns that he visions there, and not merely to mold and fashion himself, do you think he will prove a poor craftsman of sobriety and justice and all forms of ordinary civic virtue?" "By no means," he said. "But if the multitude become aware that what we are saying of the philosopher is true, will they still be harsh with philosophers, and will they distrust our statement that no city could ever be blessed unless its lineaments were traced by artists who used the heavenly model?" "They will not be harsh," he said, "if they perceive that." (500b–e)

The philosopher is connected to the realities through the faculty of vision and, relying on his vision, he creates, in the manner of the artist or craftsman, imitations of what he sees. This entire passage is filled with the language of vision and plastic, artistic creation. Not only does the philosopher mold his own soul in this manner, but when compelled to rule the polis, he "stamps out on the plastic matter of human nature" the virtues and character needed in the citizens.[23] Likewise, the Socratic project, with respect to the interlocutors,

---

23. Cf. the discussion above on the semantic and philosophical significance of "making" and "doing," Chapter 3, page 86. The objection that vision and artistic craft are mere metaphors for, respectively, the kind of knowing that the philosopher has of the realities and of the work he must do to fashion the souls of good citizens, helps to underscore my point about the need for images. Socrates' chosen way for expressing the understanding of the philosopher and the political task before him is through these images. Philosophy needs the use of images to do its work.

and the Platonic project, with respect to reader and audience, could be conceived of in similar terms as molding or making impressions on souls. Note again the subtle concessions in the passage above made to the limitations of the person whose gaze is fixed on the realities. Even that person endeavors to imitate the realities "as far as may be" and consequently that person's soul becomes ordered and divine "in the measure permitted to man."

Near the end of Book IX, Glaucon comes to understand the purpose of the images Socrates has drawn, the image of the ideal city and the corresponding soul.

> "I understand," [Glaucon] said, "You mean [the wise man] will [take part in politics] in the city whose foundation we have now gone through, the one that has its place in speeches, since I don't suppose it exists anywhere on earth."
>
> "But in heaven," I said, "perhaps a pattern (παράδειγμα) is laid up for the man who wants to see and found a city within himself on the basis of what he sees. It doesn't make any difference whether it is or will be somewhere. For he would mind the things of this city alone, and of no other." (592a–b)[24]

The image of the just city is that to which the wise person looks when modeling his or her own soul. We model our souls on the ideals, as those ideals are represented in and through images. The images' imaginary status is irrelevant for Socrates since as long as there is the ideal image to gaze at, the wise person's attention can be fixed and focused, and the just life can still be glimpsed. Glaucon's reply—"It is likely" (Εἰκός)—to Socrates' claim that the image of the city is a model to look at for the wise man, is not an insignificant end to Book IX. Glaucon's reply again links, as did the *Timaeus*, the need to look to images (εἰκών) for human understanding and the epistemological status of human understanding as merely likely or probable (εἰκός).

Not only do the wise person and the philosopher look to images in order to fashion themselves and the citizens, but the divine Creator, the demiurge (δημιουργός, but later referred to as θεός or "god") depicted in the *Republic*, also creates in this fashion. This "truly clever and wondrous man" not only creates "all implements, but he produces all plants and animals, including himself, and thereto earth and heaven and the gods and all things in heaven and in Hades under the earth" (596c). Plato expects those most capable of

---

24. Translation, Bloom (1968).

wisdom—human and superhuman—to look to images of the realities and to imitate as a means of forming, creating, or perfecting souls. Philosophy and philosophical activity are therefore artistic or creative (literally, poetic) endeavors.[25] The demiurge creates these natural objects by imitation, but by imitation of truth—whereas the painter or poet creates imitations of imitations. Thus we arrive at the infamous passages in which imitation in the arts is described as third removed from reality (595a–608b, esp. 597e ff.).

The significance of these passages, however, seems to be to help the young men to avoid confusing reality and image, to avoid being deceived about which is which. The images themselves are not (metaphysically) evil or bad since the philosopher, the wise man, and the demiurge are all image-makers. What does the philosopher do but fix the realties in his mind and create in their image—just as does the demiurge. They need both original and image to do what they do, but these figures see and understand the difference between the two. Instead of condemning images and image-making, Socrates seems to condemn the subject who mistakes images for reality. Deception is foremost on Socrates' mind:

> "When anyone reports to us of some one, that he has met a man who knows all the crafts and everything else that men severally know and that there is nothing that he does not know more exactly than anybody else, our tacit rejoinder must be that he is a simple fellow who apparently has met some magician or sleight-of-hand man and imitator and has been deceived by him into the belief that he is all-wise, *because of his own inability to put to the proof and distinguish knowledge, ignorance and imitation.*" (598d, my emphasis)[26]

Socrates' life mission, as he describes it in the *Apology*, is at its core to "put to the proof and distinguish" knowledge from ignorance. And what sets Socrates apart from others is not that he has knowledge, nor that he is not

---

25. Cf. *Laws* (817b–c). The Athenian Stranger claims that when the tragedians come to the lawgivers, asking whether their art will be allowed to visit the city, the lawgivers respond: "Most excellent of Strangers, we ourselves, to the best of our ability, are the authors of a tragedy (τραγῳδίας αὐτοὶ ποιηταὶ) at once superlatively fair and good; at least, all our polity is framed as a representation (μίμησις) of the fairest and best life, which is in reality, as we assert, the truest tragedy. Thus we are composers (ποιηταὶ) of the same things as yourselves, rivals of yours as artists and actors of the fairest drama (καλλίστου δράματος), as our hope is, true law, and it alone, is by nature competent to complete."

26. See also 598c and 598e regarding Socrates' concern with deception rather than imitation itself. Cf. *Phaedrus*, 261e–262d.

ignorant, but that he is not deceived about the difference between these two states. Socrates is not speaking in these passages simply about the dangers of painting or poetry, but more generally about those who are deceived about the nature of reality—the kind of deception that the cave dwellers epitomize. They believe that all reality dances across the cave wall in shadow. Socrates admonishes Glaucon and Adeimantus to be the sort of people who can distinguish knowledge from ignorance (or at least who are not easily deceived), to understand when they see imitation that it is imitation, and to cast their glance from the imitation to the original.

Socrates' admonishment of the two young men brings us back around again to the reason for the discussion of poetry in the city in the first place. The two boys relied heavily and exclusively on the poets to support their view that the unjust life is rewarding and fulfilling as long as one's injustices go unpunished. The particular imitators on which Glaucon and Adeimantus relied to make their case show the unjust human life to be worth living, and Socrates is warning the young men to be wary of their own deception. They need to investigate through dialectic, to "put to the proof," just what the poets say in order to find out whether it is a true imitation or not.

This is precisely what the entire conversation of the *Republic* has been. The entire discussion has been a dialectic investigation of what the just life is and whether it is worth living. Even if Glaucon and Adeimantus have been persuaded that the images that these specific poets have created are not imitations of what is true, they need not reject imitation *per se*. Instead they take up the multifarious and beautiful images created by Socrates which cast their glance at the true originals. Adeimantus and Glaucon can gaze upon the cave dwellers, the divided line, the image of the sun, the analogy of soul and city, and other images in the dialogue, and they can reconsider in light of those images, that is, philosophically, whether the just life is worth living. They are being asked to trade bad images for good ones, but images nonetheless.

The *Republic*, that behemoth work of education, learning, politics, virtue, and the role of the philosopher, is the single largest source of the most intricate and beautiful images Plato created. And it, too, portrays images as appropriate vehicles for important philosophical endeavors. Given these brief but highly significant examples from the *Republic*, it is difficult to imagine taking at simple face-value the criticisms of images and image-makers that occur in that dialogue as criticisms of image-making itself. Plainly, Socrates sees images as not only legitimate and useful, but as the human manner of proceeding philosophically.

In a consistent manner, therefore, the dialogues portray a decided emphasis on the limitations of humans. In the face of our limitation, the dialogues urge the interlocutors and the reader to philosophize and to take up the philosophical life. If we are to take that urging seriously, then there must be an avenue to philosophical insight open to limited beings such as ourselves. What that avenue might be lies right before our eyes, exemplified in the dialogues themselves: not merely arguments to higher truths, but images that attract our gaze and turn us toward philosophy.

3. The Philosophical Effect of Images and Image-Making

When we perceive images of all kinds, even images of images created by the poet, painter, or image-maker in general, we experience the same phenomena: when we see images and recognize them as such, we see similarity and dissimilarity (Cf. *Phaedo*, 76a). It is the image's very unlikeness to its intended object—its otherness—that stimulates comparison. This makes it interesting, captivating. We look also for the basic similarity that makes the image an image of something. We then move dialectically between the two, seeing further similarities and dissimilarities along the way. We are moved to consider the qualities of the image, what the corresponding qualities of the original must be, why there is this difference, what the significance of the difference is, and how the unlike could be like. Real learning comes from the deeper exploration of images (metaphors, analogies, myths) in which the several details of image and original are compared. Clearer and detailed pictures emerge from which one can gain complex understanding of both objects under view.

It is no accident that the movement here between image and original resembles basic dialectic movement. On one level, Socrates practices dialectic through question and answer and recommends it to his interlocutors in an effort to help them to ascend to higher truths. Likewise, the dialectic that Plato creates with respect to his readers requires parallel cognitive movement. The reader moves forward and backward—spatially and temporally— repeatedly through the text while making sense out of it. The phenomenology of images resembles dialectic in another important manner. Just as dialectic necessitates that learning has as its source the learning subject and not an external authority (as deductive argument might), so our viewing and learning from images necessitates this as well.[27] Neither is an image an exact likeness of its original nor are its differences from the original plainly obvious. The richness of an image, and therefore its philosophical value, are appreciated only on reflection. We must work with the image, turn it over in our minds, see it from many perspectives—some of them not our usual perspectives—and we must think about what the image is and what it is not.

Let us look at one example of an image and its original to see how the phenomenon of examining that image takes place. Late in the *Symposium*, the drunken Alcibiades relates the tale of his failed seduction of Socrates. He tells the assembled party that he will create an image of Socrates in order to praise him (οὕτως ἐπιχειρήσω, δι᾽ εἰκόνων).

> "[Socrates] is likest to the Silenus-figures that sit in the statuaries' shops; those, I mean, which our craftsmen make with pipes or flutes in their hands: when their two halves are pulled open, they are found to contain images of gods." (215a–b)

As Alcibiades draws out the details of this simple image, we see both similarity and difference. Like the Satyr, Socrates has bulging eyes and a pushed in nose; but unlike Silenus, Socrates has beauty as well. Like the Satyr, Socrates is a figure who associates himself with erotic objects—young, beautiful men; but unlike the Satyr, as Alcibiades' failure to lure him into bed indicates, Socrates' erotic liaisons are not indulged through sexual activity. Like Marsyas, Socrates has great power to enchant his listeners, although not with a flute, but rather with his words. We learn from this image that Socrates' external appearance belies what is inside, that he is complex. We learn that his grotesque face contrasts with the beauty of his soul. We learn that The Many can be deceived if they fail to open him up to see what is inside. And finally, we learn that opening him up to examine his life and his soul, might reveal glimpses of the divine.

In a brief space, this simple image manages to convey a detailed and complex picture of Socrates. It is, therefore, not at all like the image-making Socrates describes flippantly in the *Republic* as walking around holding up a mirror to everything (596d–e). A mirror of Socrates would tell us less than this rich image. Recall that an image has both likeness and unlikeness. A mirror simply reflects exactly what is put before it, whereas an image, properly constructed, can induce us to see a richness in the objects before us

---

27. This connection was suggested to me by Max Creswell.

and to gain insight into the object and its original that might not be plainly evident. Is this enough for us to hold out hope, therefore, that images can lead to truth and philosophical insight? Yes. Alcibiades says as much, in fact, just before introducing the image cited above:

> "The way I shall take, gentlemen, in my praise of Socrates, is by similitudes (δι' εἰκόνων). Probably he will think I do this for derision; but I choose my similitude for the sake of truth (τοῦ ἀληθοῦς ἕνεκα), not of ridicule." (215a)

The evidence here and elsewhere conspires to compel us to take seriously Alcibiades's view that images can serve truth.[28]

We are reminded, too, of the likeness and unlikeness between Meno and his slave, which I examined in earlier chapters. Socrates created the image of the slave speaking before large crowds, lecturing on falsehoods and misconceptions about geometry. Meno and the reader are meant to see the exact manner in which Meno's lectures on virtue are the same and yet different from this image. They are similar insofar as both are shameful acts committed by ignorant people, but they are different insofar as the geometrical falsehoods are more easily and universally correctable. In order to correct his ignorance, Meno must engage in dialectic, which is risky and personally difficult in ways that geometry lessons are not. The reader and Meno gain important insights into virtue, knowledge, and ignorance by close examination of the image of the slave's public lectures and its original instance in Meno's lectures on virtue.

That images lead to truth is argued by François Mattei in his treatment of myth in the Platonic dialogues.[29] Images are an integral part of philosophy, Mattei argues, and reason cannot be the sole avenue open for philosophical enlightenment. Beginning with the question, "Why does Plato reintroduce [myth] regularly in a serious contemplative mood at every decisive stage of his reflections?"[30] Mattei argues, contrary to the common view that they are

28. Cf. Nussbaum (1988, 185ff.). She addresses the issue directly of Alcibiades' claim to tell the truth but, contrary to my position here, she sees the telling of truth through images as disallowed by philosophy.
29. Mattei (1988).
30. Ibid., 68. Cf. Griswold (1986, 140–56). Consistent with my general thesis, and especially parallel to my argument about irony in the previous chapter, Griswold argues that "[a] myth, unlike a syllogism, has the capacity to act as a complex mirror in which people can recognize not just who they are but who they might become at their best. Platonic myth is a mirror that can not only reflect one's hopes but also seek to realize them" (147).

inferior to logico-deductive argument, that the images provided through myth are complementary to argument and necessary to philosophical insight. Myth reveals "in iconic form the initial truth of the world,"[31] which Mattei calls the Theater of Ideas. Mattei contrasts the step-by-step verification that characterizes logical reasoning with the instantaneous vision offered by myth, and he argues that mythical images complete a rich philosophical process. Myth suspends the drama momentarily and thus arrests the action of dialectic. "The suspension of human action is the necessary condition of contemplation."[32] At junctures of suspended action where myth is introduced, the dialogues create points of contemplation, vision, and cessation of dialectic. Dialectic returns later to reconstruct the vision of myth seen in the inner theater of each soul at these points. Philosophy consists in this synthesis of mythic vision and dialectic examination.[33]

Broadening philosophy to include images in a related manner, Gerald Press argues that the kind of knowledge to be found in the Platonic dialogues is best understood to be vision, that is theoria, rather than episteme.

> By theoria or vision I mean something that is in some way the opposite of the kind of knowledge that has been the focus of much Western philosophy since Aristotle. For one thing, it refers to a mental image or seeing rather than to a proposition or set of propositions.[34]

Press reasons that the knowledge Plato means to give is a "showing rather than a telling how things are."[35] Such a conception of knowledge in the Platonic dialogues, Press argues, allows us to find a third way between the traditional dichotomies that lay the ground for battles of interpreting Plato: skeptic or dogmatist, philosopher or dramatist. And against the two realm metaphysical view attributed to Plato, Press says:

31. Mattei (1988).

32. Ibid., 70. Cf. Gadamer (1991, 4): "Socratic wisdom is not confirmed by its step-by-step growth, but instead its nature is to resemble the isolatedness and unrepeatability of a vision in a dream."

33. As these paraphrases indicate, Mattei seems to equivocate in his use of "dialectic," at times using it to refer only to logico-deductive argument in contrast to myth, and at other times using it to refer to the larger process of reading and understanding the dialogues, which includes both logical argument and mythic vision. As I have defined and used "dialectic," it would be manifest in activities used to understand logico-deductive arguments, but also in activities used to understand dramatic form, character development, irony, images, etc. For example, I don't agree that our comprehension of images comes in an "instantaneous vision" but rather after reflection on those images and visions.

34. Press (1995a), 71.

35. Ibid., 72.

The picture is this: the material, changing imperfect, temporal, sensible so-called "real" world is that in and through which we gain enrapturing intellectual glimpses of an immaterial, unchanging, perfect, eternal, purely thinkable ideal world. Frustratingly, the ideal remains beyond our grasp just because we live in time and space; wherefore we must keep on striving, inquiring for it. Our only access to it in this life is through dialogue, but every dialogue is a conversation with a real, not an ideal, interlocutor and therefore is partial, from a particular point of view or orientation, and subject to the limitations and specificities of time, place, and interlocutor.[36]

For Press, too, human limitation is fundamental, and it is inseparable from Plato's art of showing. Plato's dialogues portray philosophical conversation as it takes place among human beings, and thus provide not knowledge of ideal forms, but a vision of the philosophical life.

If the Platonic dialogues urge the use of images in the service of good philosophy, then what can be concluded about the traditional view of "Platonic metaphysics"? That there are two distinct realms—of things-in-themselves and of the objects of human experience—seems clear enough. But that pure reason, leading to insight into the forms, is to be identified with philosophy, is not supported by the texts. Reason alone as an avenue to enlightenment is not a possibility for humans. Our re-vision of the metaphysics that the dialogues support must include philosophy as the very tool necessary for limited, embodied persons. Philosophy mediates between the two realms for those beings necessitated to dwell in one alone but with aspirations to understand the other. In this capacity, philosophy certainly includes arguments, but it relies as well on images in the form of myth, analogy, metaphor, and the like. Pure reason is left to the gods; philosophy is left to humans.

A renewed look at Plato's metaphysics reveals surprising results. Even the forms—the eternal, unchanging bearers of reality—and the disembodied rationality that can grasp the forms are themselves images.[37] It has perhaps escaped our notice that even these stories that are spun throughout the dialogue are imagistic, and what has traditionally passed for Plato's metaphysics and his epistemology are themselves composed of images. We have

---

36. Ibid., 81

37. Cf. Aristotle, *Metaphysics* I.ix.12: "To say that the Forms are patterns, and that other things participate in them, is to use empty phrases and poetical metaphors." τὸ δὲ λέγειν παραδείγματα αὐτὰ εἶναι καὶ μετέχειν αὐτῶν τἆλλα κενολογεῖν ἐστι καὶ μεταφορὰς λέγειν ποιητικάς. I agree with Aristotle wholeheartedly that these are poetical metaphors, but that they are empty phrases I cannot accept.

perhaps neglected to see that even these things called "forms" take shape in our imagination in ways other than their ascribed reality. They are meant to have no physical manifestation and yet they are presented to us and are taken up into our cognition as shapes, forms. Furthermore, we must imagine another world beyond our own, this realm of the things-in-themselves, this reality which is different from our lived experience and yet similar, and we must construct it from our fancy or imagination, furnish it with conceptions drawn from our own limited experience. And yet Plato expects us truly to have some access to this reality from the images he creates and from the images he compels us to create for ourselves. Ultimately, all of Plato's images are addressed to an audience firmly, and necessarily, grounded in human phenomena and are meant to turn us toward philosophy. Does this imply that ultimately we are only relegated to images? Perhaps yes. But fortunately we have philosophy. If we take seriously that this world is a mere image of the reality it imitates, then indeed we must forever deal in images. It is the human lot.[38]

We might now have a bit more insight into Plato's use of images. He is providing the link for limited humans to the realities. Just as looking at two equal stones can help us to recollect the reality of equality itself, so also other perceptions and images can aid in our recalling many other truths. Imperfect as this is, and even risky as it is, this is the avenue open for embodied beings such as ourselves. Plato faces the task of urging us to philosophy when he knows that we can only practice it as the limited beings that we are. How do you urge one to philosophy in the face of the guarantee that arguments will fail? Knowing the power of images and image-making, Plato is induced to choose them as an appropriate medium to move us in certain directions. Plato is infamous for "his" critique of poets and image-makers. Yet he is the poet and image-maker extraordinaire. While he puts warnings about the use of these devices in the mouths of his interlocutors, at the same time he places those very devices alongside the warnings. A full understanding of the dialogues cannot overlook this fact.

In order to understand the power and the risk of images, I return to the epigrams that frame this chapter. The first, from the *Sophist*, seems to warn

---

38. I have been asked on several occasions whether I am making Plato out to be a post-modern figure. Such a conjecture seems off the mark. To say that humans must always deal with images is not to say that there are nothing but images, that is, that there is no truth or reality. The purpose of images is to help us to ascend toward some higher reality or truth. There is some reality to which we aspire and of which we can fall short. Indeed, it is embedded in what it means to be an image that it is an image of *something*.

us away from resemblances by evoking a sense of danger. The wildest of animals, the wolf, might very well look to us like the tamest, the dog. Mistaking one for the other could well have dire consequences. The second epigram, from the *Timaeus*, praises our vision, which is responsible for philosophy "in all its range, than which no greater boon ever has come or will come, by divine bestowal, unto the race of mortals." There would appear to be some tension between the meaning of the two passages. On the one hand, we put ourselves in danger if our vision is not keen enough to distinguish between like things, the dog and the wolf. And on the other hand, our vision, a gift from the gods, is of the greatest benefit to us and has procured philosophy into our midst.[39] I hope that my argument has shown that these two claims are not truly contradictory, despite the tension between them; instead they convey the essence of the dialogues' presentation of vision and image. Images and vision are at the same time risky and of great benefit to us. It is our vision that casts our gaze ultimately toward philosophy, but it is also our vision that can drag us down into the mire. What accounts for the difference between these two activities is the object of our gaze. Plato's dialogues provide the kinds of resemblances that humans need in order to steer clear of danger, the images that cast our eyes toward philosophy.

4. Epi-Logos

I began this chapter asking why Plato does not rely on pure rational argumentation in his own philosophical work, as one who embraced the traditional view of his metaphysical commitments might expect. Arguments, by their very nature argue toward a conclusion. Again, I do not claim that the dialogues are void of any positive philosophical content; nevertheless the dialogues, while containing arguments, do not themselves work toward conclusions in the way we expect philosophical arguments to do. The dialogues never give us an unambiguous logos, an account, an answer to the "What is X?" questions posed in them. What the dialogues *do* give us, consistently and often, is Socrates' commitment to stories, myths, analogies, metaphors—in short, images.

---

39. Cf. *Phaedrus* (262a): "Then he who is to deceive another, and is not to be deceived himself, must know accurately the similarity and dissimilarity of things."

All of the devices whose functions I have already discussed in other terms in this book, can also be conceived in terms of Plato's use of images. For example, the dramatic form of the dialogues is a holistic way of drawing images. Each dialogue is an image of philosophical conversation and of the Socratic or philosophic life. Plato's image of the philosophical life draws us into it, in both the senses of pulling us into that life and painting us into it. The scenarios are so compelling, that they cannot but elicit our responses, whether those responses are strong attraction to the life of philosophy, adamant rejection of that life, denial about our own inabilities to participate in that life, or despair at our failures to live that life. We become actors in the drama as images of our own lives are patched onto the canvas painted so vividly by Plato; we not only see an image of the philosophical life, we can participate in the activity of philosophy when we become engaged by a dialogue, and so create our own lives in the image of the philosopher.

In a related manner, Plato's device of character portrayal involves the creation of images. Each character portrayal is a fragment of a life, portraying the essence of that life, and perhaps the consequences—good or ill—of living that life. Plato draws these images and sometimes guides our perception of them by his use of names. Each character is a image of an individual or a type, and can be used by Plato to say something about how we might want to draw our own characters. Transformation is possible when we are able to see images of ourselves in these characters. Looking back and forth from the characters to ourselves, seeing like and unlike, we make assessments and can be moved to become less like some characters and more like others. In general, the role of images and image-making helps us to see the possibility for new, better selves. Through Plato's character portrayal, we are able to imagine a possible life for ourselves that is not yet realized, and to turn toward that life.

Finally, we saw that with irony, in order for the reader to understand the irony as ironic, she must first have seen herself as different from the interlocutor. On further reflection, because the irony was about the interlocutor's mistaken self-image, about the inconsistency between the image of the interlocutor seen by the reader and the image of the interlocutor seen by himself, the reader was forced to reconsider whether she suffered from the same difficulty and therefore whether she was truly as different from the interlocutor as she thought. The reader sees two images of the interlocutor, and if all goes well, she must also confront the possible double image of herself (image and self-image). The movement of the reader in this process mimics that of our general movement in learning from images: we first see an image's difference then its similarity to its object, and we move dialectically between the two. Moreover, just as Socrates' and Plato's use of images implies that logico-deductive argumentation alone will not suffice for human philosophy, so irony compels us to different forms of understanding. Irony's inherent ambiguity leaves us epistemologically unsettled, a state that gives birth to philosophical pursuits and that reflects our inherent limits despite our desires to understand and know more than we are capable of knowing and understanding.

If Plato's entire philosophical project is to turn us toward the philosophical life, he does not give us an argument whose conclusion is that. Being the limited creatures that we are, we cannot be turned by logos alone. Plato must therefore choose to enter into another kind of relationship with us—one that grips our souls more powerfully. He turns us toward the philosophical life through all of these devices that we tend to call literary or dramatic. The dichotomy between the literary and the philosophical, which I hope to have undermined to a large extent, is rooted in the deeper division professional philosophers have created between the strictly logical and the extralogical. This deeper division identifies the philosophical with the logical and counts as unphilosophical all that falls outside those confines. The dialogues' dialectic movement—forward, back; upward, down; repelled, reconciled; engaged, offended—stands in contrast to the linear progression of logico-deductive argument. Plato's project, while wholly philosophical insofar as it aims toward the search for and investigation of truth, is nonetheless extralogical. It works through our emotions of shame, pride, and desire; it captures our attention and creates dissonance through irony, jokes, and vivid characterizations; and it captivates and focuses our imagination through stories, myths, allegories and other types of images. We need these images of ourselves, of what we could become, and what the philosophical life has to offer in order to be turned toward them. We see in several dialogues that the tools of the poets and image-makers can be corrupting influences on the soul.[40] They can be corrupting because they are devices that go directly at the human soul, can penetrate it and make a deep and lasting imprint. But by the same token, since these devices do have access to the soul, we must believe they can also be capable of—and wielded for the sake of—good. That which is capable of the greatest evil must also be capable of the greatest

---

40. As with image-making, the same argument can be made in the cases of poetry and rhetoric: Plato "commits" the very activity the dialogues seem to disparage. I treat poetry and image-making in this book, but not rhetoric. Cf. Ferrari (1987) and Roochnik (1995).

good.[41] The very danger of poetry and images is also at the heart of their effectiveness. And hence the risk and danger in human life: that we might fail to improve our souls and perhaps corrupt them. Plato is willing to take this risk and urges us to take it with him. He puts to use the devices of the poets and image-makers, harnessing their power in an effort to turn our souls toward philosophy.

41. Cf. *Crito*, 44d; *Phaedo*, 107d; *Republic*, 333e ff.; 605c–d, 607c.

Works Cited

Arieti, J. 1991. *Interpreting Plato: The Dialogues as Drama*. Savage, Md.: Rowman and Littlefield.

Aristotle. 1982. *Poetics*, translated by W. Fyfe. Cambridge, Mass.: Harvard University Press, Loeb Classical Library.

Benson, H., ed. 1992. *Essays on the Philosophy of Socrates*. New York: Oxford University Press.

Berger, H., Jr. 1987. "Levels of Discourse in Plato's Dialogues." In *Literature and the Question of Philosophy*, edited by Anthony J. Cascardi. Baltimore: The Johns Hopkins University Press.

Bloom, A., trans. 1968. *The Republic of Plato*. New York: Basic Books, Inc.

Booth, W. 1974. *A Rhetoric of Irony*. Chicago: University of Chicago Press.

Bowen, A. 1988. "On Interpreting Plato." In *Platonic Writings/Platonic Readings*, edited by C. Griswold Jr. New York: Routledge.

Brumbaugh, R. 1975. "Plato's *Meno* as Form and as Content of Secondary School Courses in Philosophy." *Teaching Philosophy* 1, no. 2: 107–15.

Bywater, I. 1945. *Aristotle on the Art of Poetry*. Oxford: The Clarendon Press.

Cascardi, A., ed. 1987. *Literature and the Question of Philosophy*. Baltimore: The Johns Hopkins University Press.

Chroust. A. 1964. *Aristotle: Protrepticus, A Reconstruction*. Notre Dame, Ind.: University of Notre Dame Press.

Cole, T., ed. 1960. *Playwrights on Playwriting: The Meaning and Making of Modern Drama from Ibsen to Ionesco*, introduction by J. Gassner. New York: Hill and Wang.

Danto, A. 1987. "Philosophy as/and/of Literature." In *Literature and the Question of Philosophy*, edited by Anthony J. Cascardi. Baltimore: The Johns Hopkins University Press.

Diogenes Laertius. 1991. *Lives of Eminent Philosophers,* vol. I, translated by R. D. Hicks. Cambridge, Mass.: Harvard University Press, Loeb Classical Library.

Düring, I. 1961. *Aristotle's Protrepticus: An Attempt at Reconstruction.* Göteborg: Elanders Boktryckeri Aktiebolag.

Eagleton, T. 1983. *Literary Theory, An Introduction.* Minneapolis: University of Minnesota Press.

Eckstein, J. 1968. *The Platonic Method: An Interpretation of the Dramatic-Philosophic Aspects of the Meno.* New York: Greenwood Publishing Corporation.

Elias, J. 1984. *Plato's Defense of Poetry.* Albany: State University of New York Press.

Ferrari, G. 1987. *Listening to The Cicadas: A Study of Plato's Phaedrus.* Cambridge: Cambridge University Press.

Fish, S. 1972. *Self-Consuming Artifacts: The Experience of Seventeenth Century Literature.* Berkeley and Los Angeles: University of California Press.

———. 1981. "Why No One's Afraid of Wolfgang Iser." *Diacritics* 11 (March): 2–13.

Frede, M. 1992. "Plato's Arguments and the Dialogue Form." In *Oxford Studies in Ancient Philosophy, Supplementary Volume,* edited by James C. Klagge and Nicholas D. Smith. New York: Oxford University Press.

Freund, E. 1987. *The Return of the Reader: Reader-response Criticism.* New York: Methuen.

Gadamer, H. 1980. *Dialogue and Dialectic: Eight Hermeneutical Studies on Plato,* translated and with an introduction by P. Christopher Smith. New Haven: Yale University Press.

———. 1986. *The Idea of the Good in Platonic-Aristotelian Philosophy,* translated and with an introduction and annotation by P. Christopher Smith. New Haven: Yale University Press.

———. 1991. *Plato's Dialectical Ethics: Phenomenological Interpretations Relating to the Philebus,* translated and with an introduction by Robert M. Wallace. New Haven: Yale University Press.

———. 1997. "Reflections on My Philosophical Journey." In *The Philosophy of Hans-Georg Gadamer,* edited by Lewis Edwin Hahn. The Library of Living Philosophers, vol. 24. Chicago: Open Court.

Gagarin, M. 1969. "The Purpose of Plato's *Protagoras.*" *Transactions of the American Philological Association* 100: 338–42.

Gonzalez, F. 1995. "A Short History of Platonic Interpretation and the 'Third Way.'" In *The Third Way: New Directions in Platonic Studies,* edited by Francisco Gonzalez. Lanham, Md.: Rowman & Littlefield.

Gooch, P. 1987. "Irony and Insight in Plato's Meno." *Laval Theologique et Philosophique* 43, no. 2: 189–201.

Gordon, J. 1991. *Is Virtue Teachable?: A Socratic View of Moral Education.* Ph.D. diss., University of Texas at Austin.

———. 1996. "Dialectic, Dialogue, and Transformation of the Self." *Philosophy and Rhetoric* 29, no. 3: 259–78.

———. 1996. "Against Vlastos on Complex Irony." *Classical Quarterly* 46, no. 1: 131–37.

Gottlieb, P. 1992. "The Complexity of Socratic Irony: A Note on Professor Vlastos' Account." *Classical Quarterly* 42, no. 1: 278–79.

Griswold, C., Jr. 1986. *Self-Knowledge in Plato's Phaedrus*. New Haven: Yale University Press.

———. 1987. "Irony and Aesthetic Language in Plato's Dialogues." In *Philosophy and Literature*, edited by D. Bolling. New York: Routledge.

———, ed. 1988. *Platonic Writings/Platonic Readings*. New York: Routledge.

Grote, G. 1888. *Plato and Other Companions of Sokrates*, vol. 2. London: John Murray.

Grube, G. M. A. 1981. *Phaedo*. Indianapolis: Hackett Publishing Company, Inc.

———. 1992. *Republic*. Indianapolis: Hackett Publishing Company, Inc.

Guthrie, W. K. C. 1956. "Introduction." In *Protagoras and Meno*. London: Penguin Books, Ltd.

———. 1971. *The Sophists*. New York: Cambridge University Press.

Haslam, M. 1972. "Plato, Sophron, and the Dramatic Dialogue." *Bulletin of the Institute of Classical Studies* 19: 17–23.

Havelock, E. 1963. *Preface to Plato*. Cambridge, Mass.: The Belknap Press of Harvard University Presses.

Hershbell, J. 1995. "Reflections on the Orality and Literacy of Plato's Dialogues." In *The Third Way: New Directions in Platonic Studies*, edited by J. Gonzalez. Lanham, Md.: Rowman & Littlefield.

Hutchinson, D. 1995. "Ethics." In *The Cambridge Companion to Aristotle*, edited by Jonathan Barnes. Cambridge: Cambridge University Press.

Hyland, D. 1968. "Why Plato Wrote Dialogues." *Philosophy and Rhetoric* 1 (January): 38–50.

———. 1995. *Finitude and Transcendence in the Platonic Dialogues*. Albany: State University of New York Press.

Irigiray, L. 1994. "Sorcerer Love: A Reading of Plato's *Symposium*, Diotima's Speech," translated by E. Kuykendall. In *Feminist Interpretations of Plato*, edited by Nancy Tuana. University Park: The Pennsylvania State University Press.

Irwin, T. 1977. *Plato's Moral Theory: The Early and Middle Dialogues*. Oxford: Clarendon Press.

———. 1979. *Plato's Gorgias*. Oxford: Clarendon Press.

Iser, W. 1978. *The Act of Reading: A Theory of Aesthetic Response*. Baltimore: The Johns Hopkins University Press.

———. 1981. "Talk Like Whales." *Diacritics* 11 (September): 82–87.

———. 1989. *Prospecting: From Reader Response to Literary Anthropology*. Baltimore: The Johns Hopkins University Press.

Jaeger, W. 1971. *Paideia: The Ideals of Greek Culture*, translated by Gilbert Highet, vol. 2. New York: Oxford University Press.

Kaufmann, W. 1979. *Tragedy and Philosophy*. Princeton: Princeton University Press.

Kerferd, G.. 1981. *The Sophistic Movement*. New York: Cambridge University Press.

King, J. 1987. "Elenchus, Self-blame, and the Socratic Paradox." *Review of Metaphysics* 41 (spring): 105–26.

Klagge, J. C., and Nicholas D. Smith, eds. 1992. *Oxford Studies in Ancient Philosophy, Supplementary Volume*. New York: Oxford University Press.

Klein, J. 1989. *A Commentary on Plato's Meno*. Chicago: University of Chicago Press.

Kosman, A. 1992a. "Acting: Drama as the Mimesis of Praxis." In *Essays on Aristotle's Poetics*, edited by A. Rorty. Princeton: Princeton University Press.

———. 1992b. "Silence and Imitation in the Platonic Dialogues." In *Oxford Studies in Ancient Philosophy, Supplementary Volume*, edited by James C. Klagge and Nicholas D. Smith. New York: Oxford University Press.

Liddell and Scott. 1985. *Greek-English Lexicon*. Oxford: The Clarendon Press.

MacIntyre, A. 1981. *After Virtue*. Notre Dame: University of Notre Dame Press.

Mattei, J. 1988. "The Theater of Myth in Plato." In *Platonic Writings/Platonic Readings*, edited by C. Griswold. New York: Routledge.

McDonald, J. 1931. *Character Portraiture in Epicharmus, Sophron, and Plato*. Sewannee: University Press of Tennessee.

McKim, R. 1988. "Shame and Truth in Plato's Gorgias." In *Platonic Writings/ Platonic Readings*, edited by C. Griswold. New York: Routledge.

McPherran, M. 1996. *The Religion of Socrates*. University Park: The Pennsylvania State University Press.

Miller, M., Jr. 1980. *The Philosopher in Plato's Statesman*. The Hague: Nijhoff.

———. 1986. *Plato's Parmenides: The Conversion of the Soul*. Princeton: Princeton University Press.

———. 1996. "'The Arguments I Seem to Hear': Argument and Irony in the Crito." *Phronesis*, 41, no. 2: 121–37.

Muecke, D. C. 1969. *The Compass of Irony*. London: Methuen.

Nails, D. 1992. "Platonic Chronology Reconsidered." *Bryn Mawr Classical Review* 3: 314–27.

———. 1999. "Mouthpiece, Schmouthpiece." In *Who Speaks for Plato? Studies in Platonic Anonymity*, edited by G. Press. Lanham, Md.: Rowman & Littlefield.

Nehamas, A., and Paul Woodruff, trans. 1989. *Symposium*. Indianapolis: Hackett Publishing Company.

Nietzsche, F. 1966. *Beyond Good and Evil: Prelude to a Philosophy of the Future*, translated with commentary by Walter Kaufmann. New York: Random House.

Nussbaum, M. 1988. *The Fragility of Goodness: Luck and Ethics in Greek Tragedy and Philosophy*. New York: Cambridge University Press.

Owen, G. E.L. 1978. "Plato on Not-Being." In *Plato I: A Collection of Critical Essays*, edited by G. Vlastos. Notre Dame, Ind.: Notre Dame University Press.

Partee, M. 1981. *Plato's Poetics: The Authority of Beauty*. Salt Lake City: University of Utah Press.

Plato. *Apology*. Translated by H. Fowler, introduction by W. R. M. Lamb. Cambridge, Mass.: Harvard University Press, Loeb Classical Library, 1990.

———. *Charmides*. Translated by W. R. M. Lamb. Cambridge, Mass.: Harvard University Press, Loeb Classical Library, 1986.

———. *Crito*. Translated by H. Fowler, introduction by W. R. M. Lamb. Cambridge, Mass.: Harvard University Press, Loeb Classical Library, 1990.

———. *Euthyphro*. Translated by H. Fowler, introduction by W. R. M. Lamb. Cambridge, Mass.: Harvard University Press, Loeb Classical Library, 1990.

———. *Gorgias*. Translated by W. R. M. Lamb. Cambridge, Mass.: Harvard University Press, Loeb Classical Library, 1991.

———. *Laws*. Translated by R. G. Bury. Cambridge, Mass.: Harvard University Press, Loeb Classical Library, 1984.

———. *Meno*. Translated by W. R. M. Lamb. Cambridge, Mass.: Harvard University Press, Loeb Classical Library, 1990.

———. *Phaedo*. Translated by H. Fowler. Cambridge, Mass.: Harvard University Press, Loeb Classical Library, 1990.

———. *Phaedrus*. Translated by H. Fowler, introduction by W. R. M. Lamb. Cambridge, Mass.: Harvard University Press, Loeb Classical Library, 1990.

———. *Protagoras*. Translated by W. R. M. Lamb. Cambridge, Mass.: Harvard University Press, Loeb Classical Library, 1990.

———. *Republic*. Translated by Paul Shorey. Cambridge, Mass.: Harvard University Press, Loeb Classical Library, vol. 1, 1982.

———. *Republic*. Translated by Paul Shorey. Cambridge, Mass.: Harvard University Press, Loeb Classical Library, vol. 2, 1987.

———. *Sophist*. Translated by H. Fowler, introduction by W. R. M. Lamb. Cambridge, Mass.: Harvard University Press, Loeb Classical Library, 1987.

———. *Symposium*. Translated by W. R. M. Lamb. Cambridge, Mass.: Harvard University Press, Loeb Classical Library, 1991.

———. *Theaetetus*. Translated by H. Fowler. Cambridge, Mass.: Harvard University Press, Loeb Classical Library, 1987.

———. *Timaeus*. Translated by R. Bury. Cambridge, Mass.: Harvard University Press, Loeb Classical Library, 1989.

Press, G., ed. 1993. *Plato's Dialogues: New Studies & Interpretations*. Lanham, Md.: Rowman & Littlefield.

———. 1995a. "Knowledge as Vision in Plato's Dialogues." *The Journal of Neoplatonic Studies* 3: 61–89.

———. 1995b. "Plato's Dialogues as Enactments." In *The Third Way, New Directions in Platonic Studies,* edited by F. Gonzalez. Lanham, Md.: Rowman & Littlefield.

———, ed. 1999. *Who Speaks for Plato? Studies in Platonic Anonymity.* Lanham, Md.: Rowman & Littlefield.

Robinson, R. 1953. *Plato's Earlier Dialectic*. Oxford: Oxford University Press.

———. 1971. "Elenchus." In *The Philosophy of Socrates*, edited by G. Vlastos. New York: Anchor Books, Doubleday & Company, Ltd.

Roochnik, D. 1995. "Socrates' Rhetorical Attack On Rhetoric." In *The Third Way, New Directions in Platonic Studies*, edited by F. Gonzalez. Lanham, Md.: Rowman & Littlefield.

———. 1996. *Of Art and Wisdom: Plato's Understanding of Techne*. University Park: The Pennsylvania State University Press.

Rorty, A., ed. 1992. *Essays On Aristotle's Poetics*. Princeton: Princeton University Press.

Rosen, S. 1983. *Plato's Sophist: The Drama of Original and Image*. New Haven: Yale University Press.

———. 1988. *The Quarrel Between Philosophy and Poetry*. New York: Routledge.

Ryle, G. 1966. *Plato's Progress*. Cambridge: Cambridge University Press.

Schleiermacher, F. 1836. *Introductions to the Dialogues of Plato*. Translated by William Dobson. Cambridge: J & J. J. Deighton.

Scolnicov, S. 1988. *Plato's Metaphysics of Education*. New York: Routledge.

Seeskin, K. 1984. "Socratic Philosophy and the Dialogue Form." *Philosophy and Literature* 8, no. 2: 181–94.

———. 1987. *Dialogue and Discovery: A Study in Socratic Method*. Albany: State University of New York Press.

Shorey, P. 1960. *The Unity of Plato's Thought*. Chicago: University of Chicago Press.

Strauss, L. 1964. *The City and Man*. Chicago: Rand McNally & Company.

Taylor, A. E. 1959. *Plato: The Man and His Works*. New York: Meridian Books.

Tejera, V. 1984. *Plato's Dialogues One By One: A Structural Interpretation*. New York: Irvington Publishers, Inc.

Teloh, H. 1986. *Socratic Education in Plato's Early Dialogues*. Notre Dame, Ind.: University of Notre Dame Press.

Thayer, H. S. 1977. "Plato on the Morality of Imagination." *Review of Metaphysics* 30 (June): 594–618.

Thrane, G. 1979. "Shame." *Journal of the Theory of Social Behavior* 9, no. 2: 139–66.

Tigerstedt, E. N. 1977. *Interpreting Plato*. Uppsala: Almqvist & Wiskell International.

Vlastos, G. 1956. "Introduction." In *Plato's Protagoras*, translated by B. Jowett, revised by M. Ostwald. Indianapolis: Bobbs-Merrill.

———, ed. 1978. *Plato I: A Collection of Critical Essays*. Notre Dame, Ind.: Notre Dame University Press.

———, ed. 1978. *Plato II: A Collection of Critical Essays*. Notre Dame, Ind.: Notre Dame University Press.

———. 1982. "The Socratic Elenchus." *Journal of Philosophy* 79: 715–21.

———. 1983. "The Socratic Elenchus." In *Oxford Studies in Ancient Philosophy*, vol. 1, edited by Julia Annas. Oxford: Clarendon Press.

———. 1991. *Socrates, Ironist and Moral Philosopher*. Ithaca: Cornell University Press.

Waugh, J. 1995. "Neither Published Nor Perished: The Dialogues as Speech, Not Text." In *The Third Way, New Directions in Platonic Studies*, edited by F. Gonzalez. Lanham, Md.: Rowman & Littlefield.

West, E. 1995. "Plato's Audiences, or How Plato Replies to the Fifth-Century Intellectual Mistrust of Letters." In *The Third Way: New Directions in Platonic Studies*, edited by F. Gonzalez. Lanham, Md.: Rowman & Littlefield.

Wiggins, D. 1978. "Sentence Meaning, Negation, and Plato's Problem of Non-Being." In *Plato I: A Collection of Critical Essays*, edited by G. Vlastos. Notre Dame, Ind.: Notre Dame University Press.

Williams, B. 1993. *Shame and Necessity*. Berkeley and Los Angeles: University of California Press.

Williams, R. 1977. *Marxism and Literature*. Oxford: Oxford University Press.

Woodruff, P. 1992. "Aristotle on Mimesis." *Essays on Aristotle's Poetics*, edited by A. Rorty. Princeton: Princeton University Press.

Xenophon. *Anabasis*. Cambridge, Mass.: Harvard University Press, Loeb Classical Library. 1980.

Index